T0338208

Islamic Finance and Economic Development

Islamic Finance and Economic Development

Risk Management, Regulation, and Corporate Governance

AMR MOHAMED EL TIBY
WAFIK GRAIS

WILEY

Published by John Wiley & Sons, Inc., Hoboken, New Jersey.
Published simultaneously in Canada.

For general information on our other products and services or for technical support, please contact our Customer Care Department within the United States at (800) 762-2974, outside the United States at (317) 572-3993 or fax (317) 572-4002.

Wiley publishes in a variety of print and electronic formats and by print-on-demand. Some material included with standard print versions of this book may not be included in e-books or in print-on-demand. If this book refers to media such as a CD or DVD that is not included in the version you purchased, you may download this material at http://booksupport.wiley.com. For more information about Wiley products, visit www.wiley.com.

ISBN 978-1-118-84726-8 (Hardcover)
ISBN 978-1-118-84718-3 (ePDF)
ISBN 978-1-118-84719-0s (ePub)

Printed in the United States of America

10 9 8 7 6 5 4 3 2 1

To my mother
To the soul of my father
To my dearest children, Mohamed, Nada, and Khaled
To my dearest friend Maha Eltiby

—Amr El Tiby

To my late parents, who taught me love, tolerance, and
perseverance. Their extraordinary humanism is for me a
constant lesson that I will always cherish.

To my wife, who remained kind and patient through the whole
process. Her support, dedication, and tolerance are continuous
reminders to me of the meaning of love.
I am greatly indebted to her.

To my children, who had to bear with my absences. Their presence
and support are a constant light and give warmth to my life.

—Wafik Grais

Contents

Preface

Islamic finance is introducing challenges to the global financial landscape. Islamic financial assets, despite the turbulence across all global financial markets, have grown from around US$55 billion in the late 1980s to around US$1.2 trillion in 2011.[1] They represent 0.5 percent of global financial assets. Deutsche Bank's *Global Islamic Banking Report* (November 2011) anticipates a 24 percent compounded annual growth rate (CAGR) in Islamic assets over the coming three years.

Islamic finance is built on different foundations from conventional finance. An institution offering Islamic financial services (IIFS) adheres to *Shari'a*-inspired principles and rules, which take precedence over profit taking. The building blocks of Islamic finance are: (1) promotion of fairness in transactions and the prevention of an exploitative relationship and of fraud; (2) sharing of risks and rewards between all parties involved in financial and commercial transactions; (3) a tangible economic purpose for each transaction, sometimes referred to as the principle of materiality; (4) the prohibition of interest; and (5) the prohibition of engaging in activities prohibited by *Shari'a* laws.

These characteristics, particularly the asset-backed nature of Islamic financial assets and risk-sharing arrangements, have played a major role in mitigating the impact of the 2008 global financial crisis on Islamic finance. These features ensure a tighter link between the growth of economic and financial transactions than would be permitted with conventional finance, and contribute to a clearer identification of where risks lie.[2] They can be expected to limit the scope for leverage. Kenneth Rogoff, a leading Harvard University economist, suggests that Islamic finance demonstrates the advantages of more equity and risk sharing over the bias in favor of debt instruments in conventional finance.[3]

---

[1] See, for example, M. Mohieldin et al. (2011).

[2] One could surmise that these features would entail a closer link between monetary and real economic expansion than in conventional finance, entailing possibly an easier control of the general price level.

[3] Rogoff states: "In the ideal world, equity lending and direct investment would play a much bigger role." He further asserts: "With a better balance between debt and equity, risk-sharing would be greatly enhanced and financial crises sharply muted." (Umer Chabbra, "International Financial Stability: The Role of Islamic Finance," Institute of Policy Studies, Islamabad, vol. 4, no. 2). www.ips.org.pk/islamic-thoughts/1006-international-financial-stability-the-role-of-islamic-finance.pdf.

Banks, conventional as well as Islamic, are subject to a wide range of risks. In general, banking risk can be categorized into four groups: financial, operational, business, and event risks. However, Islamic financial institutions face a mix of risks that are distinct from the ones faced by conventional banks. The requirement of materiality, risk sharing in earnings-bearing deposits, liquidity management, and operational risks stemming from *Shari'a* compliance highlight the distinctions. The relationship with investment account holders or depositors shapes the nature of a large portion of an IIFS's liabilities and the risks it faces. Also, the systemic liquidity infrastructure bears on the IIFS's ability to place excess liquidity or access liquidity when needed, affecting its liquidity risks. Furthermore, the risk to earnings performance of conducting non-*Shari'a*-compliant activity is specific to IIFSs.

The recent global financial crisis has highlighted the need for effective risk management and the need for international regulatory standards to foster it. The observation is equally valid for Islamic finance. Accordingly, it is crucial to understand the risk characteristics associated with Islamic finance operations to set an effective risk management framework that is sound and prudent, and to develop relevant international regulatory standards. The financial crisis has also highlighted the importance of sound corporate governance that safeguards the interests of all stakeholders, mitigates risks, and fosters growth. In this context, it is crucial to focus on the corporate governance challenges of IIFSs and establish a *Shari'a* governance framework.

This book's messages are:

- Islamic finance is an opportunity to seize to promote development, most notably in communities where conventional finance leads to the financial exclusion of large groups of society.
- Islamic finance has developed beyond infancy, and significant strides have been made in its development.
- Islamic finance faces risks that can result in specific distress, whether idiosyncratic or resulting from spillovers.
- Appropriate regulation can mitigate the mix of risks faced by Islamic finance and increase its resilience.
- Sound systemic *Shari'a* governance can strengthen the industry's stability and vibrancy as well as improve its performance.

The book contributes (1) a highlighting of the relationship of Islamic finance and economic development, (2) a blueprint for a regulatory approach to Islamic finance that promotes stability and vibrancy, and (3) an approach to the development of a systemic *Shari'a* corporate governance framework for Islamic finance.

The book contains four parts: Part One provides a primer to Islamic finance and highlights of its history. This part contributes an analysis of recent developments and a survey of the landscape of Islamic finance. Part Two is about risk, contagion, and distress; it provides a picture of how global financial crises could affect Islamic finance.

Part Three considers the regulatory framework for Islamic banking. It discusses the opportunities and challenges for regulators, policy makers, and bankers. It provides an approach that can enable the mainstreaming of Islamic finance while keeping it true to its principles.

Part Four is dedicated to the governance issue in Islamic finance. It discusses the financial fiduciary governance and the *Shari'a* fiduciary governance. It then presents an approach to the development of a systemic *Shari'a* governance framework for Islamic finance activities.

Part One: Emergence of Modern Islamic Finance

Chapter 1: History and Core Principles of Islamic Finance   This chapter provides a brief history of Islamic finance, presenting only the highlights of that history relevant to the industry's development. It does not go into the details of that history that are extensively covered in other writings. The chapter includes a primer of the foundations and modes of operation of Islamic finance.

Chapter 2: Islamic Finance: Opportunity for Egypt's Development   Egypt was an early mover in modern Islamic finance. The country offers ample opportunities for the development of Islamic finance, as well as for the contribution of the latter to Egypt's development. Islamic finance could rapidly grow beyond its current size of less than 5 percent of the country's financial assets. Islamic financial intermediation can contribute to deepening Egypt's financial system, increase the diversification of the services it offers, and improve financial inclusiveness. It can offer opportunities for financing development, whether at the state, corporate, small/medium enterprise, or consumer level. At the same time, Egypt's developmental needs and its population's values offer promising prospects for Islamic finance. However, the introduction and development of Islamic finance raise challenges to market participants, policy makers, regulators, and supervisors, as well as standard setters. These challenges need to be addressed. Dealing with them in a professional and systematic manner is the best way to ensure the success of Islamic financial services (IFS) and the opportunity the industry provides for the country's development.

Part Two: Managing Systemic Risks[4]

   Chapter 3: Risks, Spillovers, and Distress   This chapter identifies risks
   faced by Islamic financial services (IFS) and spillover and contagion
   channels across conventional and Islamic banks as well as within
   the latter group. It then looks at cases of Islamic bank distress where
   the risks and channels of transmission were at play. The focus is on
   systemic crises and not on idiosyncratic distress in a single institution offering Islamic financial services (IIFS) without risk of contamination of other financial services. Particular attention is given
   to the systemic crisis experienced by Turkey's special finance houses
   (SFHs) at the beginning of the 2000s decade triggered by the collapse of Ihlas Finance House in Turkey.

   Chapter 4: Coping with Crises: Policies, Institutions, and Markets   Chapter 4 focuses on policies, institutions, and mechanisms to promote
   financial stability and deal with crises. It deals first with the role
   of liquidity provision in periods of financial stress. It then turns
   to mechanisms of liquidity management consistent with Islamic
   finance and the setups developed in Bahrain and Malaysia. The
   chapter finally focuses on mechanisms to solve distress episodes
   when they occur. It concludes by summarizing the vulnerability of
   Islamic finance to a systemic crisis and provides recommendations
   for an increased robustness and resilience of IFS.

Part Three: Regulatory Challenges

   **Chapter 5: The Dilemma of Tailor-Made versus Mainstream Regula-
   tion**   Islamic finance offers opportunities for expanding investments, raising growth performance, and reducing poverty. It does so
   by offering new financial services, an everyday event in the realm of
   finance, whose fate is ultimately decided by market developments.
   In this permanent evolution, market participants, regulators, and the
   broader institutional environment face continuous challenges. Market
   participants' challenges lie in their ability to identify opportunities for
   profit and to pursue them while complying with *Shari'a* and managing risks. The regulators' challenge resides in their ability to provide a
   systemic governance framework that promotes financial stability while
   not stifling market vibrancy. Finally, at the broader institutional level,
   the institutional infrastructure needs to enable the expansion of investments by incorporating features that mitigate investors' risks.

---

[4]This part draws on Grais and Rajhi (2009). The authors would like to thank
Wassim Rajhi for his valuable contribution.

Chapter 6: Toward an Enabling Framework This chapter focuses on the regulators' challenges to provide a regulatory framework that enables market vibrancy, *Shari'a* compliance, market stability, and a level playing field with conventional finance. It considers an approach to avoid the "niche industry" solution as well as one that would lead to tinkering with *Shari'a* principles. It considers the rationale for regulating Islamic finance, and highlights the inconsistency of Islamic finance with general banking rules. The chapter offers an approach that would allow Islamic finance to develop without being hamstrung by the need to fit within the prevailing banking regulatory framework.

Part Four: Corporate Governance[5]

Chapter 7: Financial Fiduciary Governance This chapter focuses on the corporate governance (CG) arrangements of institutions offering Islamic financial services (IIFSs) aimed at protecting stakeholders' financial interests. Many IIFS CG issues are common with those of their conventional counterparts, whereas others are distinctive. In particular, IIFSs offer unrestricted investment accounts that share risk features with common stocks held by shareholders but without a voting right. The chapter first reviews internal and external arrangements put in place by IIFSs to protect stakeholders' financial interests. It discusses shortcomings, notably in terms of potential conflict of interest between shareholders and holders of unrestricted investment accounts. It then suggests a CG framework that combines internal and external arrangements to provide safeguards to unrestricted investment account holders without overburdening an IIFS's financial performance. The chapter uses a review of 13 IIFSs and regulatory information from countries where IIFSs have developed the most.

Chapter 8: Corporate Governance and *Shari'a* Compliance The structures and processes established within an institution offering Islamic financial services (IIFS) for monitoring and evaluating *Shari'a* compliance rely essentially on arrangements internal to the firm. By being incorporated into the institutional structure, a *Shari'a* supervisory board (SSB) has the advantage of being close to the market. Competent, independent, and empowered to approve new *Shari'a*-conforming instruments, an SSB can enable innovation likely

---

[5] Chapters 7 and 8 draw on Grais and Pellegrini (2006). The authors would like to thank Matteo Pellegrini for his valuable contribution to these chapters.

to emerge within the institution. The chapter reviews the issues and options facing current arrangements for ensuring *Shari'a* compliance by IIFSs. It suggests a framework that draws on internal and external arrangements to the firm and emphasizes market discipline. In issuing its *fatwa*s, an SSB could be guided by standardized contracts and practices that could be harmonized by a self-regulatory professionals association. A framework with the suggested internal and external features could ensure adequate consistency of interpretation and enhance the enforceability of contracts before civil courts. The review of transactions would mainly be entrusted to internal review units, which would collaborate with external auditors responsible for issuing an annual opinion on whether the institution's activities met its *Shari'a* requirements. This process would be sustained by reputable entities such as rating agencies, stock markets, financial media, and researchers who would channel signals to market players. This framework would enhance public understanding of the requirements of *Shari'a* and lead to a more effective utilization of options available to stakeholders to achieve continuing improvements in Islamic financial services.

Chapter 9: Toward a Systemic *Shari'a* Governance Framework This chapter takes a step back to consider corporate governance for Islamic financial services at the level of a jurisdiction or systemically. It outlines issues that would bear on the development and implementation of a framework for effective IFS *Shari'a* governance. It proceeds by first providing reasons underlying the need for a sound systemic *Shari'a* governance framework (SSGF) for IFS. It then considers basic criteria that one may want an SSGF to have, and identifies agents with different perspectives that would be involved in an SSGF. Then, selected SSGF experiences are reviewed and their major features highlighted. An outline of an SSGF is suggested.

Appendix: Islamic Finance: The International Landscape Islamic finance is a significant part of the financial landscape of numerous countries. Iran, Gulf Cooperation Council (GCC) countries, Malaysia, and Sudan have been at the forefront of its development. This appendix provides an overview of the international landscape of Islamic finance.

Acknowledgments

This book has benefited from numerous inputs from friends and colleagues. The common thread of humanism and tolerance in all of them has been an inspiration and encouragement for which we are most grateful.

We would like to thank Dr. Zamir Iqbal for his unique input in introducing one of us to Islamic finance and guiding his initial steps into the field. Special thanks are also due to Professor Rifaat Abdel Karim, Dr. Mohamed Nedal Al Chaar, and Mr. Ijlal Ahmed Alvi, who so kindly shared with us insights and offered multiple leads that allowed us to better grasp the extent and depth of Islamic finance and its international reach. They provided many opportunities to interact with market and academic leaders in the field. These opportunities have helped us better appreciate the tremendous progress achieved by Islamic finance, as well as the challenges it faces. We would like also to thank Dr. Ahmed El-Gebali and Dr. Dahlia El-Hawary, who kindly shared their insights on numerous occasions and have been a great support at different times. We are most grateful to Dr. Abbas Mirakhor, Dr. Ali Abdel Aziz Soliman, Mr. Adnan A. Yousif, Dr. Khalid Al Saad, and Dr. Khaled Hussein, whose humanism and support have been an inspiring and encouraging light in pursuing the effort of putting together this book. Their review and comments on the draft manuscript and previous writings on the topic are most appreciated.

The book has greatly benefited from inputs from Dr. Hussain Madzlan and Mr. Matteo Pellegrini, who have been instrumental in shaping sections of the book on corporate governance. Similarly, Dr. Wassim Rajhi has also provided significant inputs in dealing with issues of risk, distress, and contagion. We are most grateful to them for their collaboration, insights, efforts, and contributions. We owe them a great debt; they deserve all our gratitude. We are grateful to Dr. Magda Shahin, who has gracefully supported the drafting of the chapter on the opportunity that Islamic finance offers for Egypt's development.

Our thanks go also to Dr. Ahmed Kamali, Dr. Michelle Riboud, and Ms. Maha El Tiby, whose support was instrumental in the final efforts of putting together the manuscript.

Acronyms

AAOIFI	Accounting and Auditing Organization for Islamic Financial Institutions
AfDB	African Development Bank
AMC	asset management corporation
BCBS	Basel Committee on Banking Supervision
BCFS	business offering conventional financial services
BCP	Basel Core Principles
BFR	base financing rate
BHD	Bahrain dinar
BI	Bank Indonesia
BIFS	business offering Islamic financial services
BIMB	Bank Islam Malaysia Berhad
BIS	Bank for International Settlements
BMMB	Bank Muamalat Malaysia Berhad
BNM	Bank Negara Malaysia
CAH	current account holder
CAR	capital adequacy ratio
CB	central bank
CBB	Central Bank of Bahrain
CD	certificate of deposit
CFS	conventional financial services
CG	corporate governance
CGR	corporate governance rules
CIBAFI	General Council of Islamic Banks and Financial Institutions
CIPA	certified Islamic public accountant
DEJ	developing and emerging jurisdiction
DIFC	Dubai International Financial Center
DJ	developed jurisdiction
DJIM	Dow Jones Islamic Market
EGP	Egyptian pound
EMDB	Emerging Markets Data Base
FAS	Financial Accounting Standards
FDIC	Federal Deposit Insurance Corporation
FHLMC	Federal Home Loan Mortgage Corporation (Freddie Mac)

FSA	Financial Services Authority
FTSE	Financial Times Stock Exchange
GAMC	government asset management corporation
GCC	Gulf Cooperation Council
HSBC	Hong Kong–Shanghai Bank Corporation
IAH	investment account holder
IBRA	Indonesian Bank Restructuring Agency
ICFS	institution offering conventional financial services
IFC	International Finance Corporation
IFH	Ihlas Finance House
IFIS	Islamic Finance Information Service
IFRS	International Financial Reporting Standards
IFS	Islamic financial services
IFSB	Islamic Financial Services Board
IIFM	International Islamic Financial Market
IIFS	institution offering Islamic financial services
IIMM	Islamic Interbank Money Market
IIRA	Islamic International Rating Agency
IOSCO	International Organization of Securities Commissions
IRTI	Islamic Research and Training Institute
IsDB	Islamic Development Bank
KFH	Kuwait Finance House
LIBOR	London Interbank Offered Rate
LMC	Liquidity Management Center
LOLR	lender of last resort
LUTH	Lembaga Urusan Tabung Haji
MARC	Malaysia Rating Corporation
MENA	Middle East and North Africa
MII	Mudaraba Inter-Bank Investment
MOU	memorandum of understanding
MSCI	Morgan Stanley Capital International Index
NPA	nonperforming asset
NPL	nonperforming loan
OECD	Organization for Economic Cooperation and Development
OIC	Organization of Islamic Countries
PLS	profit and loss sharing
PQBC	Publicly Quoted Corporation Bank
PSIA	profit-sharing investment account
PSR	profit-sharing ratio
QIA	Qatar Investment Authority
RIA	restricted investment account

ROW	rest of the world
SAC	*Shari'a* Advisory Council
SAMA	Saudi Arabia Monetary Authority
SBP	State Bank of Pakistan
SCI	*Shari'a* Compliance Inspection
SEC	Securities and Exchange Commission
SFH	special finance house
SMEs	small and medium enterprises
SOCPA	Saudi Organization for Certified Public Accountants
SRO	self-regulating organization
SSB	*Shari'a* supervisory board
SSGF	systemic *Shari'a* governance framework
SWF	sovereign wealth fund
TBRSA	Turkish Banking Regulation and Supervision Agency
UAE	United Arab Emirates
UIA	unrestricted investment account
USD	U.S. dollar

About the Authors

Amr El Tiby earned his BA in commerce from Cairo University in 1980, majoring in business. He earned his diploma in finance from Cairo University in 1985 and his MA in economics from the American University in Cairo in 2003. In 2009 he earned his PhD from the American University in London. Dr. El Tiby has more than 30 years of banking experience in the Middle East and the Gulf region in both conventional as well as Islamic finance. His area of research focuses on banking risk and regulations, and he is published in leading journals such as that of the Global Association of Risk Professionals (GARP). He is also the author of *Islamic Banking* (John Wiley & Sons, 2011).

Wafik Grais is a senior adviser on Islamic finance, finance and private equity management, SMEs, and corporate governance. He was cofounder and chairman of Viveris Mashrek, a Cairo-based financial advisory services company specializing in private equity investments in SMEs, licensed by Egypt's Financial Services Authority. He also spent 28 years in international finance, notably with the World Bank in Washington, DC, where he held several senior positions both in operations and at corporate levels.

He was a member of the Islamic Financial Services Board (IFSB) working groups on the corporate governance of Islamic financial institutions and investment funds. He wrote on Islamic finance in the areas of SME financing, regulation, corporate governance, and microfinance. He received an award from the Accounting and Auditing Organization for Islamic Financial Institutions (AAOIFI) for his contribution to Islamic finance.

At the World Bank, he managed country and sector programs, lending, fund-raising, and policy regarding the Middle East and North Africa (MENA), Europe and Central Asia, and East Asia. He was senior adviser in the Financial Sector group, head of the Financial Sector Assessment Program (FSAP), lead resource on Islamic financial services, and director of the private-sector development and finance group for MENA; he was division chief of country operations for Ukraine, Belarus, Moldova, Georgia, and Armenia after holding the same position for the Maghreb countries. Earlier, he managed the International Bank for Reconstruction and Development (IBRD) economic policy, dialogue, and lending activities with the former

Yugoslavia. In 1997 and 1998, he was a team member in setting up the Bank for Cooperation and Development in the Middle East and North Africa in Cairo, representing the government of Egypt.

Dr. Grais holds a PhD in economics and BSc degrees in economics and political science from the University of Geneva, Switzerland. He is fluent in English, French, and Arabic.

One

Emergence of Modern Islamic Finance

Financial services are core to economic activity. Individuals and institutions need to place excess liquidity and access financial resources for investments or consumption. Also, they need financial services to settle their transactions. The financial intermediation industry has developed over time, responding to these economic needs but also to prevailing societal values. Most regulation governing finance has developed to provide public trust in an industry based essentially on information and confidence. Trust and confidence are essential values that allow societies to remain cohesive and to develop.

Thus, by its very nature, successful financial intermediation corresponds to the values of the societies where it operates. Values evolve and over time codes of conduct of business evolve with them. For example, conventional finance has gradually come to integrate environmental, social, and governance considerations in its business conduct, reflecting modern societies' evolving values.[1]

Islamic finance has emerged in modern times to provide correspondence between the conduct of financial intermediation and the values of communities wanting to abide by Islamic *Shari'a* principles. Postcolonial identity assertion and natural resource–based financial surpluses in the 1970s

---

[1]International Finance Corporation, "IFC Performance Standards on Environmental and Social Sustainability," January 2012 at www.ifc.org/wps/wcm/connect/c8f524004a 73daeca09afdf998895a12/IFC_Performance_Standards.pdf?MOD=AJPERES.

combined with the need for value correspondence to create enabling conditions for the development of *Shari'a*-compliant financial services. Chapter 1 provides a historical overview of the industry's development and highlights its core principles.

During the same period it has also become increasingly clear that financial development and economic development are significantly correlated. Financial deepening seemed to contribute to raising rates of economic growth. Moreover, financial inclusion allowing large and poor segments of a society to access financial services appeared to foster socioeconomic development.

In this context, it seems legitimate to assume that Islamic finance could be a contributor to development, as it could provide financial services to many who would otherwise refrain from dealing with conventional finance. Chapter 2 takes an initial look at the issue with a focus on the potential impact of Islamic finance on Egypt's economic development.[2]

---

[2]The issue of the potential contribution of Islamic finance to economic growth, financial inclusion, and development deserves analytical investigation.

CHAPTER 1

History and Core Principles of Islamic Finance

An often-raised question is: What actually is Islamic finance and in what way does it differ from conventional finance? Islamic financial services pledge to conduct financial intermediation in accord with a code of behavior based on Islamic values. The code's principles are enshrined in the contracts and product offerings. It happens to use the word *Islamic* to characterize its observance of the code. Possibly for that reason, in the current international context, it gathers champions and advocates, attracting many who see in it merely a business opportunity; it raises open (sometimes vehement) as well as silent opposition; and it often leaves many puzzled about its nature and value added. This leads to unnecessary mystification and often poorly based judgments. Better knowledge of its history, principles that the sector pledges to observe, the industry's compliance with market demand for transparency and truth in advertisement, and finally market developments can promote balanced views and effective dialogue. It can help assess the potential contribution of the sector to development, in a professional way.

HISTORY REVIEW

An important milestone in the development of modern Islamic finance is the establishment of Mit Ghamr local savings bank in Egypt in 1963. Although the bank provided only basic banking services, these met the requirements of the local community it served at that time. This important experience sent a clear signal in Egypt and beyond that *Shari'a*-compliant finance was feasible and relevant, notably to communities seeking alternatives to conventional finance.

Starting in the late 1970s in the wake of the sharp increase in oil prices and the considerable wealth that it channeled to the Middle East and Malaysia, Islamic banks started to spread across Muslim and non-Muslim countries.

More than 100 Islamic banks were opened and operating across the world. The Islamic Development Bank (IsDB) was established in 1975 by Saudi Arabia and other Organization of Islamic Conference (OIC) member countries.

Dubai Islamic Bank was established in 1975; Faisal Islamic Bank, Egypt, was established in 1977; and Bahrain Islamic Bank was established in 1979.

An important development in the 1980s was the transformation of the whole financial system of Iran, Sudan, and in principle Pakistan to accord with Islamic precepts.

Another important development in the 1980s was the establishment of two groups of companies: Dar al-maal al-Islam in 1981 and the Al-Baraka group in 1982. Dar al-maal al-Islam was founded in the Bahamas; it is headquartered in Geneva and operates ten Islamic banks, seven Islamic investment companies, seven trading companies, and three *takaful* (Islamic insurance) companies in 15 countries around the world. The Al-Baraka group was established in Saudi Arabia in 1982 and currently has activities in more than 43 countries. It has over 2,000 companies, including 15 Islamic banks and several Islamic insurance companies.[1] Moreover, perceiving the business opportunity, conventional banks started offering *Shari'a*-compliant products to customers through dedicated channels known as Islamic windows. From 1963 to the present, Islamic finance has gone through different stages, evolving from infant industry to maturity.

However, as in many human endeavors, the industry's development was led by champions who believed in the business model and had the vision of its practicality. Thus, the international development of Islamic finance was spearheaded by country authorities and financial entrepreneurs in Malaysia and the Gulf Cooperation Council (GCC) region.[2]

The authorities in Malaysia adopted a proactive policy to develop Islamic finance, notably in response to the country's Muslim community's aspirations. First, the Lembaga Urusan Tabung Haji (LUTH) was established in 1969 as a *Shari'a*-compliant savings institution to support people going on pilgrimage to Mecca. The first Islamic bank, Bank Islam Malaysia Berhad (BIMB), was established later, in 1983, licensed and regulated by Bank Negara Malaysia (BNM), the country's central bank. Bank Muamalat Malaysia Berhad (BMMB) came later in 1999. Malaysian authorities, in

---

[1] Saidat A. Otiti, "Evolution of Islamic Banking & Finance," Muslim Public Affairs Center, 2nd series, August 2011, at www.mpac-ng.org/archived-article/636-evolution-of-islamic-banking-a-finance.pdf.

[2] It is relevant to note that according to some estimates, the world Muslim population is expected to reach 2.2 billion by 2030, an increase of 16 percent over the 1.9 billion of 2010. Currently, the Muslim world population may account for 7.7 percent of global GDP today.

particular BNM's proactive policy, led to the development of policies and regulations that enable a steady and sound development of the industry.

In the GCC, a 1975 decree authorized the establishment of the Dubai Islamic Bank. Kuwait allowed the creation of the Kuwait Finance House (KFH) in 1977. In Bahrain and Qatar, Islamic banks were created in 1979 and 1982, respectively.[3] Of course, Saudi Arabia had Islamic finance but refrains from labeling financial activities as "Islamic"; the Saudi El Rajhi bank is the GCC's largest Islamic bank.

While Egypt was a pioneer, a disorderly early development of Islamic investment companies under weak regulation and supervision led to the development and later collapse of finance houses, most notably the El Rayan Company. It was mobilizing depositors' resources by offering highly attractive returns and claiming to be *Shari'a* compliant. In fact it instead set up a Ponzi scheme that collapsed in the late 1980s, ruining many small depositors.[4] This episode stained the reputation of Islamic finance in Egypt and beyond, led authorities to remain skeptical on the potential benefits of Islamic finance, and delayed its resurgence in the country. Cautiously, authorities permitted the existence of the first Islamic financial provider, an Islamic window set up by Bank Misr, and the establishment of the first full-fledged Islamic bank, Faisal Islamic Bank, in 1979. However, Egyptian authorities remained circumspect vis-à-vis Islamic finance for a very long time.

Various factors have contributed to the renaissance of Islamic finance. Imam and Kpodar (2010) find that the diffusion of Islamic finance is positively related to the relative size of the Muslim population in a country, income per capita, hydrocarbon exports, political stability, and trade relations with the Middle East. They also find a negative relationship between Islamic finance and interest rates.[5] Essentially, their results point out the *role of champions and resource availability* in fostering the development of

---

[3] Wilson (2009).

[4] See the Securities and Exchange Commission on Ponzi schemes: www.sec.gov/answers/ponzi.htm. A TV series on the El Rayan episode was aired on Egyptian TV during the month of Ramadan of 2012. See the *Egyptian Gazette*, July 5, 2012, http://213.158.162.45/~egyptian/index.php?action=news&id=20552&title=El-Rayan%20drama%20makes%20waves.

[5] Imam and Kpodar (2010) focus on the diffusion of Islamic banking. They find that "the probability for Islamic banking to develop in a given country rises with the share of the Muslim population, income per capita, and whether the country is a net exporter of oil. Trading with the Middle East and economic stability also are conducive to diffusion of Islamic banking. Proximity to Malaysia and Bahrain, the two Islamic financial centers, also matters. We found that rising interest rates hinder the diffusion of Islamic banking because they raise the opportunity cost for less devout individuals or non-Muslims to put their money with an Islamic bank."

Islamic finance. There is no doubt that the presence of champions has been instrumental in the renaissance of Islamic finance.[6] They have been prominent market participants like Dr. Ibrahim El Naggar in Egypt, or Mr. Salah Kamel and Prince Faisal in Saudi Arabia, founders of El Baraka and Faisal groups, respectively. Champions have also been country authorities such as Malaysia's and Bahrain's central bank governors, most notably Dr. Zeti Akhtar Aziz and Mr. Rasheed Mohammed Al Maraj, respectively, or the founders of the Islamic Development Bank (IsDB), in particular Saudi Arabia. One also has to acknowledge the role played by leaders of organizations such as the Accounting and Auditing Organization for Islamic Financial Institutions (AAOIFI), Islamic Financial Services Board (IFSB), and International Islamic Financial Markets (IIFM).[7] They endeavored to lay the ground rules for the industry and to harmonize them across countries. Champions' efforts were facilitated by resource availability or hindered by the lack thereof. The international wealth redistribution that occurred in the wake of increases in hydrocarbon prices in the early 1970s, early 1980s, and later after a lull, enabled champions (notably in the GCC region) to develop Islamic financial services. The presence of hydrocarbon resources was also a factor in Malaysia but to a lesser extent. Clearly, resource availability was less a factor in the initial renaissance of Islamic finance in Egypt, but later played a role due to the country's close geographical and cultural connection with the GCC countries.

The role of interest rates is pointed out by Imam and Kpodar (2010) as a factor influencing the industry's development. The point confirms the financial intermediation nature of Islamic finance, implying that agents do consider relative returns offered by Islamic and conventional financial services. Also, it is worth noting that periods of financial crisis and occurrences of distress in Islamic financial institutions slow down the industry's expansion. For example, the international financial crisis over 2007 and 2008 slowed down the issuances of *sukuk*s as well as the engagement of large international banks in Islamic finance.[8] Similarly episodes of collapse

---

[6]Champions mentioned here are provided as examples. These references do not diminish in any way the extraordinary role played by other champions whether at the individual level or the institutional level in national and international contexts.
[7]Other organizations were also established.
[8]The slowdown of issuance of *sukuk*s resulted also from a revisiting of the *Shari'a* compliance of previously issued *sukuk*s by AAOIFI's *Shari'a* board. Islamic banks seem to have better weathered the adverse impact on profitability of the international financial crisis in 2008. Their credit and asset growth performed better than did that of conventional banks over 2008–2009. External rating agencies assessed Islamic banks generally more favorably. See Hasan and Dridi (2010).

of Islamic financial institutions have hurt confidence in the industry and sometimes slowed its development temporarily.[9]

In summary, the development of Islamic finance can be divided into four periods:

- *The establishment period from 1963 to 1976.* The period saw the development of analytical work, international cooperation, and banking activity. Major research across the Muslim world focused on fields that concern Muslims' daily lives. Also, organizations were set up with the objective of establishing and developing cultural and religious relationships across Muslim countries.
- *The spread period from 1977 to 2002.* This period was fueled by the sharp increase in oil prices and wealth accumulation in the Middle East. It witnessed the establishment of more than 100 Islamic banks across the world, such as Dar al-maal al-Islam in 1981 and the Al-Baraka group in 1982.
- *The international recognition period from 2003 to 2009.* This period witnessed a global acceptance of the development and significance of Islamic finance by regulators across the world, including notably in China, Europe, and the United States. Also, international banks with worldwide presence showed growing interest in Islamic finance and many of them engaged in Islamic finance operations, including through Islamic windows. This is the case with banks such as Citibank (U.S.), ANZ (Australia), ABN Amro (Netherlands), Goldman Sachs (U.S.), HSBC (UK), Deutsche Bank (Germany), Société Générale (France), Saudi-American Bank (U.S.–Saudi Arabia), and Saudi-British Bank (UK–Saudi Arabia). There are to date more than 200 Islamic financial institutions in over 70 countries around the world.[10]
- *The evaluation period from 2009 to the present.* During this period, the growth momentum of Islamic financial assets that was maintained during the global financial crisis (compared to conventional financial assets) conveyed to many, including regulators, policy makers, bankers, and economists, that the asset-backed nature of Islamic finance can contribute to the stability of financial markets.

---

[9] As the collapse notably of the Ryan finance house in Egypt demonstrates, whatever were its reasons. See also, for example, Starr and Yilmaz (2007) for a Turkey 2001 distress episode. The issue is the importance of the reputation risk for the finance industry.

[10] Saidat A. Otiti, "Evolution of Islamic Banking & Finance," August 2001, http://www.mpac-ng.org/archived-article/636-evolution-of-islamic-banking-a-finance.pdf.

CORE PRINCIPLES

The primary sources of *Shari'a* are the Quran and the Sunna.[11] *Shari'a* is the body of jurisprudence accumulated over time based on interpretations of the Quran and the Sunna. These interpretations and rulings are the outcome of methods of reasoning and rules of interpretation known as *fiqh*. Accordingly, engaging in Islamic finance entails conducting business in accordance with the *Shari'a* body of Islamic jurisprudence as derived from the Quran and the Sunna using *fiqh*.

As applied to finance, *Shari'a* prohibits the charging or paying of interest (*riba*), excessive uncertainty in contracts (*gharar*), gambling and chance-based games (*qimar*), and investment in certain forbidden (*haram*) industries. This means inter alia: (1) an acquisition target industry is ethically screened, (2) debt-to-equity and income ratios are within specified *Shari'a*-accepted boundaries, and (3) *Shari'a*-compliant financing is used for the acquisition and funding of only permissible activities—that is, any activities that are not prohibited by Islamic law.

To be *Shari'a* compliant, financial transactions need be governed by shared business risks and returns and must deal with religiously acceptable services, trade, or products, with clear and transparent rights and obligations of parties to the contract. Islamic finance is limited to financial relationships involving real economy entrepreneurial activity. In particular, conventional securitization needs to feature sufficient investor ownership that incorporates an entrepreneurial stake in real economic activity within an interest-free structural arrangement. A core economic feature of Islamic finance is to have the rate of return of real economic activity drive the allocation of financial resources.

In practice, principles guiding the conduct of Islamic financial business are characterized by the following features:

- *Prohibition against the payment and receipt of a fixed or predetermined rate of interest.* This is replaced by profit and loss sharing (PLS) arrangements where the rate of return on financial assets held in banks is not known and not fixed prior to the undertaking of the transaction. The actual rate of return can be determined on the basis of actual profits accrued from real-sector activities that are made possible through the productive use of financial assets.
- *Requirement to operate through Islamic modes of financing.* These modes affect both the assets and liabilities sides of a bank's balance

---

[11] Sunna is the way of life prescribed as normative for Muslims on the basis of Prophet Mohamed's teachings and practices and the interpretations of the Quran.

sheet and can be divided into two groups: those that are based on the PLS principle (core modes) and those that are not (marginal modes).

- *Investment deposits.* Such deposits are not guaranteed in capital value and do not yield any fixed or guaranteed rate of return. In the event banks record losses as a result of bad investment decisions, depositors may lose part or all of their investment deposits. The only contractual agreement between depositors and banks is the proportion (ratio) according to which profits or losses are to be distributed.
- *Demand deposits.* Such deposits are guaranteed in capital value, although no returns are paid on them. The reason to justify the capital value guarantee is the assumption that demand deposits have been placed as *amana* (for safekeeping). Hence, they belong at any time to depositors.
- *Risk sharing.* The terms of financial transactions need to reflect a symmetrical risk/return distribution that each party to the transaction may face.
- *Materiality.* A financial transaction needs to have a "material finality" that is directly or indirectly linked to a real economic transaction.

Islamic finance has developed on the basis of the foregoing principles. They have led Islamic banks to adopt the type of balance sheet stylized in Appendix 1A. The *risk sharing* is enshrined in the use of the *mudaraba* contract, which is a contract between an owner of financial resources (*rab-ul-mal*) and someone who takes charge of managing them (*mudarib*) on behalf of the owner for a fee and a share of profit. This type of contract is extensively used in deposit taking where the bank is the manager of the resources and the depositor is the owner. It can also be used in extending financing by the bank to an economic agent or entrepreneur with the bank, this time taking the role of owner and the entrepreneur that of resource manager. Under that type of contract the bank, the owner of the funds, does not intervene in the management of the funded project. In a *mudaraba* contract, the bank is entitled to receive from the entrepreneur the principal of the sum it "invested" at the end of the period stipulated in the contract if, and only if, profits have accrued. If, on the contrary, the enterprise's books show a loss, the bank would not be able to recover its investment. For understandable risk management reasons, *mudaraba* is not a preferred contract for funding risk-bearing assets for an institution offering Islamic financial services (IIFS).

Musharaka contracts provide a better opportunity than *mudaraba* to monitor and control projects funded by the Islamic bank. Indeed, in a *musharaka*, the bank becomes an active shareholder of the project and all partners may concur in the management of the enterprise and hold direct voting rights. *Musharaka* contracts are not extensively used by Islamic banks because of their generally longer maturity and the weak institutional infrastructure found in many jurisdictions where Islamic finance is present; this similarly limits the development of conventional equity financing.

The *materiality* principle leads to the financing by the bank of a real economic transaction for the account of the economic agent needing the financing. Materiality is intrinsic to the *ijara* or leasing contracts as well as to the *murabaha*. The latter is essentially trade financing where the financier purchases the needed commodity for the account of the financed, which takes spot delivery and pays back the financier with a markup at a later date.

The *prohibition of riba* excludes the payment of interest to the *amana* depositor, basically a demand depositor who needs the guarantee of principal and forgoes remuneration for that. The *mudaraba* depositor, on the contrary, may enjoy the opportunity of a return but also may face the risk of a loss.[12] *Amana* deposit face values are guaranteed, and they are redeemable on demand.

The no exploitation principle also includes the idea of no excessive risk taking, or no risk taking in the nature of gambling. It also covers issues of asymmetric information, as benefiting from nonshared information entails an unfair contract and consequently exploitation. The prohibition against financing of harmful activities is self-explanatory.

In principle, the combination of risk sharing and prohibition of *riba* entails profit and loss sharing arrangements and a balance sheet structure as in Appendix 1A.[13] It should limit the impact of external shocks on Islamic banks' balance sheets. Indeed, an Islamic bank's balance sheet incorporates an intrinsic hedge in principle, as a loss of asset value would translate into a change of value of the pool of resources that funded it, generally mostly investment accounts. Islamic banks pool depositors' funds in providing them with professional investment management with associated returns and risks. Neither the face value of investment deposits nor their return is guaranteed. Investment depositors share in the bank's net profit (or loss) according to the profit and loss sharing (PLS) ratio stipulated in their contracts. From the perspective of investment account holders (IAHs), Islamic banks behave like mutual funds with a variable net asset value.

---

[12] The prohibition of payment and receipt of a fixed or predetermined rate of interest is replaced by profit and loss sharing (PLS) arrangements where the rate of return on financial assets held in banks is not known and not fixed prior to the undertaking of the transaction. The actual rate of return can be determined on the basis of actual profits accrued from real-sector activities that are made possible through the productive use of financial assets.

[13] See Usmani (2002) for the different modes of financing.

Fiduciary responsibility, regulatory and supervisory requirements, and risk management have led to a dominance of *murabaha* and *ijara* modes of financing in Islamic banks' balance sheets (see Figure 1.1). One could have expected *mudaraba* and *musharaka* to take a larger place because of their risk sharing features, core to Islamic finance. Mitigation of these risk sharing features requires evolved contractual, legal, and conflict resolution arrangements. However, though progress has been achieved, these arrangements are often weak in many countries and accordingly the development of equity markets and *mudaraba* and *musharaka* transactions has been slow.

In Islamic banks there are two major types of fund providers: (1) current account holders and (2) unrestricted IAHs and restricted IAHs. Islamic banks offer separate investment accounts and current accounts, the first drawable at maturity and the second drawable on demand. Current accounts are based on *qard* contracts. The investment accounts use *mudaraba* or *wakala* contracts whereby fund providers are passive partners. These account holders require a degree of liquidity to be maintained by the IIFS to meet their requirements for withdrawals. The default risk of not paying a return to depositors is eliminated under the Islamic banking model. Nevertheless, the failure to reward depositors could lead to a substantial withdrawal of deposits and the risk of bankruptcy. As current account holders do not participate in the profits of the IIFS's business activities, a sound repayment

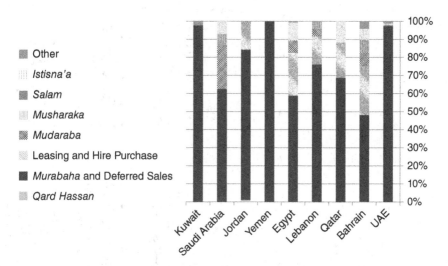

FIGURE 1.1 Murabaha and Ijara: Dominant Modes of Financing, 2008
Source: Salman Syed Ali, "Islamic Banking in the Mena Region," Islamic Development Bank, Islamic Research and Training Institute, World Bank, 2011, Figure 5.

capacity is required to meet fully cash withdrawal requests when they arise. IIFSs may rely heavily on funds provided by current account holders. Repayment by the IIFS of the principal amounts deposited by current account holders is guaranteed without any rights to share in profits, as the current account holders do not share in the risks of the IIFS. Unrestricted IAHs are investors who participate in the uncertainties of an IIFS's business; therefore, they share in profits and bear losses arising from investments made on their behalf, to the extent of their share. Apart from general withdrawal needs, the withdrawals made by IAHs may be the result of (1) lower than expected or acceptable rates of return and/or (2) noncompliance by the IIFS with *Shari'a* rules and principles in various contracts and activities. Table 1.1 shows a comparison of Islamic and conventional banking frameworks.

TABLE 1.1   Characteristics of Islamic and Conventional Banking

Characteristic	Islamic Banking	Conventional Banking
Nominal value guarantee of:		
Demand deposits	Yes	Yes
Investment deposits	No	Yes
Equity-based system where capital is at risk	Yes	No
Rate of return on deposits	Uncertain, not guaranteed	Certain and guaranteed
Mechanism to regulate final returns on deposits	Depending on banks' performance/profits from investment	Irrespective of banks' performance/profits from investment
PLS principle is applied	Yes	No
Use of Islamic modes of financing:		
PLS and non-PLS modes	Yes	No
Use of discretion by banks with regard to collateral	Possible for reducing moral hazard in PLS modes Yes in non-PLS modes	Yes always
Banks' pooling of depositors' funds to provide depositors with professional investment management.	Yes	No

Source: L. Errico and M. Farahbaksh, "Islamic Banking: Issues in Prudential Regulation and Supervision," IMF Working Paper WP/98/30 (Washington, DC: International Monetary Fund, 1998).

APPENDIX 1A: STYLIZED BALANCE SHEET OF AN ISLAMIC BANK

TABLE 1A.1 Theoretical Balance Sheet of an Islamic Bank Based on Maturity Profile

Assets	Liabilities
Short-term trade finance (cash, *murabaha*, *salam*)	Demand deposits (*amana*)
Medium-term investments (*ijara, istisna'a*)	Investment accounts (*mudaraba*)
Long-term partnerships (*musharaka*)	Special investment accounts (*mudaraba, musharaka*)
Fee-based services (e.g., *kifala*)	Reserves
Nonbanking assets (property)	Equity capital

TABLE 1A.2 Theoretical Balance Sheet of an Islamic Bank Based on Functionality

Assets	Liabilities
Cash balances	Demand deposits (*amana*)
Financing assets (*murabaha, salam, ijara, istisna'a*)	Investment accounts (*mudaraba*)
Investment assets (*mudaraba, musharaka*)	Special investment accounts (*mudaraba, musharaka*)
Fee-based services (e.g., *kifala*)	Reserves
Nonbanking assets (property)	Equity capital

Source: Iqbal and Van Greuning (2008).

APPENDIX 1B: GLOSSARY OF SELECTED ISLAMIC FINANCE TERMS

Term	Quick Definition	Full Definition
Amana	Trustworthiness, faithfulness, and honesty	*Amana* is also used to define a situation in which one party is keeping another person's property in trust. This is the way in which the term is most commonly applied, especially within the confines of Islamic commercial law. The term is also applied when referring to goods on consignment, in custody, or on deposit.

(continued)

APPENDIX 1B (*Continued*)

Term	Quick Definition	Full Definition
Arbun	Down payment	*Arbun* describes the deposit that the buyer makes to the seller at the same time as making the agreement to complete payment by a set date.
Gharar	Uncertainty	*Gharar* refers to something that is not completely set in stone within a contract. It is a fundamental disagreement between Islamic and conventional U.S./UK law, and Islam does not recognize the need for related practices such as speculation, derivatives, and short-selling contracts.
Islamic finance	Financial services specifically designed to adhere to Islamic law or *Shari'a*	Although these financial services are designed for Muslims, they are not exclusively available to Muslims. Non-Muslims can also provide and buy the services.
Ijara	Islamic leasing agreement	An *ijara* enables the financier to seek profit through the leasing of assets (house, car, etc.) rather than by actually lending money. *Ijara wa iqtina* is an extension of the concept and is a hire purchase agreement.
Maysir	Gambling	*Maysir* is forbidden in Islam and therefore the concept fundamentally disagrees with standard financial practices such as speculation, insurance, and derivative contracts.
Mudaraba	Investment partnership	This is the financial partnership between the investor (*rab-ul-mal*) and another party (*mudarib*). The contract will set out how profits will be shared, and losses are absorbed by the *rab-ul-mal*. The *mudarib* forgoes some of the expected income in case of losses.
Mudarib	Investment manager or entrepreneur partaking in a *mudaraba*	It is the *mudarib*'s responsibility to ensure that the investor's money is taken care of and is profitable in its investments. In turn, the *mudarib* gets a share of the profits. The role is very similar to a mutual fund manager or a private equity general partner.

Term	Quick Definition	Full Definition
Murabaha	Purchase and resale	The capital provider purchases the required asset or product (for which a loan would otherwise have been taken out) from a third party. The asset is then resold at a higher price to the capital user. By paying this higher price in installments, the capital user effectively gets credit without paying interest. (Also see *tawaruq*, the opposite of *murabaha*.)
Musharaka	Profit and loss sharing	This is considered the purest form of Islamic financing, because profits and losses are shared in proportion to the investment made by each investor. Each partner within the *musharaka* contributes capital and can make executive decisions; however, they are under no obligation to do so. It is basically a partnership that involves owning voting stock in a limited company.
Riba	Interest	*Riba* is forbidden by the Quran, which forbids any return of money on money, whatever type of interest it may be.
Shari'a	Islamic law	*Shari'a* refers to the law set down in the Quran and performed by example by Prophet Mohamed (PBUH). Any product purporting to be *Shari'a* must adhere to Islamic law in all respects, and to ensure this, a company will usually appoint a *Shari'a* board that will oversee the development and implementation of all *Shari'a* products to ensure they comply.
Shari'a adviser	Person who advises on Islamic financial law	A *Shari'a* adviser is generally an Islamic legal scholar who has been classically trained and has the expertise and knowledge to ensure that products comply with *Shari'a*. Some work individually to advise companies, but most are employed as part of a *Shari'a* board to ensure full compliance.
Shari'a compliant	Observing Islamic law	The *Shari'a* board ensures that products comply with *Shari'a*. Many financial products use the term *Shari'a compliant* to signal that the product has followed the law to the letter.

(*continued*)

APPENDIX 1B (*Continued*)

Term	Quick Definition	Full Definition
Sukuk	A bond	In conventional terms *sukuk*s and bonds are not quite the same, as a bond is asset backed and the term *sukuk* describes the proportionate beneficial ownership in the asset itself.
Takaful	Islamic insurance	Because the concept of insurance relates to uncertainty, which could then be related to interest and gambling, *takaful* takes a different approach. The arrangement can be summed up as a charitable collection of funds based on the idea of mutual assistance.
Tawaruq	The Islamic way of obtaining cash	This is a liquidity instrument to mobilize cash. It involves buying something on deferred credit and selling the item on to get cash. As a result, cash has been obtained without taking out a loan and paying interest.

Source: Adapted from Canadian Money Advisor at www.canadian-money-advisor .ca/archives/2006/05/islamic+finance+terms+glossary.html.

APPENDIX 1C: GLOSSARY OF ARABIC FINANCE TERMS

Term	Definition
Fatwa	Legal opinion issued by a qualified scholar on matters of religious belief and practice.
Fiqh (Islamic jurisprudence)	It refers to Islamic jurisprudence that covers all aspects of life: religious, political, social, and economic. *Fiqh* is mainly based on interpretations of the Quran and Sunna (sayings and deeds of the Prophet).
Fiqh al-Muamalat	Islamic commercial jurisprudence.
Halal	That which is permissible according to *Shari'a* law.
Haram	Unlawful according to the *Shari'a*. It indicates transactions that are not permissible under Islamic law.
Hibah	Literally, gift. A gift awarded voluntarily in return for a loan.
Ju'ala (service charge)	A party pays another a specified amount of money as a fee for rendering a specific service in accordance to the terms of the contract stipulated between the two parties. This mode usually applies to transactions such as consultations and professional services, fund placements, and trust services.

Term	Definition
Kifala	It is a pledge given to a creditor that the debtor will pay the debt, fine, or liability. A third party becomes surety for the payment of the debt if unpaid by the person originally liable.
Qard hassan (beneficence loan)	A zero-return loan that the Quran encourages Muslims to make to the needy. Banks are allowed to charge borrowers a service fee to cover the administrative expenses of handling the loan. The fee should not be related to the loan amount or maturity.
Quran	Islamic scriptures believed by Muslims to be God's revelation to the Prophet.
Sunna	Deeds of the Prophet.
Umma	Community of the faithful within Islam.
Wadiah	A safe custody contract between the depositor (customer) and the custodian (bank).
Wikala	An agency contract that may include in its terms a fee for the agent. The same contract can also be used to give a power of attorney to someone to represent another's interests.
Zakat	Religious tax to be deducted from wealth to be paid to the needy.

Source: Adapted from El-Hawary, Grais, and Iqbal (2004) and the glossary of the International Islamic Financial Market (IIFM) website (www.iifm.net).

CHAPTER 2

Islamic Finance: Opportunity for Egypt's Development

Islamic finance's renaissance did not escape international finance leaders' notice. Promptly, they understood its financial intermediation nature and the opportunities it offered for financial deepening, diversification, and inclusion. For instance, in a 1995 speech, Lord Edward George, then governor of the Bank of England, recognized the "growing importance of Islamic banking in the Muslim world and its emergence on the international stage," as well as the need to put Islamic banking in the context of London's tradition of "competitive innovation."[1] Other European countries have also identified the potential role of Islamic finance in their economies and made room in various ways for its introduction.[2]

In the United States, the country of entrepreneurship, financial entrepreneurs introduced Islamic financial products at both the retail and wholesale levels. They have succeeded in providing access to a pool of financial resources for business ventures, and have offered profitable and secure *Shari'a*-compliant placements to investors. They have also allowed many to have access to retail financial services such as mortgages, contributing to inclusion and welfare. U.S. regulators have focused on the challenges of integrating Islamic finance in the mainstream of the country's financial system. Their focus on the economic substance of transactions rather than the formality of product structures facilitated market expansion notably of retail products. U.S. financial markets do mobilize Islamic financial flows and have often led the structuring of Islamic finance products.

---

[1] September 1995, at a conference organized by the Islamic Foundation.

[2] For example, the German state of Saxony-Anhalt issued a €100 million *ijara*-based *sukuk* in July 2004, the first issued by a non-Islamic sovereign. The *sukuk* had a tenor of five years with the rate of return linked to the six-month Euribor and paid a margin of 100 basis points over the benchmark. It matured in July 2009. See IIFM (2010).

The Egyptian financial system was an early mover in modern Islamic finance. The country offers ample investment opportunities that can attract Islamic financial placements and improve the country's development prospects. Islamic finance can grow rapidly beyond its current size of less than 5 percent of the country's financial assets. Islamic financial intermediation can contribute to deepening Egypt's financial system, increase the diversification of the services it offers, and improve financial inclusiveness.[3] It can offer opportunities for financing development whether at the state, corporate, small and medium enterprise, or consumer levels. At the same time, Egypt's developmental needs and the population's values offer promising prospects for Islamic finance. However, the introduction and development of Islamic finance raise challenges to market participants, policy makers, regulators, and supervisors, as well as domestic and international standard setters. These challenges need to be addressed. Dealing with them in a professional and systematic manner is the best way to ensure that Islamic financial services are successful and deliver on the opportunity the industry provides for the country's development.

This chapter presents an overview of the broad landscape of Islamic financial intermediation and its development in Egypt. It deals with the opportunities Islamic finance offers to Egypt's development and highlights the regulatory challenges it raises.

MARKET LANDSCAPE: SIGNIFICANT BROAD-BASED PRESENCE

Today, Islamic finance is present in more than 75 countries, with worldwide assets in excess of a trillion U.S. dollars.[4] While only Iran and Sudan have fully Islamic financial systems, Islamic finance holds significant market shares in many countries, close to 50 percent in some cases. Islamic finance has diversified within and beyond banking into capital markets and insurance, as well as other nonbanking services. In parallel, the industry is now endowed at both country and international levels with an enabling

---

[3] See King and Levine (1993) for a seminal analysis of the impact of financial development on the economy. Also see Imam and Kpodar (2010): "Because Muslim populations are under banked, and given the tremendous need for infrastructure projects like roads and housing across the Muslim world, development of Islamic banking can spur growth in these regions and can be part of the solution to the slow development process."

[4] Alone, assets under management with mutual funds amounted to US$25.6 trillion at the end of the first quarter of 2011 according to Ernst & Young (2011).

regulatory framework supporting its development. Notably, the Accounting and Auditing Organization for Islamic Financial Institutions (AAOIFI) and the Islamic Financial Services Board (IFSB) have successfully developed various standards for the industry. The Islamic Development Bank (IsDB) is playing a central role in fostering the industry's expansion and providing Islamic financing for development in members of the Organization of Islamic Countries (OIC).

Islamic financial assets are concentrated in the Gulf Cooperation Council (GCC) countries, Iran, and Malaysia. The rest of the world (ROW) weight is about that of Malaysia. Out of the estimated US$1.13 trillion worldwide Islamic assets in 2010, the largest amount was held in the Islamic Republic of Iran, representing around a third of international holdings at US$406 billion. The Kingdom of Saudi Arabia's and Malaysia's financial systems had US$177 billion and US$120 billion Islamic assets, respectively, representing the second and third largest domiciliation of Islamic finance in terms of size of assets. The GCC, including Saudi Arabia, has the largest value of Islamic financial assets, ahead of Iran. Malaysia and the rest of the world have each about the same size of Islamic financial assets, on the order of US$120 billion (see Table 2.1 and Figure 2.1). Interestingly, Islamic financial assets had reached US$27 billion in the United Kingdom in 2010, placing the country eighth in terms of Islamic assets size.

Within the Middle East and North Africa (MENA), GCC countries have been at the forefront of the development of Islamic finance, in terms of number and size of banks, size of *sukuks* issuance, and development of institutional infrastructure. GCC Islamic financial institutions have also led the development of the industry in other countries of the region, notably through the establishment of local subsidiaries or acquisition of domestic ones.[5] Interestingly, the presence of Islamic finance seems to decrease from

TABLE 2.1 Islamic Financial Assets Domiciliation

	Country/Region	2007	2008	2009	2010
1	Iran	235	293	369	406
2	GCC	262	354	445	489
3	Malaysia	67	87	109	120
4	Other countries	74	89	111	125
	Total	638	823	1,034	1,140

---

[5] GCC Islamic finance institutions have also established subsidiaries beyond the MENA region, notably in South and Southeastern Asia.

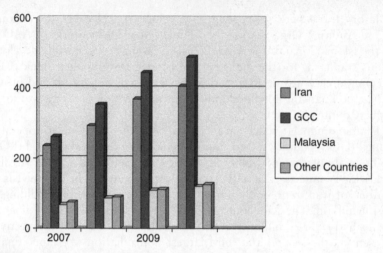

FIGURE 2.1   Islamic Financial Assets
Source: Author's calculations from Humayon Dar and Talha Ahmed Azami (2011).

the GCC region to the shores of the Atlantic Ocean, as one moves west-ward.[6] Egypt and the other North African countries are lagging behind on most aspects.

While Islamic finance assets account for 46 percent of Bahrain's finan-cial assets and have a significant share in other GCC countries except Oman, they hardly reach 5 percent in the rest of the MENA region, except in Iraq and Jordan (see Figure 2.2). West of Egypt, whose Islamic financial assets are around 4 percent, the largest share (2 percent) is in Tunisia; it is other-wise negligible.

Egypt now has 14 Islamic banking licenses, of which three are full-fledged Islamic banks, such as Faisal Islamic Bank of Egypt, and several have Islamic windows, including the National Bank of Egypt and Ahli United Bank.[7] The roughly 200 branches and 120 billion Egyptian pounds (EGP) of assets in Egypt's Islamic banking industry are dwarfed by Egypt's con-ventional banks. Total assets of the entire banking sector are about EGP 1.3 trillion, the latest central bank data show.[8]

---

[6] An exception in the GCC is the Sultanate of Oman, where Islamic finance had a late start.
[7] Part of Bahrain's Ahli United Bank group.
[8] See IFIS, "Egypt Islamists Draft Code to Boost Islamic Banks," June 12, 2012.

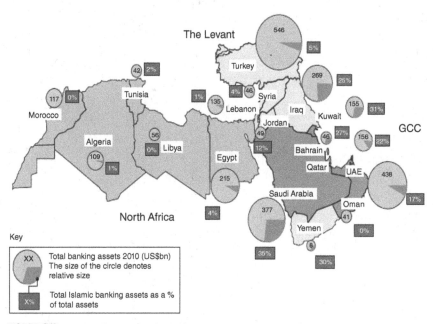

FIGURE 2.2 MENA Financial Landscape
Source: Ernst & Young (2011).

BEYOND BANKING: *SUKUKS*, FUNDS

Islamic finance has diversified beyond basic banking services, notably into capital markets and fund management, though it is still largely dominated by banking (see Table 2.2).[9]

Though *sukuk*s represent less than 8 percent of Islamic financial assets, the expansion of the *sukuk*s market has been a major development.[10] There were 803 issues of *sukuk*s for more than US$92.6 billion in 2011.[11] *Sukuk*s have provided sovereigns and corporations with access to a pool of resources

---

[9] *Takaful* is another significant segment of Islamic finance. It has also made inroads in Egypt and could fill a very important service gap that conventional insurance has not yet managed to cover. *Takaful* companies in Egypt may hold 5 percent of the Egyptian insurance market. See IFIS (2010).

[10] See AAOIFI's definition: "Certificates of equal value representing undivided shares in ownership of tangible assets, usufructs and services or (in the ownership of) the assets of particular projects or special investment activity" (AAOIFI's Shari'a Standards for Financial Institutions 2004–5, p. 298).

[11] IFIS database.

TABLE 2.2 Distribution of Islamic Finance by Asset Classes (USD Billions)

	2008	2009	2010	2011*
Banks	800	863	1,048	1,200
Funds	51	54	58	60
Takaful	8	13	21	25
Others	1	3	3	4
Total	860	933	1,130	1,289

*UK Islamic Finance Secretariat (UKIFS) estimate.
Source: The Banker, Ernst & Young, from UKIFS (2012).

whose owners seek *Shari'a*-compliant placements. There are various types of *sukuk*s. They differ by the type of the underlying Islamic financial transaction and the general purpose of its use. The first *sukuk* was issued by a non-Islamic company, Shell Malaysia, in Malaysia in 1990. It was a ringgit-denominated issue with a modest size of approximately US$30 million and based on the principle of *bai' bithaman ajil*, or deferred payment sale. Since then the market has grown, with issues expected to reach around US$100 billion in 2012 in spite of a slowdown in 2008 in the wake of the international financial crisis and a pronouncement of AAOIFI's *Shari'a* board on *sukuk*s' compliance with *Shari'a*.[12] (See Figure 2.3.)

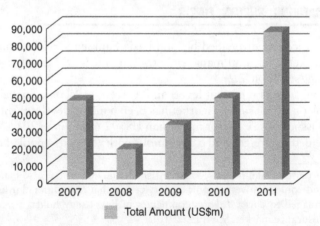

FIGURE 2.3 *Sukuk* Issuances over Five Years
Source: Islamic Finance Information Service (IFIS) database.

---

[12] See AAOIFI *Shari'a* board on *sukuk*s: www.aaoifi.com/aaoifi_sb_sukuk_Feb2008_Eng.pdf.

In contrast to the global domiciliation distribution of Islamic financial assets where Iran and the GCC dominate, *sukuks*' issuers have largely been from outside the major Islamic finance centers. More than 50 percent of the amounts issued from 2009 to 2011 originated outside Iran, the GCC countries, and Malaysia. Within traditional Islamic financial centers, Malaysia has clearly been in the lead, with issuance to date for 2012 amounting to 59 percent of the total amounts raised. Worldwide sovereigns and quasi sovereigns have been the major issuers of *sukuks*, with a share exceeding 70 percent of the total amounts issued. Corporations' shares of *sukuks* issued have generally been less than 30 percent. Within corporate issues, Malaysia and the rest of the world (ROW) have been active at more or less similar levels.

Within the MENA region, the GCC countries have dominated the *sukuks* market while Iran has a negligible presence. The share of the value of the *sukuks* issued in the GCC is reaching 15 percent of total issues for 2012, or close to US$12 billion. Sovereigns and quasi sovereigns capture the largest share of the value of issued *sukuks*, in line with the global pattern. (See Table 2.3.)

So far *sukuks* have been issued by corporations in Egypt and, interestingly, have been denominated in EGP (see Table 2.4). There have been three *sukuk* issuances in EGP worth a total of US$100.4 million, by Egypt's El Tawfeek group in 2010.[13] Still in 2010, El Baraka Egypt announced a USD-denominated issue worth US$150 million. However, the number of announced *sukuks* issuance and their value has increased since 2011 with denominations of USD and EGP. The Amer Group has announced two EGP issues worth US$447 million. Moreover, the transitional government had announced the intention of issuing a sovereign *sukuk* for an amount of US$2 billion. If all these issues materialize, Egypt would have issued the equivalent of almost US$2.7 billion, marking a significant broadening of its sources of finance at the corporate and sovereign levels.

Besides *sukuks*, nonbanking Islamic finance has seen a significant growth in Islamic funds. Assets under management stood at US$58 billion in 2010.[14] While assets under management in the global industry fell in the wake of the financial crisis, Islamic funds continued to grow at a modest pace in numbers and size of assets.[15] (See Figure 2.4.) However, institutional investors remain the dominant investors in Islamic funds, contributing about 70 percent of assets under management versus 30 percent for retail investors.

---

[13] Of this amount, two issues valued at about US$47 million have been redeemed.
[14] See Ernst & Young (2011).
[15] Assets under management in the global funds industry recovered significantly from the US$18 trillion trough of 2008 and reached US$25.6 trillion in 2010. See Ernst & Young (2011).

TABLE 2.3 *Sukuk* Issues

	2009	2010	2011	2012	2009	2010	2011	2012
Total	40,997	54,862.6	92,576	80,781	100%	100%	100%	100%
Iran			184				0%	
GCC	3,780	2,917	13,085	11,890	9%	5%	14%	15%
Malaysia	16,143	19,053	26,454	47,596	39%	35%	29%	59%
ROW	21,074	32,893	52,853	21,295	51%	60%	57%	26%
Corporate	6,731	11,582	20,803.87	24,326	16%	21%	22%	30%
Iran			183.87				1%	
GCC	393		1,747	1,373	6%	0%	8%	6%
Malaysia	1,950	5,845	9,444	18,179	29%	50%	45%	75%
ROW	4,388	5,737	9,429	4,774	65%	50%	45%	20%
Sovereign and Assimilated Corporate	34,265	43,281	71,772	56,455	84%	79%	78%	70%
Iran								
GCC	3,387	2,917	11,338	10,517	10%	7%	16%	19%
Malaysia	14,193	13,208	17,010	29,417	41%	31%	24%	52%
ROW	16,685	27,156	43,424	16,521	49%	63%	61%	29%

Source: Islamic Finance Information Service (IFIS) database and authors' calculations.

TABLE 2.4 Egypt *Sukuk* Issues

Date	Issuer	Domicile	Currency	Status	Type	US$m	Arranger	Maturity
5/28/2012	Amer Group Holding	Egypt	EGP	Announced	NA	197		N/A
5/28/2012	Amer Group Holding	Egypt	USD	Announced	NA	250		N/A
2/8/2012	Ministry of Finance (Arab Republic of Egypt)	Egypt	USD	Announced	NA	2,000		N/A
11/1/2010	Al Baraka Bank Egypt	Egypt	USD	Announced	NA	150		N/A
7/10/2010	Al-Tawfeek for Securitisation Company S.A.E.	Egypt	EGP	Outstanding	*Ijara*	52.99	CIB	7/10/2013
6/10/2010	Al-Tawfeek for Securitisation Company S.A.E.	Egypt	EGP	Redeemed	*Ijara*	40.62	CIB	7/10/2011
6/10/2010	Al-Tawfeek for Securitisation Company S.A.E.	Egypt	EGP	Redeemed	*Ijara*	6.8	CIB	6/10/2011

Source: African Development Bank (2011) and Islamic Finance Information Service (IFIS) database.

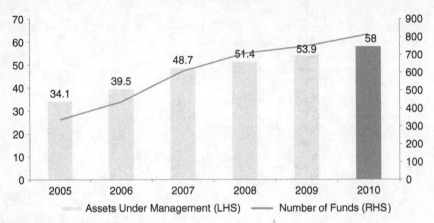

FIGURE 2.4   Islamic Funds Growth
Source: Ernst & Young (2011).

Managed Islamic mutual funds face the challenge of screening the assets
to include in their portfolio to generate returns, like their conventional
counterparts. However, in addition, they need to ensure that the assets in
their portfolio are *Shari'a* compliant. First, one can note that certificates of
equity mutual funds are intrinsically more compliant than bank deposits.
The former by construction do not have a guaranteed face value as they are
marked to market, whereas the nominal value of bank deposits is guaranteed. Accordingly, mutual fund certificates can fit more easily in an Islamic
finance framework. Second, however, Islamic mutual fund managers need to
adopt another screening layer to ensure the portfolio's *Shari'a* compliance
(see Table 2.5 and Figure 2.5).

The largest number of Islamic funds is domiciled in Malaysia and the
GCC countries, particularly Saudi Arabia. However, offshore centers continue to attract a large number of Islamic funds for their domiciliation.
More than 50 percent of Islamic funds are equity funds, investing in shares
of *Shari'a*-eligible companies.[16] These types of funds are intrinsically *Shari'a*
compliant as they combine both materiality and risk-sharing aspects. In addition, they can mitigate or even eliminate *haram* activities and *riba* through
their screening of companies eligible for investment.[17] Islamic equity funds
mobilize resources through *mudaraba* contracts and take shareholding participation (*musharaka*) when they invest.

---

[16] Ernst & Young (2011) assesses the share of Islamic equity funds at 39 percent.
[17] Hassan and Antoniou (2007).

TABLE 2.5 Financial Ratios of Alternative *Shari'a* Screens

Ratios / Screens	DJIM	FTSE*	S&P	MSCI**	HSBC	Meezan Bank***
Liquidity Ratios						
Account receivables, cash, and short-term investments over total assets					50%	
Account receivables and cash over total assets		50%				
Account receivables over total assets				70%		
Account receivables over market cap	33%		49%			
Interest Income Ratios						
Total interest income over total revenue*		5%			5%	5%
Cash and short-term investments over market cap	33%		3%			
Cash and short-term investments over total assets		33%		33.33		
Indebtedness Ratios						
Total debt over total assets	33%	33%	33%	33.33%		
Total debt over total market cap	33%	33%	33%		30%	30%
Permissible Income						
Noninterest, nonpermissible income		5%	5%			
Total investments in nonpermissible income over market cap						30%

*www.ftse.com/Indices/FTSE_Shariah_Global_Equity_Index_Series/index.jsp.
**www.mscibarra.com/products/indices/islamic/.
***For Meezan Bank the limit of 5 percent applies to interest and nonpermissible income; see M. I. A. Usmani (2002).
Source: Derigs and Marzban (2009).

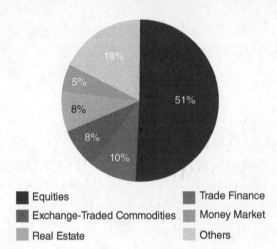

■ Equities	■ Trade Finance
■ Exchange-Traded Commodities	▦ Money Market
▦ Real Estate	▦ Others

FIGURE 2.5 Funds' Asset Allocation
Source: Islamic Finance Information Service (IFIS) database.

Egypt-based capital management companies have been active in setting up Islamic funds (see Table 2.6). With one exception, they are all equity funds reflecting the stage of development of the country's stock exchange.[18] All these funds are open ended, allowing investors to come in and withdraw at their discretion. The funds' net asset values vary with performance of the shares in their portfolios on the stock market. Islamic funds enlarge the menu of placements for private wealth management and should contribute to enhancing stock market development.

INSTITUTIONAL INFRASTRUCTURE

The regulatory arrangements and institutional infrastructure supporting Islamic finance have come a long way, but are still evolving. Their progress varies across jurisdictions. Some countries have enacted separate Islamic banking laws.[19] Others extend the general banking law to Islamic banks. Sometimes a special law is enacted for the establishment of a specific institution. In other cases, Islamic bank specificity is devolved to regulators' purview and managed through regulatory acts and circulars. Heretofore,

---

[18] Also, equity stocks represent around 70 percent of trade value, with bonds accounting for the remaining 30 percent. See IFIS (2011).
[19] Archer and Ahmed (2003) and IsDB, IRTI, and IFSB (2007).

TABLE 2.6 Islamic Funds in Egypt

Date	Fund Name	Asset Type	Currency	Fund Size	Fund Manager	Type
1/24/2012	Hilal Fund—Egypt	Equities	EGP	N/A	Cairo Capital Group	Open ended
8/18/2011	Al Wefak Fund	Equities	EGP	N/A	HC Securities & Investment	Open ended
7/21/2011	Naeem Egypt Islamic Fund	Equities	EGP	N/A	NAEEM Financial Investments	Open ended
10/17/2010	Al Hayat Fund	Equities	EGP	N/A	NBK Capital Asset Management Egypt	Open ended
8/10/2010	Al Baraka Islamic Fund (Al Mutwazin)	Mixed assets—balanced	EGP	6.79	AT—Asset Management	Open ended
2/10/2008	Bashayer Mutual Fund	Equities	EGP	42.51	National Fund Management Company	Open ended
1/8/2007	Sanabel Islamic Investment Fund	Equities	EGP	23.46	HC Securities & Investment	Open ended
10/24/2006	Banque Misr Islamic Fund (Al Hessn)	Equities	EGP	31.14	HC Securities & Investment	Open ended
10/1/2006	Al Aman Fund	Equities	EGP	N/A	CI Asset Management	Open ended
6/1/2006	El Baraka Bank Mutual Fund	Equities	EGP	22.91	EFG Hermes Egypt	Open ended
12/1/2004	Faisal Islamic Bank	Equities	EGP	47.89	EFG Hermes Egypt	Open ended

Source: Islamic Finance Information Service (IFIS) database.

Egypt had no general law for Islamic banks. It dealt with them through tailor-made legislation for specific institutions or regulations, under the general umbrella of the banking law and the supervision of the central bank.

Internationally, attention has been given since the early 1990s to the prudential framework governing Islamic financial institutions. For example, differences between Islamic and conventional banks' balance sheet structures, features of Islamic financial contracts, and associated risks have been recognized to have important implications, notably for accounting and financial reporting. Under the leadership of the IsDB and a number of central banks, standard-setting bodies have been established to address these types of issues. Bahrain-based AAOIFI was established in the early 1990s. It focuses on accounting, auditing, and *Shari'a* standards, and has taken a lead role on these matters, notably issuing standards and organizing training. Its standards have been adopted by a number of Islamic financial institutions and countries, and are used as a reference when conventional national rules are deficient for Islamic financial transactions in other jurisdictions.

In November 2002, a group of central banks established the Islamic Financial Services Board (IFSB) with headquarters in Kuala Lumpur. The IFSB has developed international standards, notably on capital adequacy, risk management, corporate governance, transparency, and market discipline and supervision. It has also provided guidance principles for systemic liquidity management. It is paying attention to prudential arrangements governing other Islamic finance nonbanking activities, including *takaful* standards as well as legal risks. Like AAOIFI's standards, IFSB's provide references for national regulatory arrangements.

Similarly, the IIFM focuses on the standardization of Islamic financial instrument structures, contracts, product development, and infrastructure, as well as the issuance of guidelines and recommendations for the enhancement of Islamic capital and money market globally. In addition, these international bodies provide a useful interface with global organizations focusing on conventional finance such as the International Accounting Board, Basel Committee for Banking Supervision, or International Organization of Securities Commissions (IOSCO). With the AAOIFI, IFSB, IIFM, and various national efforts aimed at providing a framework governing Islamic financial intermediation, the essential building blocks for the formulation and implementation of public policy are coming into place, though still evolving.

Rating agencies are also focusing on IFSB as well as Islamic capital market instruments. They have developed approaches to assessing Islamic financial institutions' risks as well as rating *sukuk*s. They also have focused on legal risk issues, related notably to dispute settlement.[20] Prominent Islamic financial

---

[20] Fitch Ratings (2005, 2007), Moody's (2006), and Standard & Poor's (2006).

institutions such as the IsDB, Al Rajhi, or Kuwait Finance House (KFH) receive ratings. The gradual involvement of rating agencies has led to the rating of *sukuk* issues and has brought a degree of direct market discipline. Malaysia's global *sukuk* and the Kingdom of Bahrain *sukuk* notes were among the first to be rated in 2002. The increased number of ratings helps mainstream Islamic financial services increase confidence and limit spreads. More than half of the corporate *sukuk*s issued in the first half of 2007 are rated.[21]

ISLAMIC FINANCE: OPPORTUNITY TO FINANCE EGYPT'S DEVELOPMENT

Countries with deeper financial systems achieve higher economic growth rates (see Figure 2.6). Also, inclusive financial systems that permit access to financial services to more people and companies promote social inclusion and equity.[22] While Egypt has made significant progress in deepening and developing its financial sector, it still has some way to go in terms of increased depth, diversification of services, and regulatory and supervisory arrangements. Moreover, financial inclusion remains limited, with only 44 percent and 8.5 percent of adult population having a deposit bank account and a loan account, respectively.[23] Furthermore, access to insurance services, most notably life insurance, remains limited (see Table 2.7). The development of *takaful* could help expand these services, improve risk management for businesses and individuals, encourage entrepreneurship, and enhance intergenerational equity.[24] Thus, further development and diversification of financial services can foster a healthy economy and equitable society. Islamic finance can contribute to the development and diversification of Egypt's financial services, increase financial inclusion, and promote social equity.[25]

---

[21] IFIS website, August 15, 2007.

[22] See, for example, Honohan (2004a).

[23] Reported in Pearce (2011), Annex I.

[24] For example, Arena (2006) reports: "Using the generalized method of moments for dynamic models of panel data for 56 countries and for the 1976–2004 period, we find robust evidence of a causal relationship between insurance market activity and economic growth."

[25] See Pearce (2011) who reports that an IFC-commissioned market study in the MENA region found that "between 20 and 60 percent of those interviewed (micro-enterprises, low income individuals) indicated a preference for *Shari'a* compliant products. For some the lack of *Shari'a* compliant products is an absolute constraint to financial access, while for others this is a preference and they continue to use conventional financial services in the absence of competitive Islamic ones."

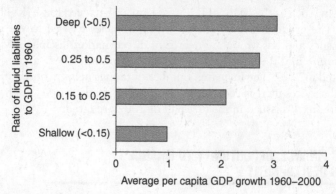

FIGURE 2.6 Financial Deepening and GDP Growth
Source: Honohan (2004b).

The following subsections highlight Islamic finance's potential contributions to household, project, corporate, and SME financing.

Household Finances

A performing financial system should provide households with the services to: (1) efficiently settle their financial transactions, (2) manage their lifelong finances, and (3) cope with unanticipated adverse events, all without facing catastrophic consequences. Islamic finance can contribute in two ways: It can offer financial services needed by households that do not wish to deal with conventional finance, and can diversify the menu of available financial services. Thus, Islamic finance can enhance financial inclusion, as it allows more Egyptian households to find services consistent with their religious beliefs. Moreover, Islamic finance can make available to all households a larger menu of financial services, allowing them to more efficiently settle

TABLE 2.7 Insurance Penetration (% of GDP)

	Non-Life Premium	Life Premium	Assets
Egypt	0.42	0.37	3.9
High-income OECD	2.3	4.0	45
East Asia and Pacific	0.97	2.8	4.9

Source: Lester (2011), based on AXCO reports, Swiss Re, Sigma, IMF/World Bank databases, national sources.

financial transactions, manage their lifelong finances, and cope with unanticipated adverse events.

The availability of *amana* and investment accounts can provide households with instruments for conducting their current financial transactions and to hold some of their savings. Islamic funds can provide other placement opportunities to retail investors and contribute to the vibrancy of capital markets. Similarly, Islamic financial institutions can extend *murabaha*, *ijara*, or *musharaka*—for instance, to support households in acquiring durable goods and equipment as well as to finance mortgages to enlarge access to home ownership. Without the availability of these resources, many households would remain outside the financial system, entailing a loss of welfare, a drag on economic growth, and a missed opportunity for social inclusion. Besides, these services can be available to all groups of society irrespective of their religious affiliation, enlarging the menu of financial services.

Financing Corporations and Projects

In the normal course of business, corporations have recourse to financial facilities to fund their short-term needs or longer-term investments, to manage invoices, or to extend financing to clients. Islamic finance can provide resources to enable corporations to conduct these activities. However, generally these corporate finance decisions have been based on analyses where interest rates play a critical role. Accordingly, corporations that seek to access Islamic finance need to recast their operations and decisions on a framework that is *Shari'a* compliant. Similarly, Islamic finance providers are constantly innovating to offer their corporate clients facilities that suit their needs and are *Shari'a* compliant. In addition, advisory services are available to support firms making their financial management *Shari'a* compliant.[26]

Economic growth is driven by investments in projects, most notably in infrastructure. Because of their material nature, these activities are particularly suited to Islamic finance. These projects are funded based on various degrees of possibilities of recourse to the balance sheet of the sponsor. Egypt has benefited from Islamic finance for a number of projects, principally supported by the IsDB and mostly based on *ijara* operating leases or *murabaha* contracts.[27] The IsDB was the financier for the three *ijara* deals and the government the funding recipient. In the case of the Benha Power Plant, the government of Egypt rents the facilities from the IsDB from the fourth year after the project is completed with revenues from the sale of the electricity.

---

[26] See, for example, Ayub (2007).
[27] See African Development Bank (2011).

TABLE 2.8 Islamic Project Finance in Egypt

Date	Project	Sector	Financial Instrument	Amount (USD Millions)
January 2011	Saudi Al Batterjee	Hospital	*Ijara*	10.0
January 2011	Suez Steam Power	Energy	*Ijara*	60.0
September 2010	Benha Power Plant	Energy	*Ijara*	120.0
December 2009	ENPC Fertilizers	Manufacturing	*Murabaha*	15.0
October 2009	Abu Qir Power	Energy	*Mudaraba*	73.8

Source: African Development Bank (2011), based on Islamic Finance Information Service (IFIS).

The *ijara* rents are paid over a 15-year period to the IsDB, after which the government purchases the plant. Islamic funding in the form of *mudaraba* was made available for the power plant of Abu Qir Power from the Faisal Islamic Bank of Egypt. The *mudaraba* facility provided partnership finance in return for a share of the profits accruing to the West Delta Electricity Company. It was part of a syndicated financing deal arranged by the Arab African International Bank.[28] (See Table 2.8.)

SME Financing

SMEs are the mainstay of most economies, including Egypt's. However, they have limited access to external finance. This constrains their contribution to employment, growth, and social inclusion.

Within an adequate regulatory and institutional framework, Islamic financial products can make a significant contribution to easing SME access to finance. However, there is a need to deal with basic challenges that limit the menu of Islamic financial products to SMEs and their ability to contribute to Egypt's economic and social success.[29]

On average, SMEs contribute 67 percent to formal manufacturing employment in high-income countries and 45 percent in developing countries. Their contribution to gross domestic product (GDP) amounts to 49 percent in high-income countries and 29 percent in developing countries.[30]

---

[28] Ibid.
[29] These challenges include clear and transparent regulation, adequate risk management practices, availability of reliable market information, competent Islamic finance professionals, and other broad institutional infrastructure.
[30] Consultative Group to Assist the Poor (CGAP) (2010).

In Egypt, SMEs are estimated to be on the order of 6.4 million, with about 6 percent of them formal.[31]

In spite of their significant role in Egypt's and MENA countries' economies, SME access to financing from banks remains limited. In Egypt, their share in total lending does not exceed 5 percent (see Figure 2.7).[32]

Various reasons underlie SMEs' limited access to finance. Of course SMEs expect that returns will be a major driver of bankers' lending to them. But bankers perceive SMEs as riskier than established corporations and find significant obstacles in extending lending to them (see Figure 2.8). In particular, issues regarding SMEs' transparency and collateral reliability are considered major obstacles. Apparently, bankers do not perceive *Shari'a* compliance as an important obstacle to lending to SMEs. However, this reported perception is a response to a direct question on the issue. Bankers' sense of a poor demand by SMEs for lending may reflect the absence of *Shari'a*-compliant offerings and SMEs' reluctance to seek conventional funding.

Currently, in non-GCC MENA only a limited number of banks offer or plan to offer *Shari'a*-compliant products to SMEs (see Figure 2.9). However, an expanded menu of well-structured Islamic finance offerings

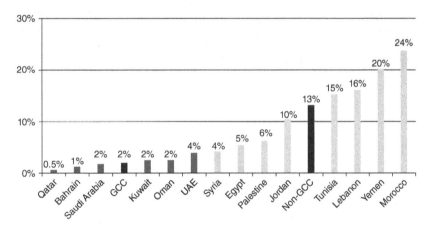

FIGURE 2.7   MENA: Share of Loans to SMEs in Total Lending
Source: Rocha, Aravai, and Farazi (2011).

---

[31] See McKinsey-IFC (2011).
[32] The non-GCC average includes Iraqi banks whose share is not separately reported. From Rocha, Aravai, and Farazi (2011).

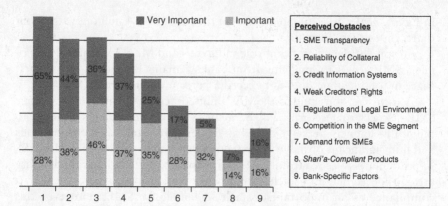

FIGURE 2.8   Bankers' Perceptions of Obstacles to Lending to SMEs—Percentage of Bankers' Responses, Non-GCC MENA
Source: Rocha, Aravai, and Farazi (2011).

can contribute to an increase in financial resources acceptable to SMEs that are reluctant to seek conventional finance. It can also mitigate risks of lending to SMEs as perceived by bankers. In particular, the reliability of collateral may be less of an issue in Islamic financing, as the financier retains ownership title to the asset or commodity financed until it is fully repaid. Furthermore, Islamic finance could expand leasing facilities that are offered by only 26 percent of non-GCC MENA banks to SMEs.[33]

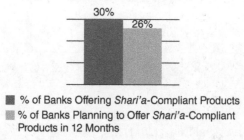

FIGURE 2.9   Supply of *Shari'a*-Compliant Products—Non-GCC MENA
Source: Rocha, Aravai, and Farazi (2011).

---

[33] Rocha et al. (2011).

REGULATORY CHALLENGES

Financial services are essentially an information-based industry where public trust is critical. Accordingly, these services are highly regulated and subject to supervision by public authorities.[34] Adequate regulation promotes prudent conduct without stifling entrepreneurial initiative; it is critical to the stability and vibrancy of financial intermediation. Similarly, sound and vibrant Islamic finance also requires an adequate regulatory framework and effective supervision, which can instill public confidence in the industry and encourage innovation.

So far, the international response to the regulation of Islamic finance has been along two tracks.[35] The first stems from the view that Islamic finance is financial intermediation. It adds to the menu of financial services and can be regulated in the same way that any financial innovation is dealt with. Accordingly, the laws, regulations, and supervision arrangements applying to financial intermediation should extend to Islamic finance. Adjustments and additions may be necessary, as they would be in the normal course of other financial innovations.[36] Heretofore, the position adopted by the Egyptian banking regulator appears to have been in line with this view. However, there are currently efforts to develop an appropriate legal and regulatory framework to govern Islamic finance activity.[37]

---

[34] The recent crisis following 2007 brought to the forefront these issues and highlighted their international dimension, leading to a renewed emphasis on international financial standards and codes, as well as subjecting financial organizations to stress testing.

[35] It is interesting to note the view of Ben Bernanke, U.S. Federal Reserve chairman: "I will argue that central banks and other regulators should resist the temptation to devise ad hoc rules for each new type of financial instrument or institution. Rather, we should strive to develop common, principles-based policy responses that can be applied consistently across the financial sector to meet clearly defined objectives." See Bernanke (2007).

[36] According to the Central Bank of Nigeria: "Islamic banking as one of the models of non-interest banking, serves the same purpose of providing financial services as do conventional financial institutions save that it operates in accordance with principles and rules of Islamic commercial jurisprudence that generally recognizes profit and loss sharing and the prohibition of interest, as a model."

[37] In 2010, the Egyptian Financial Supervisory Authority (EFSA) had already announced the preparation of the first draft of *sukuk* regulations to be implemented by the first quarter of 2011 (IFIS 2011). However, the events of early 2011 derailed that schedule. The parliament elected in 2011 also prepared legislation to establish a framework governing Islamic finance activity. It was, however, not discussed (IFIS 2012).

Another view is that Islamic financial intermediation is intrinsically different from conventional finance. Accordingly, it would be difficult to extend to Islamic finance a conventional finance framework; Islamic finance requires specific laws, regulations, and supervision arrangements to allow Islamic banks to operate. The previous Egyptian authorities appear to have adopted this view.[38]

Thus, policy makers face the choice of either extending conventional regulation to Islamic finance or designing separate regulation for the industry. The first option raises conceptual challenges whereas the second runs the risk of containing the industry in a niche status. Alternative organizational arrangements could help the industry flourish and play an effective economic role without forcing it into the straitjacket of conventional regulation or circumscribing it to a niche activity.

The following considers first the challenge of conceptual inconsistencies between *Shari'a* compliance and conventional banking regulations. It then outlines a blueprint of an alternative organizational arrangement that can help overcome the challenges and facilitate the development of a vibrant Islamic finance industry.[39]

Inconsistencies between Conventional Regulation and Islamic Finance Principles

Islamic banking offers services provided by both conventional banking and nonbanking financial intermediation services.[40] Accordingly, it can be awkward to apply conventional banking regulation directly to Islamic banks as it would entail extending banking regulation to nonbanking financial intermediation. The following highlights the challenges to bridge the

---

[38] See IFIS, "Egypt Islamists Draft Code to Boost Islamic Banks," June 12, 2012: "Ahmed al-Najjar, a member of the Freedom and Justice Party's economic committee, told Reuters that the proposals envisaged a new Islamic banking section being added to the law, which now has no specific regulations covering Islamic banks. Draft amendments to the law have been presented to parliament but no date has been set to discuss them, he said."

[39] The following focuses on Islamic banking regulation as a separate area from Islamic nonbanking finance activities, notably *takaful* and capital markets activities. Nonbanking Islamic finance can more easily fit within conventional frameworks with minor adjustments. Also, it does not deal with issues related to systemic liquidity management that present significant challenges to the operation of Islamic financial institutions.

[40] For example, investment account deposits are akin to mutual fund certificates; restricted investment accounts are close to services offered by private banking to high net worth individuals.

requirements of the principles of risk sharing, materiality, and no *riba* with those of conventional banking regulation.

In principle, a revenue-earning deposit in an Islamic financial institution should be consistent with *risk sharing* and accordingly would not correspond to the prevailing definition of a deposit in a conventional bank where (1) the deposit should be retrievable by the depositor at its face value, and (2) the depositor is a priority senior creditor of the financial institution in case of its liquidation.[41] The *materiality* principle requires Islamic banks to bundle the associated real and financial transactions, entailing that the bank may enter into partnership with its clients or own the assets that they seek to finance.[42] It would conflict with the prevailing prohibition for conventional commercial banks to enter into partnerships with clients or have ownership of real estate and common stock. The prohibition of earning or charging interest, or no *riba*, is a central tenet of Islamic finance.[43] The remuneration resulting from a placement should not be preset or linked to the value placed. It should rather be the result of the efforts made in the economical use of the resources and accordingly should not be set a priori. In a dual conventional and Islamic financial system, the prohibition to transact in interest-bearing debt instruments constrains the ability of (1) Islamic deposit-taking institutions to compete in attracting deposits; (2) Islamic deposit-taking institutions to manage liquidity, placing their own excess resources or accessing resources when needed, notably on conventional money markets; or (3) monetary authorities governing dual Islamic and conventional financial system, in particular central banks, to conduct monetary policy, injecting or withdrawing resources from the financial system.[44]

CONCLUSION

Over the past 30 years, Islamic finance has experienced a tremendous expansion in the size of assets and their diversification, number of Islamic finance institutions, and geographic scope. Noteworthy is Islamic finance

---

[41] Bollen (2006).

[42] For example, the bank could not lend money to an individual (lending contract) who would use the money to purchase a house (house purchase contract). In principle the lender would need to hold some ownership in the house until it is fully paid.

[43] There are different types of *riba*, generally understood as interest. The prohibition of *riba* has generally carried over to the prohibition of charging or receiving interest. A minority interpretation is that *riba* refers to usury rates and not to reasonable rates charged. See Mahmoud El-Gamal (2003). See also www.islamic-finance.com/item5_f.htm.

[44] Davies (2011).

development in non-OIC member countries such as the United Kingdom or the United States. In the United States the industry developed in response to two types of needs: (1) local communities' retail finance needs, notably for mortgages, and (2) foreign investors' needs to invest in the U.S. market in a *Shari'a*-compliant way. Worldwide, Islamic financial assets exceed US$1.2 trillion and are growing.

An early mover in the modern development of Islamic finance, Egypt has lagged behind Malaysia, Bahrain, and GCC countries since the 1970s. The country's Islamic financial assets are estimated around 5 percent of the total financial system. It includes a number of Islamic mutual funds, besides banking. Moreover, the country has managed to mobilize some Islamic funds for large-scale projects, mainly with the support of the IsDB. Egypt has remained largely outside of the *sukuk* market, though some corporate activity is taking place and there are intentions of issuing sovereign *sukuk*s.

This limited development goes hand in hand with the financial system's overall development. However, it also reflects the regulatory and institutional challenges of integrating Islamic finance within the overall financial system. This limited development of Islamic finance in the country has excluded many from access to financial services, as they are reluctant to deal with conventional finance either to place their resources or to secure funding for their ventures. As a result, Egypt has missed opportunities of access to financial resources and increased social inclusion and social equity.

However, there is the opportunity to set up a legal, regulatory, and institutional framework to enable Islamic finance entrepreneurs to respond to market demand and give access to financial services to those who do not wish to deal with conventional finance. An appropriate and effective legal, regulatory, and institutional framework is essential. It can provide an enabling framework for the industry to grow beyond a niche activity or avoid an unwieldy development. Ultimately, Islamic finance will be market tested and develop if it responds to market demand and efficiently offers the services needed.

A specific legal, regulatory, and institutional framework runs the risk of maintaining Islamic finance in a niche status separate from the mainstream of finance even if it can adequately handle the industry's specificity. A joint effort by *Shari'a* finance scholars and mainstream finance regulators can address that challenge. It needs to focus on the substance of the activities and transactions rather than on their formal structures to overcome the pitfalls of niche status or unwieldy development. An organizational structure of a finance holding group with subsidiaries dealing with the substance of Islamic finance can overcome the conundrum of squaring the principles of Islamic finance with the requirements for conducting banking activity.

Egypt could once more take a leading role in Islamic finance by set-ting up a legal, regulatory, and institutional framework that does not twist *Shari'a* principles or conventional banking rules by forcing the industry to operate in the conceptual setup of banks. *Amana* banking and mutual funds can play a core role in deposit taking while not departing from either *Shari'a* principles or conventional finance rules. Leasing, project finance, private equity, and *sukuk*s can be effective instruments for funding business activity, investments, and sovereign needs while complying with *Shari'a*.[45]

APPENDIX 2A: SIZE OF ISLAMIC FINANCE IN USD BILLIONS

Country	2007	2008	2009	2010
Iran	235	293	369	406
Saudi Arabia	92	128	161	177
Malaysia	67	87	109	120
UAE	49	84	106	116
Kuwait	63	68	85	94
Bahrain	37	46	58	64
Qatar	21	28	35	38
United Kingdom	18	19	24	27
Turkey	16	18	22	25
Bangladesh	6	8	9	10
Sudan	5	7	9	10
Egypt	6	6	8	9
Pakistan	6	5	6	7
Jordan	3	5	6	6
Syria	1	4	5	5
Iraq	–	4	5	5
Indonesia	3	3	4	5
Brunei	3	3	4	4
Other countries	7	7	9	10
Total	639	822	1,036	1,139

Source: Humayon Dar and Talha Ahmed Azami (2011).

---

[45] See Part Three on regulatory issues for an elaboration of the organizational framework.

APPENDIX 2B: LARGEST GCC ISLAMIC BANKS
(USD MILLIONS)

Rank	Bank	Country	Year	Assets	Profits	Deposits	Loans	Equity
1	Al-Rajhi Bank	Saudi Arabia	2010	49,286	1,805	38,155	32,020	8,085
			2009	45,525	1,804	32,761	29,909	7,664
2	Kuwait Finance House	Kuwait	2010	44,800	379	27,259	na	4,598
			2009	40,237	424	25,036	na	4,281
3	Dubai Islamic Bank	UAE	2010	24,539	262	17,272	15,564	2,607
			2009	22,952	330	17,479	13,591	2,443
4	Abu Dhabi Islamic Bank	UAE	2010	20,499	279	15,386	13,500	2,205
			2009	17,452	21	13,123	11,293	1,399
5	Al-Baraka Banking Group	Bahrain	2010	15,879	193	2,906	1,538	1,818
			2009	13,166	167	2,607	1	1,736
6	Qatar Islamic Bank	Qatar	2010	14,204	366	8,291	9,721	2,500
			2009	10,761	362	5,579	7,481	2,467
7	Masraf Al Rayan	Qatar	2010	9,503	488	354	6,867	1,953
			2009	6,610	361	403	4,864	1,633
8	Emirates Islamic Bank	UAE	2010	8,916	450	6,595	3,982	797
			2009	6,885	413	5,287	4,548	782
9	Bank Al-Jazira	Saudi Arabia	2010	8,804	8	5,904	4,987	na
			2009	7,993	7	5,581	4,134	na
10	Alinma Bank	Saudi Arabia	2010	7,111	4	2,217	4,158	na
			2009	4,614	161	400	300	na
11	Ithmaar Bank	Bahrain	2010	6,743	−139	4,657	5,123	654

Rank	Bank	Country	Year	Assets	Profits	Deposits	Loans	Equity
			2009	6,105	−251	4,185	4,478	711
12	Bank Al-Bilad	Saudi Arabia	2010	5,631	25	4,515	3,277	na
			2009	4,643	−66	3,658	2,936	na
13	Qatar International Islamic Bank	Qatar	2010	4,981	243	777	2,514	1,046
			2009	4,252	214	672	2,485	1,041
14	Boubyan Bank	Kuwait	2010	4,802	22	3,434	3,007	876
			2009	3,518	−190	2,583	2,102	325
15	Sharjah Islamic Bank	UAE	2010	4,538	72	2,826	2,628	1,184
			2009	4,349	71	2,685	2,728	1,161
16	Kuwait International Bank	Kuwait	2010	4,163	na	3,448	3,740	715
			2009	4,160	66	3,452	na	631
17	Kuwait Finance House Bahrain	Bahrain	2010	3,838	24	1,849	1,698	470
			2009	3,641	16	1,949	1,747	470
18	Arcapita	Bahrain	2010	3,457	−559	na	na	na
			2009	4,372	−88	na	na	na
19	Bahrain Islamic Bank	Bahrain	2010	2,482	−105	1,966	1,703	265
			2009	2,419	−51	1,804	1,589	373
20	Al-Salam Bank	Bahrain	2010	2,273	19	1,687	1,450	536
			2009	2,082	37	1,524	1,496	533

Source: Islamic Finance Information Service (IFIS), September 19, 2011.

APPENDIX 2C: ISLAMIC FINANCE IN THE UNITED STATES

In the United States, one can identify four major developments for Islamic finance: (1) regulatory opinions on the consistency of Islamic finance products with existing regulations; (2) introduction of Islamic retail finance, especially for home mortgages; (3) establishment of Islamic mutual funds and introduction of Islamic indexes, particularly the Dow Jones Islamic Market Index; and (4) emergence of wholesale finance focusing on foreign investors wanting to invest in the United States in compliance with *Shari'a* structures.

A major breakthrough in the introduction of Islamic finance to the U.S. market occurred with the request by the United Bank of Kuwait (UBK) for an opinion on the permissibility to offer *ijara*-based mortgages and securitize the products in 1997. Later, in 1999, UBK requested an opinion on the permissibility of *murabaha* home, inventory, equipment, and construction financing. In both cases, the Office of the Comptroller of the Currency (OCC) provided the opinion of admissibility of the transactions based on the substance of their economic outcome rather than on their formal structure, guided by precedents from the courts. The approach taken by the U.S. regulator is noteworthy. It does not seek to establish a separate regulatory framework to accommodate *Shari'a* rules applying to Islamic finance. It rather seeks to check whether Islamic finance products are admissible within existing regulations and their potential interpretations. The resulting principle and practice are that most Islamic finance activities can develop with the existing regulatory framework. The aspect that appears difficult to accommodate is to square the notions of conventional and Islamic deposits. The former has a guaranteed face value whereas the latter cannot if it generates returns.[46]

Nonbank financial institutions have dominated the Islamic finance market in the United States. Offers of Islamic mortgages (see Table 2C.1) and *Shari'a*-compliant mutual funds developed in response to local community needs. A major development in the Islamic mortgage business was Freddie Mac's approval to finance mortgages originated by the American Finance House (LARIBA) in 2001. This approval, later replicated with other Islamic finance mortgage companies, gave the industry the means to expand significantly. A group of Muslims started an investment pool in 1984. When the demand grew beyond a size the pool could accommodate, its members called on a professional fund manager to help them set

---

[46] See Yasaar Media (2009). The OCC was able to declare permissible "impermissible forms under a literal interpretation of the banking laws so long as they create the economic outcome of permissible types of financing. This broad ability to interpret non traditional financing methods makes U.S. regulations quite flexible in accommodating Islamic financial products, but only in so far as they are 'functionally interchangeable' with permissible products." See later sections of this chapter for a discussion of these issues and an approach to deal with them.

TABLE 2C.1 Noteworthy Islamic Finance Retail Activities in the United States

Financial Institution	Location	Activity	Highlights
American Finance House (LARIBA)	Early 1980—Pasadena, California	Islamic home and small business finance	Approval to receive financing from the Federal Home Loan Mortgage Corporation (FHLMC or Freddie Mac) in 2001
Guidance Financial (now called Guidance Residential)	2002—Washington, D.C., and Maryland and Virginia	Islamic home finance using a diminishing *musharaka*	Agreement with Freddie Mac to finance $200 million in home purchases; rose to more than $1 billion by the middle of 2007
Devon Bank	2003—Chicago	Small community bank offering Islamic mortgages following a demand from the local community	Has sold its Islamic mortgages to Freddie Mac since 2005
University Islamic Financial Corporation	Ann Arbor, Michigan	Home finance and a deposit product that pays returns based on the return on the company's home finance products	Only wholly *Shari'a*-compliant Islamic banking subsidiary in the United States
African Development Center	Minneapolis–St. Paul, Minnesota	Provides business and entrepreneurial training and *Shari'a*-compliant financing for American Muslim immigrants from Africa, primarily Somalia; *murabaha* product with financing from Freddie Mac and Fannie Mae	Has a nonprofit mortgage origination firm ADC Financial Services, financing from Freddie Mac and Fannie Mae, and expanded program working with the Minnesota Housing Finance Agency

Source: Adapted from Yasaar Media (2009).

TABLE 2C.2 Wholesale Islamic Finance in the United States

Financial Institution	Establishment Location	Activity
Arcapita	Since 1998; with the Arcapita name since 2005, based in Atlanta, Georgia	Private equity, asset purchase, and venture capital; United States is the destination for *Shari'a*-compliant investments.
Gulf Investment House (GIH) with Gulf Finance House (GFH) through Innovest Capital and TransOcean Capital	Since 2003, based in Cleveland, Ohio, and in Boston, Massachusetts	Private equity and real estate funds.
Codexa Capital through Calyx Financial	Calyx Financial is owned by venture capital. In 2004, the firm transitioned from the hedge fund business to *Shari'ab*-compliant asset management. Based in New York.	Operates for offshore *Shari'a*-compliant investments; between 2002 and 2008, Calyx Financial refocused its activities on structuring offshore products to connect businesses needing financing with investors looking for *Shari'a*-compliant investment opportunities.
Unicorn Investment Bank, through UIB Capital	Since 2004, based in Chicago, Illinois	Private equity firm.
Anchor Finance Group	Since 2005, based in New York	Business finance, product arranging, and consumer financing (e.g., providing financing for investment properties in their home countries owned by expatriate South Asians living in the United States).
Zayan Finance	Since 2007, based in New York, with offices nationwide	Commercial real estate investments, ranging from $500,000 to $2.5 million.

Source: Adapted from Yasaar Media (2009).

up a mutual fund, the Amana Income Fund. Later the Amana group and other managers launched other funds.[47] The industry received a significant push with the introduction of the Dow Jones Islamic Market Index. It permitted the introduction of systematic screening as well as benchmarking-facilitating transparency. Other indexes followed. Besides retail market institutions catering to the needs of the local community, a number of financial institutions developed their activities in the United States focusing on funds seeking to be invested in the country but being *Shari'a* compliant. Naturally, these institutions were nonbank financial intermediaries and mostly private equity or broader capital management companies, two types of activities that are intrinsically more in line with *Shari'a* principles (see Table 2C.2).[48]

---

[47]Yasaar Media (2009) reports that "the Iman Fund, known as the Dow Jones Islamic Fund until 2008, and the Azzad Ethical Income and Ethical Mid Cap Funds were launched in mid-2000."

[48]There are also *Shari'a*-compliant boutique investment companies that operate internationally from a U.S. base such as The DateStone Group, a financial advisory and alternative asset management firm, at www.thedatestonegroup.com.

Two

Managing Systemic Risks

With hindsight, it seems that every 10 to 12 years an international financial crisis erupts. The East Asia crisis erupted in 1997, hit Thailand, and spread to many countries of the region and beyond. Following each crisis, 10 years are spent assessing and analyzeing what happened and living with the consequences of the measures taken to contain it. Reforms are pursued with the aim of avoiding a repeat episode of distress. In the meantime, the next crisis is already in the making, and soon it erupts where radar screens had not anticipated it. Unlike previous modern crises, the 2007–2008 crisis erupted in the world's financial center, not in emerging markets, and rapidly spread to its periphery with devastating effects. Thus the cycle of boom and bust resumes merrily, while humanity suffers great financial loss, grief, and tragedies. But efforts to stabilize the system, or at least to limit the most damaging effects of its volatility, cannot be abandoned, if not for the sake of maintaining growth, at least for limiting the human dramas that are the natural corollary of financial crises.

The risk of a systemic crisis affecting Islamic financial services (IFS) and the way to cope with it if it occurs have gained relevance in the wake of the

This part draws on Grais and Rajhi (2009). The authors would like to thank Dr. Rajhi for his contribution and the insights he has brought to this work.

2008 worldwide financial tsunami that spread from the United States to the rest of the world.[1] The international financial crisis naturally prompts the question of whether IFS are robust and resilient or may be swept into crisis by a global wave and, if so, through what channels. A corollary is whether relevant public authorities and market participants have tools at their disposal to deal with a systemic crisis affecting IFS.

In May 2008, conventional banking units in the Middle East were estimated to be exposed to subprime-related assets in the order of as much as US$1 billion. Four regional banks suffered from the fallout. Bahrain-based Bank of Bahrain & Kuwait announced write-downs of US$62 million. Abu Dhabi Commercial Bank made provisions of US$152 million of bad debt, while the Arab Banking Corporation (ABC) reported that it had taken a hit of US$230 million. In the largest write-down in the region, Gulf International Bank (GIB) declared a US$757.3 million net loss in 2007.[2] Gulf Bank's problems do not directly threaten to undermine the banking system in Kuwait. The losses, estimated at up to 200 million Kuwaiti dinars, led to a run on the bank as customers scrambled to withdraw their cash. However, this amount is small compared to the bank's equity. The bank lost money when clients used currency derivatives to bet against the dollar's value, but suffered huge losses when the dollar strengthened. In contrast to their conventional counterparts, Islamic banks have been shielded from the direct impact of the U.S. mortgage crisis mainly because subprime-linked debt spread through securities that would not comply with *Shari'a* law.[3] However, the ensuing economic downturn, in particular its effects on the real estate sector, was bound to impact their performance eventually.

This part has two chapters. Chapter 3 identifies risks faced by IFS and spillover and contagion channels across conventional and Islamic banks as well as within the latter group. It then looks at cases of Islamic bank distress where the risks and channels of transmissions were at play. The focus is on systemic crises and not on idiosyncratic distress in a single institution offering Islamic financial services (IIFS) without risk of contamination of other financial services. Particular attention is given to the systemic crisis

---

[1] Islamic financial services (IFS) is used to refer to essentially Islamic banking. The more general IFS expression is used as Islamic banks also provide nonbank financial services and cannot be considered to fall into a category such as conventional commercial banks.

[2] Zawya, Middle East Business Information, May 3, 2008, "Islamic Banks Are Sub-Prime Winners," http://cm3.zawya.com/marketing.cfm?zp&p=/Story.cfm/sidEIU20080401223346006.

[3] Islamic finance scholars prohibit the trading of debt (*bai al-dayn*) at market value or negotiated value, but allow it only at face value.

experienced by Turkey's special finance houses (SFHs) at the beginning of the 2000s decade triggered by the collapse of Ihlas Finance House in Turkey.

Chapter 4 focuses on policies, institutions, and mechanisms to promote financial stability and deal with crises. It deals first with the role of liquidity provision in periods of financial stress. It then turns to mechanisms of liquidity management consistent with Islamic finance and the setups developed in Bahrain and Malaysia. The chapter then focuses on mechanisms to solve distress episodes when they occur. It concludes by summarizing the vulnerability of Islamic finance to a systemic crisis and provides recommendations for an increased robustness and resilience of IFS.

CHAPTER 3

Risks, Spillovers, and Distress

In most jurisdictions, Islamic and conventional banks operate side by side. Both types of institutions mobilize financial resources and intermediate them to fund economic activities. It can be expected that both types of institutions are susceptible to shocks. For example, one can imagine a failure of a conventional bank that induces a crisis of confidence that spreads to other banks, conventional or Islamic, or to the entire financial system. One can also imagine a macroeconomic failure in the form of unsustainable fiscal or current account deficits that hits the whole economy and shocks both Islamic and conventional banks. For example, the combination of macro-economic imbalances and idiosyncratic stress affected Ihlas Finance House (IFH) in Turkey and spread to the country's institutions offering Islamic financial services (IIFSs) in the early 2000s.[1] One can also anticipate that some banks in the Arab countries in transition may be adversely affected by the downturn in economic activity in the wake of regime changes.

However, it is legitimate to ask whether the effects of shocks hitting conventional or Islamic banks would spill over to the other group or remain circumscribed. A related question is the degree of vulnerability and resilience of the two groups of banks. These two questions stem from the premise that Islamic and conventional banks have different features even if they perform essentially similar functions.

The following discussion reviews various types of risks financial institutions face and whether IIFS features mitigate those risks or compound them. The chapter then surveys spillover risks across conventional and Islamic financial institutions. The basic outcome is that spillover risks are essentially idiosyncratic to each category of banks. However, spillovers can occur across these two groups of banks through effects on the broader economy. If a particular shock profoundly distresses one category of banks, affecting their markets to the point of depressing the whole economy, then the other

---

[1] Discussed later in the chapter.

category of banks would be affected. Given the relative size of the two types of banking groups, one would expect that spillovers might be more pronounced from the conventional to the Islamic banks. However, the latter's modes of operation where risk sharing and materiality of transactions are prevalent can be expected to mitigate the impact.

FINANCIAL RISKS AND THEIR IMPACT ACROSS CONVENTIONAL AND ISLAMIC FINANCIAL INSTITUTIONS

Conventional and Islamic financial institutions face credit, market, and operational risks. Each type can be at the origin of a shock that may remain circumscribed to one institution, or spill over within one group or across groups.

Credit risk is the risk of loss due to a debtor's nonpayment of a loan or other line of credit. Fatemi and Fooladi (2006) argue that it arises principally from uncertainty about a given counterparty's ability to meet its obligations. Increasing variety in the types of counterparties (from individuals to sovereign governments) and forms of obligations (from auto loans to complex derivatives transactions) means that credit risk management is at the forefront of risk management challenges facing financial services firms. Important factors determining credit risk assessments include: (1) rating of the counterparties, (2) nature of the legal and judicial system, (3) quality of collateral, (4) maturity of the credit facility, (5) size of banking and trading books, (6) use of credit derivatives, and (7) internal control systems. IIFSs and conventional financial institutions address the foregoing factors in conducting business, extending financing, and assessing their own vulnerability to adverse events.

Chapra and Khan (2000) argue that IIFSs face other risks arising from their inability to reschedule debts on the basis of a higher markup rate, from differences of opinion among *fiqh* schools, and from the dearth of *Shari'a*-compliant hedging instruments, notably credit derivatives. *Shari'a* forbids debt rescheduling with increased markup rates. This prohibition may represent an incentive to debtors to be lax in meeting debt service obligations, thus increasing financial institutions' credit risk. However, the asset-based nature of Islamic finance transactions mitigates the risks by providing banks an ownership title to marketable collateral.[2]

---

[2] In this way Islamic banking may be compared to collateral-based mortgages, which have less risk in comparison to commercial loans and are, therefore, given a lower risk weight of 50 percent whereas the latter are given 100 percent.

Differences of opinion among *Shari'a* scholars create another risk specific to IIFSs. For example, some scholars consider the *murabaha* contract binding only for the seller, but not for the buyer.[3] Others consider it binding on both parties, and most Islamic banks function on this basis. But the OIC Fiqh Academy believes that the party that defaults has the overall responsibility for the compensation of any losses to the wronged party. In another example of differences of opinions, some scholars have challenged the compliance of *ijara* ending in ownership, a type of transaction implemented by most Islamic institutions. This difference of opinion raises the degree of risk in the *ijara* contract. Finally, non-*Shari'a* compliance of most hedging instruments, notably credit derivatives, limits IIFSs' access to effective methods of credit risk mitigation.

In addition to the foregoing, Islamic financial instruments incorporate specific credit risk features. The *salam* contract may face a counterparty risk associated with a failure to supply on time, or at all, and failing to supply the agreed-upon quality or quantity. When an Islamic bank participates in an *istisna'a* contract, it functions as supplier, manufacturer, constructor, and builder. As none of these roles are the bank's normal business, subcontractors must be used. Thus the bank is exposed to two-way counterparty risk. The risk of default of the customer is one of these, but there is also the risk of the subcontractors failing to carry out their duties effectively and on time.

IIFSs indirectly face *market risk* through the markup price of deferred sale and lease-based transactions. Market risk may result in losses in on- and off-balance-sheet positions arising from movements in market prices. These would include volatility of market rates or prices such as profit rates, foreign exchange rates, and equity prices. A typical loss would be a decrease in the value of an investment due to changes in market factors.[4] The fact that IIFSs operate under the principles of risk sharing and no interest and in compliance with *Shari'a* principles does not remove market risk.

Islamic banks often benchmark the pricing of their instruments to the London Interbank Offered Rate (LIBOR). Thus, a change in LIBOR affects

---

[3]They include the OIC Fiqh Academy.

[4]Equity price risk arises from fluctuations in equity indexes and prices. The nontrading equity price risk exposure arises from the bank's investment portfolio. Currency risk is the risk that the value of a financial instrument will fluctuate due to changes in foreign exchange rates. The bank takes an exposure to the effect of fluctuation in prevailing foreign currency exchange rates on its financial position. Commodity risk refers to the uncertainties of future market values and of the size of the future income caused by the fluctuation in the prices of commodities. Quémard and Golitin (2005) argue that most conventional bank failures and banking problems historically have been attributable to poorly managed exposures to market risk.

an IIFS's income statement in the same way it does with a conventional bank, depending on the share of the balance sheet linked to the benchmark. An increase in the LIBOR leads to an increase in the markup charged on new transactions and expected returns by investment account holders, compared to the earnings from the bank's long-term investments. Furthermore, IIFSs' balance sheets are exposed indirectly to variations of rates of return linked to LIBOR. The value of assets such as a deferred sale and lease transaction will vary with the wedge between the price at which they were issued and market changes in the benchmark.[5]

Basel Accords and national regulators have shown increasing concern about *operational risks*. The Basel Committee defines operational risk as "the risk of loss resulting from the inadequate or failed internal processes, people and systems or from external events. This definition includes legal risk." In addition, "legal risk includes, but is not limited to, exposure to fines, penalties, or punitive damages resulting from supervisory actions, as well as private settlements."[6] Operational risk in IIFSs would include *Shari'a* noncompliance, in addition. [7] One particular feature is that an IIFS may conduct business that is later considered not *Shari'a* compliant. In this case the IIFS will have to forgo the income earned. In addition, if this becomes a frequent occurrence, the IIFS would incur reputational damage that would undermine its franchise as a *Shari'a*-compliant financial institution. Moreover, the profit and loss sharing (PLS) modes of operation may be intrinsically more complex to run, compounding operational risk.[8]

SPILLOVERS AND CONTAGION

In the wake of the 2008 financial crisis, observers noted that IIFSs may have been less affected than conventional banks. The foregoing pointed out that the risk-sharing and materiality features of IIFS transactions have the potential of mitigating risks. However, IIFSs and conventional banks perform essentially similar financial intermediation functions. Therefore, both groups of institutions face credit, market, and operational risks. They also

---

[5] In PLS modes, the rate of return on financial assets is unknown or fixed prior to undertaking the transaction. In purchase-resale transactions, a markup is determined based on a benchmark rate of return, typically LIBOR.
[6] Operational risk factors incorporate mismanagement, inadequate staffing, malfunctions in information processing systems, weak control systems, fraud, and catastrophic events (Basel Committee on Banking Supervision, 2005).
[7] See El-Hawary, Grais, and Iqbal (2006); Grais and Pellegrini (2006c).
[8] Čihák and Hesse (2008).

face reputational risks and macroeconomic risks. They may be affected to different degrees, however. IIFSs also face a particular type of risk related to the nature of their franchise, namely the pledge to conduct their business in compliance with *Shari'a* principles. This difference not only entails an idiosyncratic operational risk in each IIFS, but may also spill over to other IIFSs through damaging the reputation of the industry.

Table 3.1 provides an overview of the potential contagion channels that may affect IIFSs and conventional banks. It considers that a general economic slowdown has the potential of significantly affecting both groups. At the other end of the spectrum, a *Shari'a* operational risk may moderately affect other IIFSs but have a negligible impact on a conventional bank. It would be negligible but still present because of the involvement of a number of conventional banks in Islamic financial intermediation. To the extent that monetary policy and systemic liquidity management have an impact,

TABLE 3.1 Overview of Contagion Effects across Islamic and Conventional Banks

Risk of Contagion to From	Islamic Banks	Conventional Banks
Islamic Banks		
Reputational shock	High	Negligible
Idiosyncratic risks (credit, market, operational)	Moderate	Negligible
Tight interbank liquidity	Low	Low
Tight financing (lending) policies	Low	Low
Shari'a pronouncements	Moderate	Negligible
Conventional Banks		
Reputational shock	Moderate	High
Idiosyncratic risks (credit, market, operational)	Negligible	Moderate
Interbank liquidity	Low to moderate	High
Tight lending policies	Moderate	High
Economic Slowdown		
Commodity market weakness	High	Moderate
Monetary policy	Low	High
General economic slowdown	High	High
Bear stock markets	Low to moderate	Moderate to high

it would be high on conventional banks but low on IIFSs; this is due to the limited tools available to monetary authorities to manage IIFS liquidity. Based on features of both groups of banks and types of risks, the table highlights expected impacts.

CASES OF ISLAMIC BANK DISTRESS

There have been episodes of Islamic bank distress. They include the closing of Bank Taqwa in 2001 on anti–money laundering/combating the financing of terrorism (AML/CFT) grounds; Faisal Islamic Bank closing its operations in the United Kingdom for regulatory reasons; the Kuwait Finance House engulfment in 1986 in the Souk al Manakh crash (1982); the liquidation of the International Islamic Bank of Denmark due to excessive financing exposure to a single client (1986); and the failure of the Islamic Money Management Companies in Egypt (1988–1989) for engaging in Ponzi-like schemes. The Islamic Bank of South Africa (IBSA) failed in November 1997 with debts between R50 million and R70 million and went under registrar of banks curatorship.[9] It has emerged that bad management and improper accounting and management systems caused the bank to fail. A large amount of insider unsecured lending had taken place, which resulted in a large proportion of nonperforming assets (NPAs) on the balance sheet.[10]

Dubai Islamic Bank experienced a fraud believed to be worth almost US$300 million, leading to its partial ownership by the state in 1998. The fraud caused a run on deposits, endangering the bank's stability and forcing the government to underwrite the losses and take a 30 percent stake in the bank. A number of high-profile persons were detained in Dubai as part of a fraud investigation, though the precise circumstances were not disclosed.

Bank Islam Malaysia, a *Shari'a*-compliant financial institution, had incurred losses of RM 457 million (US$120.2 million at that time) in the year ending June 30, 2005, whereas the provisions for bad loans and investments were RM 774 million.[11] Most of these had been incurred by the bank's Labuan branch, which had been converted from a subsidiary to a branch only the previous December. The bank had a gross nonperforming

---

[9] Okeahalam (1998).

[10] The Reserve Bank has agreed to compensate the investors up to a maximum of R50,000 per depositor. This covers 80 percent of depositors since the primary depositor base of IBSA is small depositors.

[11] "Islamic Finance: Why Islamic Banks Must Offer a Cushion against Collapse," *Asiamoney* 19, no. 8 (September 2008), 09589309.

loan portfolio of around RM 2.2 billion.[12] Bank Negara Malaysia became involved, allowing suitors (initially Bahrain's Unicorn Bank and then Malaysia's own Commerce Tijari Bank) to open talks about taking stakes in the bank. Bank Negara also set up a special purpose vehicle with Bank Islam Malaysia to manage and restructure the debt and loan portfolio, ring-fencing RM 1.6 billion, with the remainder, comprised mainly of Islamic home financing loans, staying on the bank's books. By October 2006, a recapitalization had been completed. Bank Islam issued 845 million new shares for a cash injection of RM 1.01 billion. In all, 40 percent of the bank, or 690 million shares, went to Dubai Financial, part of the Dubai Investment Group, for RM 828.2 million. Another chunk, worth 9 percent, went to Lembaga Tabung Haji, a fund designed to help Malaysian Muslims with their pilgrimages. Bank Islam returned to profitability in 2007/2008 financial year.[13]

THE CASE OF TURKEY'S SPECIAL FINANCE HOUSES

Turkey's banking and financial crisis of 2000–2001 provides a dual conventional–Islamic financial system context to consider the stability of the country's Islamic banking sector. It presents an episode where stresses on the liquidity of the largest Islamic bank in conjunction with a broader economic crisis propagated to other IIFSs. The experience provides an opportunity to identify channels and factors that can contribute to the propagation of financial distress in times of crisis.[14]

Turkey's special finance houses (SFHs) offered *Shari'a*-compliant financial services based on a decree of December 1983 on the "Establishment

---

[12]The precise reasons for these losses have, in some people's eyes, never been adequately explained, yet they threatened the bank's future.

[13]The bank delivered a net profit of RM 253.68 million (US$78 million) in the first nine months of its 2007/2008 financial year.

[14]As in many emerging-market banking crises, the runs on the SFHs occurred during a period of macroeconomic and financial crisis. In 1999, Turkey had embarked on a stabilization program supported by the International Monetary Fund (IMF) that was intended to bring inflation down using a crawling exchange-rate peg, while reducing fiscal imbalances through privatization. However, by late 2000, continued heavy government borrowing created doubts about whether the peg could be sustained; the central bank ran down $7 billion of its reserves to support the lira, and the crisis abated only when a $10 billion loan was arranged with the IMF. The pressure on it became so severe that government had to let the lira float. It immediately depreciated by 30 percent.

of Special Financial Houses." The SFHs were *Shari'a*-compliant financial institutions in which costs of borrowing and returns to financing were based on risk participation rather than interest payments. In Turkey's dual banking system, Islamic banks were competing with conventional banks that charged and offered interest. However, SFHs were not covered by deposit insurance and accordingly were less susceptible than their conventional counterparts to moral-hazard problems that may occur in the presence of deposit insurance.

For the most part, they adopted conservative conduct in their approach to risk. SFHs held 90 percent of their assets in short-term facilities (typically four to five months in duration) provided mainly to small and medium-sized companies. This sort of financing was extended in the form of *murabaha*. Kuran (1995) points out that the concentration of lending in this low-risk form implies that returns, if not guaranteed, are highly predictable.[15] SFHs also offered financial leasing and full or partial funding for long-term business projects in the form of *mudaraba* and *musharaka* participations. Following the general practice in *mudaraba* contracts, SFHs kept 20 percent of the income received from their financing activities and distributed 80 percent to account holders. While the SFH sector had been growing consistently, it constituted a tiny sliver of the banking sector, holding less than 3 percent of its total deposits, as of 2000.[16]

Although SFHs were initially governed by a separate regulatory framework from that applying to conventional banks, the 1999 bank law brought them under the same regulatory umbrella. They were required to meet the same minimum capitalization as conventional banks, and the same reserve ratios and liquidity ratios. SFHs had similar reporting requirements to the central bank as commercial banks, notably on foreign-currency positions. However, SFHs were not covered by deposit insurance, with the rationale that *Shari'a*-compliant profit-and-loss accounts involved no guarantee of return of principal. Also, unlike commercial banks, a failed SFH would not be transferred to the Savings Deposit Insurance Fund for reconciliation. The SFHs could engage in all commercial banking activities, as well as leasing and commodity trading. However, in compliance with *Shari'a*, they could not take deposits and make loans in ways that involved payment or receipt

---

[15] Indeed Kuran (1995, 162), among others, argues that *murabaha* financing does not effectively involve risk sharing and so should instead be seen as a "cumbersome form of interest." See Martha A. Starr and Rasim Yilmaz (2007).

[16] As of December 31, 2000, 2.65 percent of the total deposits of the banks displaying activity in Turkey was collected by the special finance houses; see www.ifk.com.tr/detay.asp?ContentID=754&lang=eng.

of interest. Their main source of funds was profit-and-loss participation accounts.[17]

Ihlas Finance House (IFH) was Turkey's largest SFH, with close to 38 percent of the total deposits collected by the six SFHs at the end of 2000.[18] The decision to liquidate IFH was made in February 2001 following a run on deposits amounting to US$270 million out of a total deposit base of US$1.17 billion. Liquidation procedures started on August of the same year.

IFH's failure revealed how poor idiosyncratic corporate governance can lead to crisis in an institution and become contagious and propagate to other IIFSs whose challenges are compounded by the difficulty of managing liquidity in the absence of *Shari'a*-compliant money markets. Lack of decisive early action against failing banks on the part of the regulators also contributed to compounding the problems.

IFH had been a well-regarded market leader but was liquidated by the Turkish Banking Regulation and Supervision Agency (TBRSA) because it had illegally appropriated almost $1 billion through connected lending to shareholders, virtually the entire value of the deposit base. When the bank was liquidated, the misappropriation of funds was so large that the bank was unable to pay back its 220,000 deposit accounts.[19] Thus IFH became insolvent following irregular use of funds that hindered its ability to cope with a run on deposits triggered by the general macrofinancial crisis and by a loss of confidence, and its problems were compounded by the lack of short-term interbank Islamic financial facilities and instruments.[20] IFH's difficulties induced runs on other SFHs, resulting in a sizable loss of deposits in the sector.[21]

Assets of all SFHs declined 63 percent in 2001; the assets of the five remaining houses fell by more than one-third (see Table 3.2). Many depositors sought to withdraw their funds before maturity, and initially the SFHs

---

[17] Profit-and-loss accounts represent 90 to 95 percent of the value of SFH deposits; these are also called unrestricted investment accounts (UIAs). The remaining 5 to 10 percent are special current accounts, which are demand deposits that pay no return.

[18] "Ihlas Finansin Liquidation," www.ifk.com.tr/detay.asp?ContentID=754&lang=eng.

[19] Starr and Yilmaz (2007).

[20] In 2000, 10 banks had failed, eight of them state owned. They were transferred for liquidation or refloatation to the Savings Deposit Investment Fund (SDIF).

[21] The category "loans" for the special finance houses (SFHs) includes certain commodity-related transactions in which SFHs place part of their liquid assets with foreign banks in special arrangements. For example. Citibank-England owns stock in the London Metal Exchange market; SFHs buy these stocks from Citibank, and then immediately sell them back on deferred payment terms. This enables the SFHs to earn a safe, fixed, short-term return from commodity buying and selling.

TABLE 3.2 Percentage Decline in Deposits at the Special Finance Houses, December 31, 2000, to June 30, 2001

Special Finance Houses	Percentage Decline
Al Baraka Turkish Finance House	42.1
Family Finance House	29.4
Kuwait Turkish Evkaf Finance House	22.3
Anadolu Finance House	55.0
Ihlas Finance House	100.0
Asya Finance House	34.2
Total special finance houses	63.6
Total excluding Ihlas Finance House	36.4

Source: Martha A. Starr and Rasim Yilmaz, "Bank Runs in Emerging-Market Economies: Evidence from Turkey's Special Finans Houses," *Southern Economic Journal* 73, no. 4 (2007): 1112–1132.

accommodated such requests. But as the runs continued, some had to restrict early withdrawals. On February 21, 2001, the SFHs published advertisements in newspapers announcing their intention to set up a private insurance fund to cover deposits, with government approval but not financial support. However, it is unclear that this measure had any effect in stemming the outflow of deposits.

Martha A. Starr and Rasim Yilmaz (2007) delve into depositors' behavior during bank runs.[22] They find that both informational and self-fulfilling types of dynamics were at work.[23] The authors interpret their findings as being consistent with Chen's (1999) argument that there are both first-come, first-served and informational elements involved in bank runs. They argue that, while there were valid reasons for depositors to be concerned about the safety of their funds, their sense of urgency about getting their money out of the SFH was out of proportion with the risk, and is best interpreted as a reaction to noisy bad news that escalated into a panic. Increased withdrawals by moderate-sized account holders tended to boost

---

[22]They analyzed detailed data on withdrawals from a financially strong SFH.

[23]The authors investigated how depositors of different sizes reacted to each other's withdrawals, using a vector autoregressive (VAR) framework. The framework allowed them to distinguish between informational and self-fulfilling elements of runs. Data cover the 48 business days of the run, starting on February 12, 2001, and ending on April 25.

withdrawals by smaller counterparts, suggesting that the latter viewed the behavior of the former as informative with respect to the SFH's financial condition. However, the opposite also appeared to be true, with increased withdrawals by smaller account holders inducing withdrawals by moderate-sized account holders, and the latter spilling over to withdrawals by large account holders, effects consistent with concerns about self-fulfilling elements of runs. This suggests a role of deposit insurance to mitigate inefficient aspects of runs. As much as overly generous deposit insurance may contribute to excessive risk taking by banks, some amount of insurance may be important for ruling out risks of inefficient runs by reducing uninformed depositors' incentives to rush to withdraw in periods of macrofinancial uncertainty.[24]

[24]This implies a possibility that some level of partial insurance is enough to cover average depositors, but not so generous as to cause moral hazard problems that could contribute to bank instability in emerging-market economies.

CHAPTER 4

Coping with Crises: Policies, Institutions, and Markets

The case of Lehman Brothers strikingly illustrates the dilemma authorities may face in dealing with a liquidity squeeze of a systemically important financial institution. In that event, policy makers decided not to provide liquidity support, letting market discipline punish Lehman Brothers, triggering a crisis of confidence and the financial intermediation's collapse that ensued. History and numerous analyses will judge the role of that decision. For our purpose, the case illustrates public financial authorities' challenges, namely: (1) to be able to judge whether a liquidity shortage in a financial institution is merely a short-term liquidity problem or a deeper solvency issue; (2) to be able to judge the impact on the rest of the financial system of a decision to provide or not liquidity to a financial institution facing a shortage; (3) to have available financial instruments to provide liquidity without distorting markets, if the authorities decide to do so; and (4) to have in place mechanisms to resolve in an orderly fashion not only single but even more importantly a series of distressed financial institutions.

The chapter first reviews monetary and systemic liquidity management policies that essentially aim at containing crises and limiting their spread. Core issues are the *Shari'a* compliance of policy instruments targeting liquidity management, and their insertion in a policy framework that can apply to dual systems without inducing distortions. Switching from crisis containment to resolution, another section reviews available mechanisms to solve distressed financial institutions and their relevance to institutions offering Islamic financial services (IIFSs).

The chapter proceeds to review the experience of the Gulf Cooperation Council (GCC) countries in coping with the 2008 financial stress. It then considers theoretical predictions on the impact of monetary policy in a dual system. The experiences of Bahrain and Malaysia in developing a monetary policy and systemic liquidity management framework for their jurisdictions are assessed. Finally, an outline of a road map to develop a framework relevant to dual systems is suggested.

PROVISION OF LIQUIDITY AND CRISIS CONTAINMENT

Confronted with an emerging stress in the financial system, public authorities generally provide liquidity to banks through the extension of credit lines or by purchasing banks' assets. Generally these operations are interest-based and would be out of IIFSs' reach. Public authorities also seek to increase public confidence in banks by announcing guarantees of bank deposits. These measures seek to stem depositors' rush to withdraw their funds and to encourage banks to extend financial facilities to each other.

RECENT EXPERIENCE IN THE GCC COUNTRIES BUILDING PUBLIC CONFIDENCE

During the 2008 financial turmoil, GCC financial authorities provided liquidity, capital increases, and guarantees to strengthen confidence and stabilize both Islamic and conventional financial institutions operating under their jurisdiction.

The central bank of the United Arab Emirates (UAE) injected cash into the financial system. In addition to the AED 50 billion (US$13.6 billion) liquidity fund, a further AED 70 billion injection was subsequently announced by the Ministry of Finance.[1] The UAE government guaranteed all deposits with local and foreign-owned banks for three years, including the country's two largest lenders, Emirates NBD and National Bank of Abu Dhabi, to ensure that credit continued to flow.[2] The measure also includes a guarantee of all interbank lending in the UAE. The central bank

---

[1] The charge for banks to draw on these funds has also been eased from 5 percent to 3.5 percent. "UAE: Government Moves to Shore Up Banking Sector," *Emerging Markets Monitor* 14, no. 28 (October 20, 2008), 19 (AN 34881789); Economist Intelligence Unit Limited, *Country Monitor* 16, no. 37 (October 26, 2008), 10 (AN 34905428).
[2] Abu Dhabi injects Dh 16 billion of tier 1 capital for five banks; the emirate has allocated 2 billion dirhams each for Union National Bank and Abu Dhabi Islamic Bank, and 4 billion dirhams each for the National Bank of Abu Dhabi, First Gulf Bank, and Abu Dhabi Commercial Bank. The liquidity support made by the emirate will be in the form of tier 1 capital qualifying nonvoting, noncumulative perpetual securities. It relates the factors that affected the Gulf banking sector. *Euroweek*, no. 1090 (February 6, 2009), 64.

of the UAE urged banks operating in the country to reduce lending and to boost deposits as part of efforts to shore up the country's banking system. It also advised banks that from June 2009 on they would be required to have a capital adequacy ratio (tier 1 capital) of 11 percent and to reach 12 percent by June 30, 2010, compared with the 8 percent required under the Basel Accords.[3] According to most bank analysts, almost all banks have already met the deadline. The average ratio for the UAE banks was 20.3 percent at the end of first quarter of 2010, according to central bank data.[4]

The Saudi Arabia Monetary Authority (SAMA) provided about US$3 billion in liquidity to the banking system in the form of deposits to ease liquidity pressures and made a $40 billion lending facility available to domestic banks needing funds.[5] SAMA made a rare benchmark repurchase interest rate cut by a total of 350 basis points to 2 percent and also lowered reserve requirements to 7 percent from 13 percent to give increased liquidity to banks.[6]

Over a large part of 2008, the four largest banks by total assets, Qatar National Bank, Commercial Bank of Qatar, Doha Bank, and Qatar Islamic Bank, saw the prices of their shares decline by 18.8 percent, 55.5 percent, 48.1 percent, and 35.3 percent, respectively.[7] Fears over their future earnings were being driven by concerns over the global economic slowdown, the trend in hydrocarbon prices, and the risks of a contagion effect from a Dubai property price crash spreading to Qatar. Qatari banks are heavily exposed to the domestic real estate sector and vulnerable to the sector's performance. Real estate loans make up 13.2 percent of total bank lending.[8] The government offered assistance through its sovereign wealth fund (SWF), the Qatar Investment Authority (QIA). Under a plan unveiled in October 2008, the Commercial Bank of Qatar and Qatar International Islamic Bank have sold stakes to the QIA, and Doha Bank sought shareholders' approval for a similar deal, which would raise its capital by up to 20 percent. QIA announced that it would take between 10 and 20 percent of the equity of all banks in Qatar.

---

[3] Martin (2008, 19).
[4] Shveta Pathak, "UAE Banks Achieve June CAR Target, Cushioned Banks Have No Trouble Meeting Capital Adequacy Ratios," *Emirates 24/7*, May 25, 2010.
[5] Shamseddine and Critchlow (2008).
[6] Arabianbusiness.com, "Saudi Banks Post Lower Q4 Profits," January 19, 2009. www.arabianbusiness.com/544145-saudi-banks-post-lower-q4-profits.
[7] "Qatar: Little Danger of Systemic Failure," *Emerging Markets Monitor* 14, no. 32 (November 24, 2008), 18.
[8] Ibid.

In Kuwait, the government agreed to buy part of Gulf Bank if shareholders do not provide enough capital to shore it up. It has announced that it would guarantee all banks' deposits, including savings accounts and certificates of deposit. The Ministry of Finance provides liquidity from the state's general reserve funds with oversight by the Central Bank of Kuwait (CBK).

IMPACT OF MONETARY POLICY IN DUAL SYSTEMS

In principle, most IIFSs' resources would be only indirectly linked to changes in the cost of funds induced by conventional monetary policy to tighten or loosen credit. Accordingly, the latter may have only a limited impact on the cost of financial facilities extended by IIFSs to the economy. Indeed, the bulk of IIFS resources is mainly mobilized through UIA. UIA holders would be expected to have low substitution elasticity in their demand choice between conventional and Islamic deposits. Thus, IIFSs should not face significant shifts in their deposit base as a result of changes of relative costs of funds induced by monetary policy. Consequently, conventional monetary policy on its own should not have a significant effect on the cost of financing extended by IIFSs to the economy.

Moreover, *Shari'a*'s prohibition of conventional borrowing and absence or shallowness of active interbank *Shari'a*-compliant money markets restrict IIFS options in managing liquidity. Wherever countries have Islamic and conventional finance operating side by side, monetary authorities generally do not have at their disposal a menu of liquid *Shari'a*-compliant instruments to inject or mop up liquidity and reduce or raise, respectively, the cost of funds to IIFSs. The use of central bank certificates or treasury bills bearing interest can deal with liquidity only in the conventional segment. They present an opportunity for conventional banks to hold risk-free government paper, an opportunity that escapes IIFSs. Furthermore, the introduction of *Shari'a*-compatible instruments may lead to market segmentation, limit liquidity, and compound the efficient transmission of monetary policy.[9]

TOOLS FOR SYSTEMIC LIQUIDITY MANAGEMENT

The Bahrain Monetary Authority established a Liquidity Management Center (LMC), and Bank Negara Malaysia established the Islamic Interbank Money Market (IIMM) based on *Shari'a* principles with the goal of allowing Islamic banks to handle their liquidity needs and develop an active secondary market that would be *Shari'a* compliant on the basis of profit

---

[9]Sundarajan (2006).

and loss sharing (PLS) arrangements.[10] Bahrain and Malaysia have been forerunners in developing bond markets[11] that can also support the conduct of monetary policy and systemic liquidity management[12] in dual systems. One of the objectives in the Islamic bond issues is to create a dynamic secondary market. Islamic bonds, which comply with *Shari'a* principles, have played a major role in Malaysia's capital market development, contributing to the significant growth of the country's Islamic financial system.[13]

In 2001, the Bahraini authorities introduced two types of *sukuk* to satisfy the needs of Islamic banks. The intention was to replace some of the sovereign's conventional borrowing with Islamic instruments, so that (1) Islamic banks would face a level playing field with conventional banks in terms of investment opportunities, and (2) the authorities could engage Islamic banks in the conduct of monetary policy. Consequently, *ijara* and *salam sukuk*s were issued as long-term and short-term sovereign instruments, respectively.[14]

---

[10]The Bahrain Monetary Authority (BMA) later became the Central Bank of Bahrain (CBB). The International Islamic Financial Market (IIFM) was also founded with the support of the central banks and monetary agencies of Bahrain, Brunei, Indonesia, Malaysia, Sudan, and the Islamic Development Bank based in Saudi Arabia, as an infrastructure institution with the mandate to take part in the establishment, development, self-regulation, and promotion of the Islamic capital and money market.

[11]Oh and Park (2006) and Park and Rhee (2006) have proposed a package of three policy measures to develop regional bond markets: namely, a regional credit guarantees agency, a regional bond rating facility, and a regional clearing and settlement capacity. Combined, these elements are seen as the necessary infrastructure components on which to build a regional bond market. Similar developments could take place in the GCC region after the creation of the monetary union planned for 2010. (The introduction of a single currency, officially targeted for 2010, was not achieved as scheduled. Oman and the UAE have officially withdrawn from the common currency project.) In fact, the efforts already under way to harmonize several areas of the economy (financial regulations, tax codes, accounting conventions, as well as payment systems) that are important from the perspective of the monetary union are also beneficial for the creation of a regional bond market.

[12]Sudan has developed *musharaka* certificates linked to the ownership of state-owned enterprises.

[13]Malaysia is the largest issuer of Islamic financial products in East Asia. In 2008, Islamic bonds accounted for nearly 38 percent of total local currency bonds outstanding. "Systemic Liquidity Management: Bahrain's Experience," http://asianbondsonline.adb .org/islamic_finance/structure/overview.php.

[14]*Sukuk salam* are created and sold by a special purpose vehicle (SPV) that mobilizes funds from investors as an advance in return for a promise to deliver a commodity at a future date. The SPV appoints an agent to market the promised quantity at the time of delivery, perhaps at a higher price. The difference between the purchase price and sale price is the profit to the SPV and hence to the holders of the *sukuk*.

Mirroring the use of treasury bills in conventional systems to manage systemic liquidity, the Central Bank of Bahrain (CBB) uses short-term (91-day) *salam sukuk*s to engage Islamic banks in its monetary operations. The special deposit facilities available for conventional banks are not available to IIFSs, as these are not *Shari'a* compliant. Thus, IIFSs rely on non-interest-bearing excess reserves held in their current accounts with the CBB, and have access to *ijara* and *salam sukuk*s for their liquidity management.

The CBB manages the government's *ijara* and *salam sukuk*s and treasury bill programs.[15] All Islamic securities are backed by the government-owned underlying assets as the government's agent. The government directly guarantees the Islamic leasing securities via a binding promise to buy the asset at original par value at maturity. It also guarantees to continue renting the asset according to the rental contract until the end of the rental period. The securities are issued at 100 percent of their face value, and the rate of return is set by the Monetary Policy Committee. Apart from being the guarantor, the CBB is also acting as the issuing agent.[16]

The *salam sukuk* is a short-term Islamic security, denominated in Bahrain dinar (BHD), with a maturity of 91 days and issued once a month. At any time, there are three *salam sukuk* outstanding issues. The return is preset by the Monetary Policy Committee and is paid upon maturity. The Ministry of Finance decides the amounts to be issued each year in advance. Commercial banks (Islamic and conventional), the General Organization for Social Insurance, the Pension Fund Commission (military and civilian), financial institutions, and national insurance companies are permitted to subscribe to the *salam sukuk*. The allotment amount is determined on a pro rata basis in relation to the total amount subscribed to by participants. Hence, all participants receive a part of the issue. The *salam sukuk* is used to affect the level of Bahrain dinar current account balances of banks with the CBB, and thereby to influence monetary conditions, while also serving as a tool of public debt management.

There are two types of *ijara sukuk*s: (1) short-term (182 days) denominated in BHD only, and (2) long-term (between three and 10 years) denominated in USD or BHD. The short-term *sukuk al-ijara* is issued once a month and with the same issue amount for all issues during the same calendar year. There is no secondary market for the short-term Islamic securities. The long-term *ijara sukuk* is issued on an ad hoc basis, and the issue amount varies across issues. The *ijara sukuk*s are listed on the Bahrain Stock Exchange, and the CBB provides buy-back facilities at the maturity date. The return

---

[15] www.cbb.gov.bh/page-p-issuance_of_govt_securities.htm.
[16] These are government issues, but the CBB issues them on behalf of the government and does not charge the government for the issuance cost.

for these securities is either fixed or floating and is paid semiannually. The issue amount is decided by the Ministry of Finance each year in advance, and the Banking Services Directorate is responsible for publishing an issuance calendar for each year, which is available on the CBB website. All commercial banks, the General Organization for Social Insurance, the Pension Fund Commission (military and civilian), financial institutions, and national insurance companies are eligible to participate in the USD-based *ijara sukuk*.

SYSTEMIC LIQUIDITY MANAGEMENT: MALAYSIA'S EXPERIENCE

Malaysia's experience appears to indicate a significant degree of substitutability in the demand choice between Islamic and conventional deposits, contrary to theory-based predictions.

Bank Negara Malaysia (BNM) established an interbank investment facility where IIFSs may obtain short-term funds from one another on the basis of PLS arrangements. The Islamic interbank market is a mechanism known as the *mudaraba* interbank investment (MII) scheme. The mechanism allows Islamic banks to borrow and lend to each other. As the name suggests, the financing is *mudaraba* based with a negotiated profit-sharing ratio (PSR). The minimum amount of investment in the MII is RM 50,000. The term of investment can vary from overnight to 12 months. In the early years of the Islamic interbank market, the rate of return on the MII used to be based on the gross profit rate on one-year investments that the receiving (borrowing) bank was paying to depositors.[17] Conventional financial institutions have access to the Islamic Interbank Money Market (IIMM); there are no limits on the participation of conventional financial institutions in buying Islamic money market instruments or selling the ones they own. They cannot issue their own Islamic papers. By 2011, 55 banks were registered to participate in the Islamic money market and the annual trading volume exceeded RM 1 trillion, reflecting its depth and vibrancy.[18]

---

[17] Currently the scheme would operate as follows: "The period of investment is from overnight to 12 months, while the rate of return is based on the rate of gross profit before distribution for investments of 1-year of the investee bank. The profit-sharing ratio is negotiable among both parties. The investor bank at the time of negotiation would not know what the return would be, as the actual return will be crystallised towards the end of the investment period. The principal invested shall be repaid at the end of the period, together with a share of the profit arising from the used of the fund by the investee bank." See www.bnm.gov.my/index.php?ch=&pg=en_ib_all&ac=374.

[18] See Bank Negara Malaysia (2011): "Financial Stability and Payments Systems Report."

Obiyathulla (2008) observes three channels of transmission between Islamic and conventional money markets: (1) pricing in interbank rates, (2) pricing of Islamic money market instruments, and (3) the central bank's money market operations. Evidence of strong correlation between the interbank rates means that changes in interest rates in the conventional money market are simply transmitted to Islamic banks when they use the IIMM for their liquidity management. Similarly, since IIMM instruments are priced using discounting, interest rate changes cause repricing risk with discount rate changes. As a result of the possibility for pure arbitrage, prices and yields of IIMM and conventional money market instruments will invariably converge. Accordingly, IIFSs issuing IIMM instruments will face higher cost if conventional interest rates rise. A third transmission channel arises from central bank intervention. Regardless of whether the intervention is a routine open market operation to influence liquidity or execution of new monetary policy, the central bank's actions in the IIMM must reflect its actions in the conventional money market.

Over the period 2003–2006, profit rates in the Islamic money market have been generally lower than in the conventional money market.[19] However, movements in the Islamic profit rates follow closely changes in the conventional money market interest rates, and the base financing rate (BFR) of two major Islamic banks moves fairly closely with the base lending rate (BLR) of conventional banks. Therefore, monetary operations to manage liquidity in both the conventional and the Islamic banking system do seem to have a similar impact.

THE ROAD AHEAD: DEALING WITH SYSTEMIC LIQUIDITY IN ISLAMIC FINANCIAL SERVICES

To cope with systemic liquidity risk within Islamic financial services (IFS), public financial authorities need to develop an effective systemic liquidity management framework that factors in both conventional and Islamic finance. In particular, liquid money markets offering a level playing field to Islamic and conventional financial institutions are needed. In dual systems, it is important to develop a uniform monetary operations framework covering both Islamic and conventional financial institutions. This requires the "design and use of neutral instruments that can be widely held by both conventional and Islamic banks."[20] A lot can be learned from the experiences of

---

[19] Bank Negara Malaysia (2006). www.bnm.gov.my/files/publication/ar/en/2006/ar2006_book.pdf.
[20] Sundarajan (2006).

Bahrain and Malaysia and work done by the International Islamic Financial Market (IIFM) and the Islamic Financial Services Board (IFSB).[21]

Operations in central bank and government paper, once developed, would greatly facilitate the use of lender of last resort (LOLR) arrangements, providing authorities with instruments to deal with possible liquidity problems affecting IIFSs. The IFSB's guidelines offer a design for the development of appropriate money market instruments and the needed systemic liquidity infrastructure. The IFSB encourages the adoption of programs to develop Islamic money markets nationally, and to promote their integration regionally and globally.[22] Components of systemic liquidity infrastructure would include: (1) payment/securities settlement systems; (2) monetary policy instruments and monetary and exchange operations (lender of last resort, open market operations, etc.); (3) public financing and foreign exchange reserve management arrangements; and (4) microstructure of money, exchange, and securities markets.[23]

The design and features of these four infrastructure components are interlinked. Accordingly, a comprehensive approach is needed to develop Islamic money markets. For example, the scope and structure of monetary and exchange operations by the central banks will affect the structure and liquidity of money and exchange markets and vice versa. The operational features of

---

[21] Reserve requirements are blunt instruments of monetary policy. Remunerated reserve requirements applied equally to conventional and Islamic deposit-taking institutions would penalize the latter relative to the former. In the case of Islamic banks in Bahrain, the profit-sharing investment accounts (PSIAs) are also subject to cash reserve requirements. In Sudan, the reserve requirement does not apply to PSIAs, while Bahrain's central bank does not pay interest on reserve requirements; the special deposit facilities available for conventional banks are not available to IIFSs, as these are not *Shari'a* compatible. Thus, IIFSs rely only on non-interest-bearing excess reserves held in their current accounts with CBB. No special deposit facilities are available to banks in Malaysia (conventional or Islamic), other than the current account for holding the required and excess reserves. No return is paid on excess reserves. BNM has developed several Islamic financial instruments to facilitate effective management of liquidity in the Islamic financial system. Among others, it has developed mechanisms for the acceptance and placement, respectively, of interbank deposits that are based on the *Shari'a* contracts of *wadia* and *mudaraba*.

[22] The more recently established International Islamic Liquidity Management Corporation (IILM) can play a significant role in promoting cross-border integration of money markets. The IILM was established in October 2010 with headquarters in Kuala Lumpur (www.iilm.com/index.html).

[23] Islamic Financial Services Board (IFSB), "Technical Note on Issues in Strengthening Liquidity Management of Institutions Offering Islamic Financial Services: The Development of Islamic Money Markets," 2008, www.ifsb.org/docs/mar2008_liquidity.pdf.

monetary policy will depend upon the structure of money markets and the features of the payment system. The development of market-based monetary operations, in turn, can have a first-order impact on the evolution and liquidity of money markets. These infrastructure elements taken together not only influence the day-to-day conduct of monetary, public financing and fiscal policy, and the pace of development of money and securities markets, but also affect the profitability and efficient operations of financial institutions.[24]

DISTRESSED INSTITUTIONS RESOLUTION

If shocks are not too severe, if also balance sheets, income statements, and cash flow statements are robust and the institutions resilient, monetary policy and systemic liquidity management should permit the stabilization of the financial system. However, in many instances, and notably the post-2007 episodes of financial turmoil, shocks create victims in the form of distressed financial institutions that may well run into insolvency. In these cases, more is required than effective systemic liquidity management and monetary policy.

Most cases of financial distress are generally resolved with some kind of public authority intervention. However, the latter tend to expect and rely on cooperation between concerned private-sector agents and their ability to engage in efficient mergers and to seek outside capital injections. The financial crisis of 2008 is no exception in this respect. Examples of such reliance include Merrill Lynch and Bank of America's merger, as well as the numerous capital injections to strengthen banks' capital whether on banks' own initiative or at the behest of public authorities.[25] Sovereign wealth funds (SWFs) form an essential transmission belt within the engine of financial globalization[26] in dealing with crises.[27] These state-backed asset management pools have become pivotal actors in the provision of liquidity to minimize the solvency dilemma posed by declared cumulative losses

---

[24] Ibid·

[25] On June 11, 2009, Bank of America's CEO Kenneth D. Lewis affirmed earlier reports that he was pressured by public authorities to conclude the merger with Merrill Lynch. A number of institutions sought and secured capital increases from sovereign funds.

[26] Commission of the European Communities, A Common European Approach to Sovereign Wealth Funds, February 27, 2008.

[27] Evidence to House Committee on Financial Services, United States Congress, Washington, D.C., March 5, 2008 (G. Alvarez); see also M. Allen and J. Caruana, "Sovereign Wealth Funds: A Work Agenda," International Monetary Fund, Washington, D.C., February 29, 2008.

TABLE 4.1 Sovereign Wealth Fund Investments (U.S. Billions)

Investment Bank	Subprime Losses	SWF Injection	Equity Stake
Merrill Lynch	31.7	11.0, including:	
		4.4 (Temasek, Singapore)	9.4
		2.0 (Korea Investment Fund)	3.0
		2.0 (Kuwaiti Investment Fund)	3.0
		0.3 (New Jersey Division of Investment)	
Citigroup	40	20.0, including:	
		7.5 (Abu Dhabi Investment Authority)	4.9
		6.8 (Singapore Investment Corporation)	3.7
		3.0 (Kuwait Investment Authority)	1.6
		0.4 (New Jersey Division of Investment)	
UBS	38	9.7 (Singapore Investment Corporation)	9.8
Morgan Stanley	12.6	5 (China Investment Corporation)	9.9

Source: Justin O'Brien, "Barriers to Entry: Foreign Direct Investment and the Regulation of Sovereign Wealth Funds," 2008. This paper derives from presentations at the University of California at Berkeley; University of Cambridge; University of Glasgow; University of New Hampshire; Dayton Symposium on Accountability, Ohio; International Monetary Fund, Washington, D.C.; and Lowy Institute for International Policy, Sydney. www.cama.anu.edu.au/Events/swf2008/swf2008_papers/O'Brien_SWF_paper.doc.

across the global banking sector (see Table 4.1). Significant investment banks have secured immediate survival by turning to sovereign wealth funds operating out of the Middle East and out of East and Southeast Asia.

Distress and insolvency imply a negative net worth and an inability to pursue operations on market terms. Under the circumstances, public financial authorities may envisage the following actions.[28] *Liquidation* is a legal mechanism under which an insolvent institution is closed, its license is withdrawn, and its assets are sold or collected over time to meet the claims of depositors and other creditors.[29] *Assisted acquisition* is a mechanism under which an insolvent institution's license is withdrawn, and some of its

---

[28] See Scott (2002). This presumes the legal framework to conduct these actions is in place.

[29] The applicable legal regime may be the general bankruptcy law or a special regime for financial institutions. The extent of court involvement varies from country to country. Where deposits are insured, the deposit protection entity pays insured claims in advance of the sale or collection of the assets.

assets and liabilities are sold to one or more other financial institutions.[30]
Nationalization is a mechanism under which the government assumes temporary ownership of an insolvent institution. The institution's license is
not withdrawn, and it remains open for business.[31] *Conservatorship* is a
period of temporary government control during which management may
be removed and shareholder rights at least partially and temporarily constrained. It is not a resolution mechanism, but rather an interim step. In
suspension, an institution is closed for business (perhaps with limited exception, for example, for limited deposit withdrawals), yet its license is not
withdrawn pending further analysis of its solvency. In this sense, suspension
is not a resolution mechanism, but only an interim step.[32]

Whatever the action envisaged, implementation requires an institutional and organizational infrastructure. Furthermore, funding to acquire
and dispose of distressed assets has to be identified and secured. The process
needs to be administered and an allocation of losses across stakeholders
determined. Within a clear legal and regulatory framework, implementation
can be driven by the private or the public sector.

The Bank of England encouraged private-sector-driven out-of-court
negotiations to restructure the finances and operations of distressed companies (workouts). These have been widely used and frequently successful
since promoted in the mid-1970s. Often known as the "London approach,"
workout proceedings may be used as an alternative to court-supervised
insolvency or appointment of a trustee (or receiver) to administer the distressed entity. The London approach sets principles and processes for guiding out-of-court workouts, including also the need to address potential tax,
legal, and regulatory factors that may impede corporate restructuring and
the need to consider constraints in implementation capacity in a systemic
crisis.[33] Workouts may seem a preferable alternative to potentially more
costly and time-consuming court proceedings or the only alternative in

---

[30] Assisted acquisition is also known as business transfer (South Korea) and purchase
and assumption (United States). Most commonly, insured deposits are transferred to
(assumed by) the other institution, with payment to that institution made in the form
of cash or official debt (for example, bonds issued by the deposit protection entity and
guaranteed by the government). This resolution mechanism can minimize or eliminate potential disruption of service to depositors. Depending on the development of
the markets and the extent of preplanning by the authorities, it is possible to arrange
the sale of a large portion of a failed bank's assets and liabilities in this manner.

[31] Nationalized banks were considered "intervened" in Thailand and "taken over" in
Indonesia in the 1997–1998 East Asia crisis.

[32] Suspension in the Asia crisis involved limited numbers of banks. In other countries,
suspension has involved all banks (sometimes referred to as a general bank holiday).

[33] Mako (2003).

a systemic crisis when many simultaneous cases of distress might place a heavy burden on courts, administrators, and other insolvency professionals.

The following reviews basic features and experiences of an approach that relies on setting up an asset management corporation (AMC) with a leading role of the public sector. It then considers the relevance of the model to deal with IIFSs.

Experiences with Asset Management Corporations

An often-used mechanism to finance rehabilitation or sale of distressed assets is the establishment of an asset management corporation (AMC).[34] In the context of a systemic crisis, a government asset management company (GAMC) is often viewed as an effective way to resolve inevitable differences over loss sharing among financial institutions' creditors and public shareholders.[35] A GAMC is basically a sovereign asset management company whose purpose is to clean up the financial sector by buying, managing, and selling distressed assets of troubled financial institutions. It may also be considered a means of placing government at arm's length from the implementation of the process and reducing the cost to government of crisis resolution.[36]

A GAMC can maximize the value of a bank's assets by reducing the burden on the bank's management, reducing risks, and improving information. The sale of nonperforming assets (NPAs) to an AMC relieves bankers of further responsibility for debt restructuring, eliminates future risk of loss arising from these assets, and makes transparent the losses inherent in them. Accordingly, bankers are able to devote their attention to other tasks and to focus on the resumption of business. Moreover, eliminating the risks associated with the assets sold reduces uncertainty regarding the bank's finances, which can accelerate the process of recapitalizing and restructuring, reduce recapitalization requirements, and improve the prospects for raising private capital for recapitalization.

However, a number of issues bear on the decision to set up an AMC and the mandate it is given. They include the depth and spread of a banking problem, the political determination to deal with it, political consequences and technical difficulties of asset valuation, and the urgency of restoring confidence and encouraging the resumption of normal financial intermediation.

---

[34] Individual banks may set up privately managed AMCs (PAMCs).

[35] Fung, George, Hohl, and Ma (2004).

[36] In Turkey, the estimated net cost of the crisis (2000–2001) in terms of gross national product (GNP) was –25.33 percent in 2001, with GNP (in billions of U.S. dollars) contracting by $201.3 to $150.3 (IMF source). The estimated net cost of this crisis to the state as a percentage of GDP was 30.5 percent by June 2002 (Hoelscher and Quintyn 2003).

These factors will affect the AMC's business discretion as to the volume, type, and quality of transferred assets and will define to a large extent the complexity of the task it faces. An AMC's core charter needs to emphasize transparency and set clear guidelines for the type of assets the AMC takes over and approaches to their valuation.

The underlying *quality and type of transferred assets* affect an AMC's resolution and recovery performance. Indonesia's IBRA not only accepted nonperforming loans (NPLs), but also took over a wide range of assets, including equity interests in corporations acquired from former shareholders who pledged equity to settle claims for violating prudential norms or to obtain liquidity support from Bank Indonesia (BI) and ownership in closed banks and other financial institutions. Some AMC deal with distressed assets only, while others acquire both performing and nonperforming assets.[37] For example, the Indonesian Bank Restructuring Agency (IBRA) received whole banks, thus accepting both performing loans and NPLs. South Korea's, Malaysia's, and Thailand's AMCs dealt exclusively with problem assets. China's four AMCs took over a large number of NPLs, as well as some supposedly performing loans from the big four state banks. All in all, clarity of mandates and policy objectives is an important consideration to guide an AMC in a decision about whether to take over performing assets.

AMCs face the tremendous challenge of *valuation of the assets* that they take over. In distressed cases, relying on the notion of fair market value to price assets becomes elusive, albeit the pricing of assets to be transferred to an AMC is critical to its performance. Market value may incorporate distortions associated with the crisis, and may penalize the banking institution forced to sell assets in distressed markets. On the other hand, transferring assets at prices above their fair value subjects the AMC and possibly taxpayers to potential losses.[38] The U.S. Supreme Court recognized the dilemma when it defined fair market value as "the price at which the property would change hands between a willing buyer and a willing seller, neither being under any compulsion to buy or to sell and both having reasonable knowledge of relevant facts."[39] Some AMCs have used option-like profit- or

---

[37] One complicating factor in this respect is the evolving and inconsistent definitions and criteria used to classify nonperforming assets, both over time and across economies.

[38] Most of the NPL acquisitions by AMCs are financed through bonds, often issued by the AMC to the transferring bank.

[39] United States Supreme Court: *United States v. Cartwright*, 411 U.S. 546, 93 S. Ct. 1713, 1716–17, 36 L. Ed. 2d 528, 73-1 U.S. Tax Cas. (CCH) ¶ 12,926 (1973) (quoting from U.S. Treasury regulations relating to federal estate taxes, at 26 C.F.R. sec. 20.2031-1(b)). The issue has long concerned the accounting profession, with some arguing that marking to market and fair value are procyclical, compounding crises uselessly. In the wake of the recent crisis, accommodations to IFRS standards have been made.

TABLE 4.2   Approaches to Asset Transfers by AMCs

	China	Indonesia*	Japan	South Korea	Malaysia	Thailand
Average acquisition price (as a % of book value)	100	100	7.2	36.1	46.0	33.2
Pricing approaches used:						
- Book value	Yes	Yes	No	No	No	No
- Fair value	No	No	Yes	Yes	Yes	No
- Others	No	No	Yes	No	Yes	Yes
Incentives/ penalties:						
- Statutory requirements	Yes	Yes	Yes	Yes	Yes	Yes
- Gain or loss sharing (options)	No	No	No	Yes	Yes	Yes

Source: B. Fung, J. George, S. Hohl, and G. Ma, "Public Asset Management Companies in East Asia," Occasional Paper no. 3, Bank for International Settlements (BIS), 2004. www.bis.org/fsi/fsipapers03.pdf.

*For Indonesia, NPLs were transferred from banks at zero value. However, the government recapitalized or took over these banks through the issuance of government recapitalization bonds. Thus, one can interpret that these NPLs were acquired at book value.

loss-sharing agreements in acquiring NPLs from banks, which facilitates NPL transfers and contains AMC losses (see Table 4.2).[40] Losses accruing to the AMCs owing to the difficulty of asset valuation raise challenges in considering AMCs' funding, the ability to perform on bonds issued, and the potential burden on public finances.

Asian AMCs were expected to recover between 20 percent and 50 percent of the book value of the loans, figures that are comparable to the experiences of public AMCs created in banking crisis situations in other parts of the world.[41]

---

[40]To facilitate rapid asset transfers, profit and loss sharing between AMCs and the selling financial institution has been arranged. Profit and loss sharing is defined as the amount recovered from asset resolution in excess of the acquisition price (Fung, George, Hohl, and Ma 2004).

[41]Fung et al. (2004).

Relevance of an Asset Management Corporation for Islamic Financial Services

The Bank for International Settlements (BIS) identifies key factors that contribute to the successful operation of an AMC.[42] They include:

- *Strong political will.* There should be a strong commitment from the government to address the NPLs in the system, and the AMC should have independence and freedom from political interference.
- *Supportive legal and judicial infrastructure.* There should be effective laws, particularly in bankruptcy and foreclosure, and special legal powers to allow the AMC to achieve quicker resolution and higher recoveries.
- *Efficient market environment.* There should be well-functioning capital markets to facilitate asset sales. If the local market is immature, allowing foreign participation would speed up asset disposition.
- *Clear AMC mandate.* The AMC needs to be clear on its mandate, the types of assets to be acquired, and the resolution methods it can use. It should focus on asset sales and not be overly burdened by corporate restructuring.
- *Well-defined AMC life span.* The tenure of an AMC should generally be limited to prevent it from warehousing acquired assets in an attempt to prevent realization of large losses.
- *Adequate governance.* There should be a sound system of internal control and effective external supervision, with regular audits by an independent auditor.
- *Good transparency.* An AMC should periodically disclose the results of its operations, as well as its audit results, in a manner that will be easily understood by the market.
- *Realistic asset pricing.* Generally, assets should be transferred to an AMC at market-based prices, with proper incentives to facilitate transfers.
- *Speedy resolutions.* An AMC should aim for speedy disposition of acquired assets, as waiting for an economic turnaround to increase recovery often leads to slower resolution progress and larger losses.
- *Implementation capability.* It is reasonable to add the availability of trained staff with the administrative and financial skills to manage effectively an AMC; a weak implementation capability can undermine the ability of the best designed AMC to achieve its objectives.

Table 4.3 reviews the foregoing characteristics in two stylized jurisdictions, developing and emerging jurisdiction (DEJ) and developed jurisdiction (DJ). For the sake of presentation, IIFSs are assumed to operate

---

[42] Ibid·

TABLE 4.3   Conditions for a Successful GAMC

	Developing and Emerging Jurisdictions Where IIFS Are Present	Developed Jurisdictions with Dominant Presence of Conventional Banks
Strong political will	Possible	Possible
Supportive legal and judicial infrastructure	Generally poor but improving	Generally supportive
Efficient market environment	Generally distorted but improving	Generally good but with instances of excesses
Clear AMC mandate	Achievable	Achievable
Well-defined AMC life span	Issue of credibility	Likely credible
Adequate governance	Generally poor but improving	Good governance credible
Good transparency	Generally difficult to achieve	Generally not perfect but reasonable
Realistic asset pricing	Difficult	Difficult
Speedy resolutions	Possible	Possible
Implementation capability	Generally weak	Generally reasonable

in the DEJ, while conventional banks operate in the DJ. Though generic and accordingly overlooking specificities, this approach can be justified by the existence of a body of standards and codes applying to conventional finance and espoused by most jurisdictions. Though Islamic financial services (IFS) have made significant progress in this regard with the work undertaken by notably the AAOIFI and the IFSB, as well as national jurisdictions, the body of regulations governing IFS and their implementation has not yet received the same broad support as in the case of conventional financial services.

On the basis of judgments incorporated in Table 4.3, it would appear that a GAMC approach may be particularly challenging in most DEJs with significant presence of IIFSs. Strong political will, the definition of a clear mandate, and speed of resolution are features the DEJ can achieve. However, the other features may pose a greater challenge, even if wide variations exist and significant progress is occurring. Transparency, adequate governance, efficient market environment, and supportive legal and judicial framework are, in most DEJs, works in progress. Accordingly, a GMAC may not be the most effective instrument to deal with systemic financial distress affecting IIFSs under most institutional frameworks governing their operations.

Whether an AMC is or is not a preferred approach to dealing with a case of systemic distress in IFS, the foregoing review points out the need to anticipate the possibility of such occurrence and prepare the institutional and organization infrastructure to deal with the situation. In particular, it entails the existence of an insolvency and creditors' rights framework relevant for IIFSs, with clear laws and regulations. Also, public financial authorities need to dedicate resources to envisage scenarios of distress and approaches to deal with them, as well as train personnel and assign them to such undesired occurrences.

CONCLUSION

Islamic financial services are certainly not more prone to distress and crisis than conventional financial services.[43] Most banking failures are precipitated by liquidity shortages, though their troubles may have been building up earlier. The case of Ihlas Finance House (IFH) in Turkey reflects a sequence of poor management decisions, including nonprudent intragroup financing, and poor crisis management strategy that made the institution vulnerable to shocks. When the latter occurred with the macroeconomic crisis and the subsequent run on deposits, IFH could not meet demands on its deposits. Its problems spilled over to other special finance houses (SFHs) and created distress in the sector. The contagion could not be contained due to the shallowness of inter-SFH money markets and the dearth of instruments to inject liquidity in the system.

IFH's distress points to the need of ensuring a highly *professional management* with an effective information system to allow both higher management and supervisors to monitor developments in an institution's risk profile. Regulatory and supervisory capability of IIFSs needs strengthening. This entails the ability of *regulators and supervisors* to fully understand Islamic finance operations, and the allowance for a regulatory regime that is adapted to their risk profile without creating distortions. It is not sound to let IIFSs operate in a regulatory twilight zone, nor is it sound for the regulator and the market to lack the necessary information to monitor each institution and the sector as a whole. The progress made to date to develop *money markets* accessible to IIFSs is commendable; it is not yet sufficient, however. Licensing IIFSs in dual financial systems entails a public authority responsibility linked to the authorities' accountability for the conduct of monetary policy and systemic liquidity management. Licensing an IIFS

---

[43] They may even be less susceptible to financial distress due to the basic requirement of materiality in their transactions. Nevertheless, their governance and risk management may deserve greater attention.

entails acknowledging the responsibility of being able to manage a system that includes IIFSs. This is feasible and possible, but the issue needs to be addressed directly. In a crisis, monetary policy and systemic liquidity management will be at the forefront of the stabilization efforts.

Beyond managing systemic liquidity to promote financial stability, it is essential to put in place a framework for dealing with cases of distress if and when they emerge. Such a framework needs to be prepared in anticipation of episodes of distress and not in reaction to the latest one. It will include a legal, regulatory, and organizational infrastructure adapted to the nature of the jurisdiction concerned. It will also require anticipation of the way to secure the resources that need to be devoted to deal with the issues. Finally, such a framework will entail scenario creation and management exercises. While a GAMC may not be the most appropriate instrument in a DEJ, there may be cases where it is. It is better to anticipate the issue and not argue the pros and cons at the time of action. While the London approach may be attractive, it entails the existence of a decentralized ability to handle distress and an inclination for cooperation between entities in crisis. That also may be a considerable challenge that can be better faced with sufficient preparation.

APPENDIX 4A: TYPES OF INSTRUMENTS IN ISLAMIC INTERBANK MONEY MARKET OF MALAYSIA

Mudaraba Interbank Investment (MII)	*Mudaraba* interbank investment (MII) refers to a mechanism whereby a deficit Islamic banking institution (investee bank) can obtain investment from a surplus Islamic banking institution (investor bank) based on *mudaraba* (profit sharing). The period of investment is from overnight to 12 months, while the rate of return is based on the rate of gross profit before distribution for investment of one year of the investee bank. The profit-sharing ratio is negotiable between both parties. The investor bank at the time of negotiation would not know what the return would be, as the actual return will be crystallized toward the end of the investment period. The principal invested shall be repaid at the end of the period, together with a share of the profit arising from the use of the fund by the investee bank.
Wadiah Acceptance	A *wadiah* acceptance is a transaction between Bank Negara Malaysia (BNM) and the Islamic banking institutions. It refers to a mechanism whereby the Islamic banking institutions placed their surplus funds with BNM based on the concept of *al-wadiah*. Under this concept, the acceptor of funds is viewed as the custodian for the funds and there is no obligation on the part of

(*continued*)

the custodian to pay any return on the account. However, if there is any dividend paid by the custodian, is perceived as *hibah* (gift). The *wadiah* acceptance facilitates BNM's liquidity management operation, as it gives flexibility for BNM to declare a dividend without having to invest the funds received. Under the liquidity management operation, BNM uses the *wadiah* acceptance to absorb excess liquidity from the IIMM by accepting overnight money or fixed-tenure *wadiah*.

Sell and Buy-Back Agreement (SBBA)

A sell and buy-back agreement (SBBA) is an Islamic money market transaction entered by two parties in which an SBBA seller sells Islamic assets to an SBBA buyer at an agreed price, and subsequently both parties enter into a separate agreement in which the buyer promises to sell back the said asset to the seller at an agreed price.

Commodity *Murabaha*

Often used as a liquidity management tool by financial institutions, the commodity *murabaha* is today the mainstay of the Islamic interbank short-term liquidity market. In these transactions, the commodity, usually a London Metal Exchange (LME) metal-based structure, is sold on a deferred basis and the markup is close to conventional money market levels.

Government Investment Issue (GII)

Government Investment Issues (GIIs) are long-term non-interest-bearing Government securities based on Islamic principles issued by the Government of Malaysia for funding developmental expenditures. Similar to Malaysian Government Securities (MGSs), GII is issued through competitive auction by Bank Negara Malaysia on behalf of the Government. The GII issuance program is preannounced in the auction calendar with issuance size ranging from RM 1 billion to RM 3.5 billion and original maturities of three years, five years, seven years, and 10 years. GII is based on *Bai' Al-Inah* principles, part of the sell and buy-back concept in Islamic finance. Under this principle, the Government will sell a specified nominal value of its assets and subsequently will buy back the assets at their nominal value plus profit through a tender process. The profit rate is based on the weighted average yield of the successful bids of the auction. The nominal value of buying back the assets will be settled at a specified future date or maturity, while the profit rate will be distributed half-yearly. The obligation of the Government to settle the purchase price is securitized in the form of GII and is issued to the investors. At maturity, the Government will redeem the GII and pay the nominal value of the securities to the GII holders. GII is one of the financial instruments that are actively traded in the Islamic Interbank Money Market (IIMM). When the first Islamic bank in Malaysia began operations in 1983, the bank could not, among other things, purchase or trade in Malaysian Government

Securities (MGSs), Malaysian Treasury bills (MTBs), or other interest-bearing instruments. However, there was a serious need for the Islamic bank to hold such liquid papers to meet the statutory liquidity requirements as well as to park its idle funds. To satisfy both requirements, the Malaysian Parliament passed the Government Investment Act in 1983 to enable the Government of Malaysia to issue non-interest-bearing certificates known as Government Investment Certificates (GICs), now replaced with the Government Investment Issue (GII). The GII was introduced in July 1983 under the concept of *qard al hasan*.

The concept of *qard al hasan* does not satisfy the GIIs as tradable instruments in the secondary market. To address this shortfall, BNM opens a window to facilitate the players to sell and purchase the papers with the central bank. The price sold or purchased by the players is determined by BNM, which maintains a system to record any movement in the GII. On June 15, 2001, the Government of Malaysia, with the advice of Bank Negara Malaysia, issued a three-year GII of RM 2.0 billion under a new concept of *Bai' Al-Inah*. The move therefore added depth to the IIMM, as the GII is now tradable in the secondary market via the concept of *Bai al-Dayn* (debt trading). On March 16, 2005, the Government of Malaysia, with the advice of Bank Negara Malaysia, issued the first Profit-Based GII with five-year tenure of RM 2 billion. It is coupon-bearing paper on which the Government pays half-yearly profit to the investors. On June 17, 2005, the Government has amended the Government Funding Act of 1983 (previously known as the Government Investment Act of 1983) to increase the issuance size limit of GIIs from RM 15 billion to RM 30 billion. At the end of 2005, the outstanding amount of the GIIs issued was RM 10.1 billion.

Merdeka Savings Bond	Merdeka Savings Bonds have a bond structure based on *Shari'a* principles with the purpose of providing assistance to retirees who depend primarily on interest income from deposits placed with the banking institutions.
Bank Negara Monetary Notes–i (BNMN-i)	Bank Negara Monetary Notes–i (BNMN-i) are Islamic securities issued by Bank Negara Malaysia replacing the existing Bank Negara Negotiable Notes (BNNNs) for purposes of managing liquidity in the Islamic financial market. The instruments will be issued using Islamic principles that are deemed acceptable to *Shari'a* requirements. The maturity of these issuances has also been lengthened from one year to three years. New issuances of BNMN-i may be issued on either a discounted or a coupon-bearing basis depending on investors' demand. Discount-based

(continued)

BNMN-i will be traded using the same market convention as the existing BNNN and Malaysian Islamic Treasury bill (MITB) while the profit-based BNMN-i will adopt the market convention of the Government Investment Issue (GII).

Malaysian Islamic Treasury Bill (MITB)	Malaysian Islamic Treasury bills (MITBs) are short-term securities issued by the Government of Malaysia based on Islamic principles. MITBs are usually issued on a weekly basis with an original maturity of one year. Normal auction day is Thursday, and the results of successful bidders will be announced one day after, on Friday. Both conventional and Islamic institutions can buy and trade MITBs. The MITBs are structured based on the *Bai' Al-Inah* principle, part of the sell and buy-back concept. Bank Negara Malaysia on behalf of the Government will sell the identified Government assets on a competitive tender basis, to form the underlying transaction of the deal. Allotment is based on highest price tendered (or lowest yield). Price is determined after profit element is imputed (discounting factor). The successful bidders will then pay cash to the Government. The bidders will subsequently sell back the assets to the Government at par based on credit terms. The Government will issue MITBs to bidders to represent the debt created. MITBs are tradable on yield basis (discounted rate) based on bands of remaining tenure (Band 4 = 68 to 91 days to maturity). The standard trading amount is RM 5 million, and the MITB is actively traded based on the *Bai al-Dayn* (debt trading) principle in the secondary market.
Cagamas Mudaraba Bond (SMC)	The Cagamas Mudaraba Bond was introduced on March 1, 1994, by Cagamas Berhad to finance the purchase of Islamic housing debts from financial institutions that provide Islamic house financing to the public. The SMC Mudaraba Bond is structured using the concept of *mudaraba* where the bondholders and Cagamas will share the profits according to the agreed profit-sharing ratios. In July 2005, Cagamas also raised funding with its first Islamic mortgage-backed issue of *mudaraba* bonds in the amount of RM 2.05 billion (US$532 million), which was issued to regional investors and added a new asset class to the local debt market. In 2007, 43 percent (or RM 4.16 billion) of Cagamas's outstanding residential mortgage-backed securities comprised Islamic residential mortgage-backed securities. Malaysia has stepped up efforts to broaden the investor base, announcing a slew of measures to overhaul the exchange market (Capital Market Plan) and foster greater asset diversity in the securitization market with the release of revised Guidelines on Asset-Backed Securities in March 2005. In the same year, Malaysia's central bank launched the first regular issue of *ijara*

leasing securities. After having successfully placed US$750 million worth of local currency–denominated Islamic bonds, the largest convertible bond issues in Asia in 2006, Malaysia's state investment agency, Khazanah Nasional Berhad, planned to debut the first U.S. dollar–denominated Islamic bond issue in the course of 2007 in a bid to attract Middle Eastern investors who previously have avoided similar sales due to different interpretations of Islamic law.

When Issue (WI)	When issue (WI) refers to a transaction of sale and purchase of debt securities before the securities are issued. The National Sharia Advisory Council stated that the WI transaction is allowed based on the permissibility to promise for sale and purchase transactions.
Islamic Accepted Bills (IAB)	The Islamic Accepted Bill, also known as an Interest-Free Accepted Bill (IAB), was introduced in 1991. The objective of introducing IAB is to encourage and promote both domestic and foreign trade by providing Malaysian traders with an attractive Islamic financing product. The IAB is formulated on the Islamic principles of *al-murabaha* (deferred lump-sum sale or cost-plus) and *Bai al-Dayn* (debt trading). *Al-murabaha* refers to the selling of merchandise at a price based on a cost-plus profit margin agreed to by both parties. *Bai al-Dayn* refers to the sale of a debt arising from a trade transaction in the form of a deferred payment sale. There are two types of financing under the IAB facility, namely:

Imports and local purchases: The financing would be financed under a *murabaha* working capital financing mechanism. Under this concept, the commercial bank appoints the customer as the purchasing agent for the bank. The customer then purchases the required goods from the seller on behalf of the bank, which would then pay the seller and resell the goods to the customer at a price inclusive of a profit margin. The customer is allowed a deferred payment term of up to 200 days. Upon maturity of *murabaha* financing, the customer will pay the bank the cost of goods plus profit margin. The sale of goods by the bank to the customer on deferred payment terms constitutes the creation of debt. This is securitized in the form of a bill of exchange drawn by the bank on and accepted by the customer for the full amount of the bank's selling price payable at maturity. If the bank decides to sell the IAB to a third party, then the concept of *Bai al-dayn* will apply whereby the bank will sell the IAB at the agreed price. *Exports and local sales:* The bills created would be traded under the concept of *Bai al-Dayn*. An exporter who had been approved for IAB facility prepares the export documentation as required under the sale contract or letter of credit. The export documents

(continued)

are sent to the importer's bank. The exporter draws on the commercial bank a new bill of exchange as a substitution bill, and this will be the IAB. The bank purchases the IAB at a mutually agreed price using the concept of *Bai al-Dayn*, and the proceeds will be credited to the exporter's account. Domestic sales are treated in a similar manner.

Islamic Negotiable Instruments (INI)	The INI covers two instruments: In an Islamic Negotiable Instrument of Deposit (INID), the applicable concept is *mudaraba*. It refers to a sum of money deposited with the Islamic banking institutions and repayable to the bearer on a specified future date at the nominal value of INID plus declared dividend. In a Negotiable Islamic Debt Certificate (NIDC), the transaction involves the sale of a banking institution's assets to the customer at an agreed price on a cash basis. Subsequently, the asset is purchased back from the customer at principal value plus profit and is to be settled at an agreed future date.
Islamic Private Debt Securities	Islamic Private Debt Securities (IPDS) has been introduced in Malaysia since 1990. At the moment, the IPDS which are outstanding in the market were issued based on the *Shari'a*-compliant concept of *Bai' Bithaman Ajil*, *murabaha*, and *al mudaraba*.
Ar Rahnu Agreement–I (RA-I)	Under RA-I, the lender provides a loan to the borrower based on the concept of *qard al hasan*. The borrower pledges its securities as collateral for the loan granted. However, in the event that the borrower fails to repay the loan on maturity date, the lender has the right to sell the pledged securities and use the proceeds from the sale of the securities to settle the loan. If there is surplus money, the lender will return the balance to the borrower. BNM will use RA-I as a liquidity management tool for its money market operations. Return from the RA-I will be in the form of a gift (*hibah*) and is determined based on the average interbank money market rates.
Sukuk Bank Negara Malaysia Ijara (SBNMI)	SBNMI is issued based on the *ijara* or sale and lease back concept, a structure that is widely used in the Middle East. A special purpose vehicle, BNM Sukuk Berhad, has been established to issue the *sukuk ijara*. The proceeds from the issuance will be used to purchase Bank Negara Malaysia's assets. The assets will then be leased to Bank Negara Malaysia for rental payment consideration, which is distributed to investors as a return on a semiannual basis. Upon maturity of the *sukuk al-ijara*, which will coincide with end of the lease tenure, BNM Sukuk Berhad will then sell the assets back to Bank Negara Malaysia at a predetermined price.

BNMN-Istithmar	In June 2011, BNM announced the introduction of BNMN-Istithmar. It is based on the *istithmar* (investment) concept, which refers to portfolio investments into a combined structure of sale and lease back of assets (*ijara*) and commodity markup sale transaction (*murabaha*). The main objective of issuing BNMN-Istithmar is to increase efficiency and flexibility of liquidity management in the Islamic money market by expanding the *Shari'a* concept used in Bank Negara Malaysia's Islamic monetary instruments. BNMN-Istithmar would contribute toward expanding investment instruments and the investor base, as well as promote greater liquidity in the Islamic money market. BNMN-Istithmar will be traded using current market conventions and is accorded the same regulatory treatment as all Bank Negara Monetary Notes Issuance. The issuance of BNMN-Istithmar will be conducted through competitive auction via the domestic Principal Dealer network.

Source: Adapted from Islamic Interbank Money Market, http://iimm.bnm.gov.my.

Three

Regulatory Challenges

The existence, nature, and extent of financial regulation have been long-debated issues. There are those who believe that there are no major differences between financial and commercial activity and, accordingly, the former need not face more regulation than the latter. Then there are those who believe that the nature of financial activity calls for specific regulation and supervision to ensure orderly operations. It is sometimes a debate between views on fostering market vibrancy and concerns for financial stability.[1]

Whatever the debates, increased regulation and supervision and periodical financial crises have been the hallmark of financial system history. Within countries and across the world, financial regulation has spread, especially in the wake of financial crises. However, markets have continued to lead financial innovation, leaving regulators in a permanent catch-up phase. Over certain periods, too stringent regulation has stifled financial development and accordingly prevented societies from benefiting from the beneficial impact of regulation on economic development. On other occasions, unbridled financial activity has led countries and sometimes the international economy to crashes.

Increasing internationalization of finance, contagion, and spillovers across borders have led the international community to seek to monitor financial developments and harmonize financial regulations across countries. The Basel agreements on banking regulation and supervision are the

---

[1] D. Llewellyn, "The Economic Rationale for Financial Regulation," Financial Services Authority, April 1999, at www.fsa.gov.uk/pubs/occpapers/op01.pdf; J. Barth, G. Caprio, and R. Levine, *Rethinking Bank Regulation: Till Angels Govern* (New York: Cambridge University Press, 2006).

highlights of those efforts that extend by now to most segments of financial systems.[2]

The emergence of Islamic finance posed a challenge to regulators wherever it was introduced. The debate was on how to license and regulate Islamic financial institutions and products. Concerned policy makers and regulators faced the compounded challenge of calibrating regulation of conventional finance and enabling the development of a mode of finance with its own specific rules. Chapter 5, on the dilemma of regulating Islamic finance, looks at the various dimensions of financial regulation and how they are dealt with in various jurisdictions. Chapter 6 suggests an organizational framework that could help address the dilemma. It could help in complying with *Shari'a* principles while avoiding constraining Islamic finance to a niche activity with its own separate regulations.

---

[2] See, for example, World Bank on the Financial Sector Assessment Program for an overview at http://web.worldbank.org/WBSITE/EXTERNAL/TOPICS/EXTFINANCIALSE CTOR/0,,contentMDK:22142161~menuPK:6459396~pagePK:210058~piPK:210062 ~theSitePK:282885,00.html.

CHAPTER 5

The Dilemma of Tailor-Made versus Mainstream Regulation

Islamic finance offers opportunities for expanding investments, raising growth performance, and reducing poverty. It does so by offering new financial services, an everyday event in the realm of finance in which their fate is ultimately decided by market developments. In this permanent evolution, market participants, regulators, and the broader institutional environment face continuous challenges. Market participants' challenges lie in their ability to identify opportunities for profit and the ability to pursue them while complying with *Shari'a* and managing risks. The regulators' challenge resides is their ability to provide a systemic governance framework that promotes financial stability while not stifling market vibrancy. Finally, at the broader institutional level, the institutional infrastructure needs to enable the expansion of investments by incorporating features that mitigate investors' risks.

For the opportunities it offers to materialize, Islamic finance needs to address the aforementioned challenges squarely without compromising the tenets on which it is founded. A requirement for that purpose is the availability of adequate information and analysis that provide market participants and policy makers with sound foundations for their decisions. Information and knowledge are at the core of progress. Islamic financial services providers, consumers, and the financial authorities that govern them all need to invest in that intangible but critical factor of development that is knowledge. The investment in the knowledge of Islamic finance will allow all concerned to have a better sense of the potential and limits of Islamic financial services, and avoid ideological posturing for and against that is damaging for the economic performance and welfare of the region.

The following focuses first on policy makers' and regulators' challenges, and on issues related to the broad institutional infrastructure. It then briefly turns to market participants' challenges.

POLICY MAKER AND REGULATOR CHALLENGES

Most countries of the region have dual financial systems where Islamic and conventional financial services are both present. This duality presents financial authorities with the challenges of managing systemic liquidity, adopting an approach to the regulatory framework to govern the financial system, and introducing regulation that deals with idiosyncratic features of Islamic financial services without entrenching market segmentation and reducing competition.

Managing Systemic Liquidity

The challenges of managing systemic liquidity are compounded in dual financial systems. In a number of countries, inflation is rising. The windfall from the increase in hydrocarbon prices is finding its way to the economy and non-traded goods, putting pressure on domestic prices. Fiscal policy could play a role in moderating aggregate demand. In countries with an exchange rate peg, the scope for active monetary policy may be constrained. However, monetary authorities could mop up liquidity and mitigate the heating up of the economy.

Wherever countries have Islamic and conventional finance operating side by side, monetary authorities generally do not have at their disposal instruments compliant with *Shari'a* to mop up liquidity and raise the cost of funds. The use of central bank certificates or treasury bills bearing interest can deal with liquidity only in the conventional segment. They present an opportunity for conventional banks to hold risk-free government paper, an opportunity that escapes institutions offering Islamic financial services (IIFSs). Furthermore, the introduction of *Shari'a*-compatible instruments may lead to market segmentation, limit liquidity, and complicate the efficient transmission of monetary policy.[1]

In fact, systemic liquidity management needs liquid money markets that offer a level playing field to Islamic and conventional financial institutions. In dual systems, it is important to develop a uniform monetary operations framework covering both Islamic and conventional financial institutions. This requires the "design and use of neutral instruments that can be widely held by both conventional and Islamic banks."[2] A lot can be learned from the experiences of Bahrain and Malaysia and the work done by notably the International Islamic Financial Market (IIFM) and the Islamic Financial Services Board (IFSB).[3] Bahrain has developed short-term *sukuk*s that

---

[1]V. Sundarajan (2006).
[2]Ibid.
[3]Reserve requirements are blunt instruments of monetary policy. Remunerated reserve requirements applied equally to conventional and Islamic deposit-taking institutions would penalize the latter relative to the former. While Bahrain does not remunerate required reserves, Yemen does so for domestic currency reserves.

in principle should provide a basis to manage systemic liquidity. However, there seems to be a limited secondary market for such instruments, as they are generally held to maturity. Accordingly, an interbank money market that would help IIFSs to access or place liquidity needs to be developed. Each national jurisdiction may not have sufficient depth in such instruments to see a liquid secondary market develop, which would point to the need for cross-jurisdiction cooperation. Similarly, it is unlikely that secondary markets would develop without the presence of market makers, preferably other than monetary authorities. The latter, along with market participants, may want to assess the capital, regulatory, and skill requirements that would enable the development of market makers on the *sukuk* market.

Enabling Regulatory Framework

The nature of the regulatory framework that should govern dual financial systems poses an equal challenge. As pointed out, regulatory approaches to Islamic financial services, whether banking, financial markets, or *takaful*, vary across the region's jurisdictions. In some countries, like Bahrain and the United Arab Emirates (UAE), Islamic financial services are governed by regimes separate from that of conventional finance. For example, separate licenses are needed in Bahrain and Kuwait to engage in Islamic financial services. In others, like Lebanon, special chapters of laws are dedicated to Islamic financial services, but under the general umbrella of conventional financial services. In still other jurisdictions, such as Saudi Arabia or Egypt, Islamic financial services are considered part and parcel of conventional financial services and are subject to the same licensing, regulation, and supervision. In connection with the foregoing, authorities' positions vary also as to allowing or not conventional financial institutions to have windows that offer Islamic financial products.

While diversity with clarity is not an issue, diversity is often associated with confusion in approaches and rules, if not in its reality at least in the perception it conveys. Three adverse consequences of unmanaged diversity of approaches can be pointed out. They are the assessment of sovereign risk, cost and competitiveness of cross-jurisdiction investments, and a nonlevel playing field between conventional and Islamic financial services within jurisdictions.

1. *Sovereign risk.* In the absence of generally recognized international benchmarks of what constitutes good regulatory and supervisory practices of Islamic financial services, sovereign risk assessors of jurisdictions with significant Islamic financial services may err on the side of caution and penalize otherwise sound financial jurisdictions. This is likely to be compounded by the relative unfamiliarity of a number

of international market participants with Islamic financial services generally. While risk rating agencies have strengthened their ability to deal with Islamic financial services, other players may not have reached that point.[4]

2. *Relative cost and competitiveness of cross-jurisdiction investments.* At this stage, conventional finance has developed generally accepted standards that are used as references and facilitate cross-border assessments, and accordingly financial flows and investments.[5] While the IFSB and the Accounting and Auditing Organization for Islamic Financial Institutions (AAOIFI) have developed standards for Islamic financial services, these have not yet received the general recognition to be references that facilitate cross-border information sharing and financial flows. Accordingly, diversity without a set of common references is likely to compound the challenges of cross-border comparisons and may put Islamic financial services at a competitive disadvantage.

3. *Nonlevel playing field between conventional and Islamic financial services within jurisdictions.* In the diversity of approaches followed, sufficient attention may not have been given to the neutrality of regulatory and supervisory arrangements across Islamic and conventional financial services. An example is a requirement to have both conventional and Islamic banks hold remunerated reserves with the monetary authority. Other examples are regulations related to the holding of real assets, deposit protection, or capital adequacy sometimes simply extended from conventional finance to Islamic finance and possibly distorting the playing field between them.

AAOIFI, IFSB, IIFM, and the Islamic Development Bank (IsDB) are endeavoring to promote some consensus, but the road may be long. Efforts to expand the recognition of the standards already developed would go a long way in overcoming the foregoing challenges. In moving in that direction, one may want to consider the approaches of the U.S. Federal Reserve or the UK Financial Services Authority (FSA). Federal Reserve chairman Ben Bernanke pointed out in a 2007 speech: "I will argue that central banks and other regulators should resist the temptation to devise ad hoc rules for each new type of financial instrument or institution. Rather, we should strive to develop common, principles-based policy responses that can be applied consistently

---

[4]Unfamiliarity with the industry and a bias toward risk aversion may, for example, attribute macroeconomic instability to the high liquidity present with IIFSs.

[5]These are standards such as the Basel Core Principles for Banking Supervision (BCPBS), the International Financial Reporting Standards (IFRS), as well as the other financial standards such as for capital markets or insurance.

across the financial sector to meet clearly defined objectives."[6] He was thus arguing for clarity of policy objectives and consistency of approach that is principles based and risk focused. However, Chairman Bernanke's point does not mean that there should not be rules but rather that these rules should implement the principles and not develop in an ad hoc manner.

Benchmarks for the regulatory approach should facilitate the development of an international consensus on the main features of a regulatory and supervisory framework for Islamic financial services. This is not a suggestion to aim for uniformity, which would be elusive and also not necessary. It is rather a suggestion to develop a consensus on a benchmark approach to the regulation of Islamic financial services. This could build upon the work of existing international standard setting bodies such as the AAOIFI, IFSB, and IIFM. These institutions could be natural forums to develop such benchmarks with the support of the IsDB and national authorities.

In the context of the regulatory approach adopted, financial authorities need to deal explicitly with specifics of IIFSs. Among those, two critical dimensions deserve attention, as they bear on the reputation of the industry and its impact on overall financial stability and the ability to mobilize resources and channel them to investment activity. These two dimensions relate to the implementation of the risk-sharing and materiality principles.

1. Risk sharing leads IIFSs to mobilize deposits, where depositors share the risks of investments made by the IIFS.[7] Accordingly, the deposit amount is not protected, a feature that generally conflicts with most treatments of bank deposits in conventional banking. This risk-sharing principle renders these deposits in IIFSs akin to mutual fund shares and less similar to traditional deposits. Placing these deposits under the umbrella of banking regulation creates an intrinsic ambivalence that needs to be made transparent to enhance confidence in the financial system.

2. The requirement of materiality requires also specific attention. Generally, conventional banks hold only the real assets necessary to their operations, like their own buildings or equipment. The principle there is the distinction between commercial and financial intermediation activities. A core feature of Islamic finance is the bundling of the real transaction with the financing of it. It entails that IIFSs need to hold the title to real

---

[6] Remarks by Chairman Ben S. Bernanke to the Federal Reserve Bank of Atlanta's 2007 Financial Markets Conference, Sea Island, Georgia, May 15, 2007.

[7] These investment account deposits are generally governed by a *mudaraba* contract whereby the depositor (owner) uses the services of a financial manager (IIFS) to manage his or her resources. The owner and the IIFS share the profit and loss of managing the resources according to a specified share.

assets in the form of commodities or real estate. As a corollary, the IIFS is at the same time a financial and a commercial venture, which will generally be inconsistent with conventional banking regulation. The IIFS's risks would thus cover inventory or title risks.

Strengthening the Broad Institutional Infrastructure

An often-overlooked dimension affecting the performance of financial systems is the quality of the broad financial institutional infrastructure. This refers especially to the quantity, quality, and timeliness of financial information, stakeholders' trust in market rules and reliability of institutions, and the existence of a mechanism to settle disputes efficiently and with predictability. Islamic and conventional financial services rely on the broad institutional infrastructure. Progress has been achieved in the region, but it does still lag in comparison to best-performing jurisdictions. Notable are the existence or lack thereof of alternative dispute resolution, the cost and time frame of a court decision, and legal precedence that may guide predictability.[8] Countries that have made significant progress may suffer from a neighborhood effect often implicit in international investors' risk assessments. In addition, most of the attention has been directed to the institutional infrastructure in relation to conventional finance, with only recently a shift to issues specific to Islamic finance.

Financial Information Infrastructure An effective financial information infrastructure would be expected to have two pillars: (1) reliable and timely financial reporting statements and (2) service providers that process and disseminate the information. The first pillar refers primarily to accounting and auditing standards and their use by market participants. The second pillar refers to diverse ancillary services.[9] It would help mitigate institution-specific and systemic risks and shift responsibility with market participants away from the collectivity. It enables an environment that would allow depositors and investors to exercise their monitoring and market discipline roles in an affordable manner.[10] Market developments will see the gradual

---

[8] A notable success is the mechanism of settling banking disputes under SAMA's jurisdiction.

[9] These would include financial media, financial advisory services, and credit information bureaus.

[10] An effective information infrastructure promotes access to finance and social inclusion, benefits that may be paramount to United Nations Economic and Social Commission for Western Asia (ESCWA) economies; see Grais and Maglione-Piromallo (2005).

emergence of ancillary services as business opportunities arise. However, reliable and timely financial information reporting can be fostered by policy action, though driven by industry participants.

Of particular relevance to financial information infrastructure is a charter of accounts that IIFSs would use to organize and produce credible financial statements. The accounting profession has gradually developed standards at the national and international levels, generally with official support. Existing accounting standards, including International Financial Reporting Standards (IFRS), are designed mainly for conventional finance. The nature of IIFS products, their practice to set up reserve funds to smooth profit distribution and protect risk-sharing depositors' principals, and the commitment to distribute *zakat* are IIFS features that may not directly find a home in IFRS. This sense has led to the establishment in the early 1990s of AAOIFI, which gradually developed standards dealing with IIFS specificities.[11] While AAOIFI has achieved major progress, the accounting pillar of the financial information infrastructure for IIFSs continues to present challenges. Wherever IFRSs are the only rule, they may not permit the establishment of financial statements reflecting IIFSs' genuine performance and may give a false sense of reliability. AAOIFI's standards may deal adequately with IIFS specificities. However, they may not always allow for cross-sector comparability.

Dispute Settlement Mechanisms   Efficient and predictable dispute settlement mechanisms will bear notably on the ability of Islamic financial services to mobilize and channel resources competitively. Whether mobilizing resources or extending financing in one jurisdiction or across different ones, participants enter into contracts. The latter need to be clear on the legal jurisdictions governing the contract and on the dispute mechanisms that the parties intend to follow. These issues are paramount to the development of Islamic finance, the cost of conducting the business, and its ability to compete. They bear importantly on the financing of international trade as well as the issuance of *sukuk*s and development of their markets.

The relevance of legal certainty was highlighted by the dispute between Shamil Bank of Bahrain and Beximco and the Bangladesh Export Import Company following *murabaha* contracts entered into in 1995.[12] The case raised the issue of the relative precedence of *Shari'a* and the national law, in this case English law, in settling the dispute between the parties. It

---

[11] AAOIFI's standards are mandatory for the following markets: Bahrain, Jordan, Sudan, Qatar, and Dubai International Financial Center. Syria is considering their adoption. The standards are used as guidelines in Saudi Arabia, Kuwait, Malaysia, Lebanon, and Indonesia. Most IIFS *Shari'a* supervisory committees use AAOIFI standards as guidelines.

[12] Beximco is Pharmaceuticals Limited. See Dutton and Vause (2006).

highlighted the importance of clarity in the drafting of contracts for Islamic financial transactions.[13]

MARKET PARTICIPANT CHALLENGES

Market participant performance in driving the growth of Islamic financial services is impressive. Opportunities have been seized and actions have been pursued, even in uncharted waters. Market participants are continuously adapting to the changing environment, notably to the pressures of competition and globalization.

Two Strategic Challenges

Without dwelling on the issues, from a macro perspective, two considerations appear of pervasive importance. They are the size of IIFSs in the context of globalization and the depth and liquidity of markets for both macroeconomic and risk management reasons. Size calls for consolidation through mergers and acquisitions in addition to natural growth. Market liquidity entails that banks' liquid portfolio managers have incentives to actively manage their liquidity and develop markets of short-term instruments. Without options for recontracting, accessing, and placing short-term liquidity, the potential for growth may not be realized as fully as hoped for.

On the backdrop of the foregoing strategic challenges, three areas deserve particular attention: namely, corporate governance, risk management, and product and service diversification.

Corporate Governance

Sound IIFS corporate governance (CG) can be expected to strengthen business confidence, foster investments, and improve performance.[14] Two broad sets of CG issues facing IIFSs require specific treatment.[15] The first one revolves around the need to reassure stakeholders that IIFSs' financial activities fully comply with the precepts of Islamic jurisprudence.[16] Ultimately, the core mission of an IIFS is to meet its stakeholders' desire to conduct their

---

[13] See also McMillen (2007) regarding securities laws, trusts, enforceability, and *sukuks*.
[14] Claessens (2003).
[15] Archer and Abdel Karim (2007) and IFSB (2007a). See also Grais and Pellegrini (2007).
[16] Islamic jurisprudence is also known as *fiqh*. It covers all aspects of life: religious, political, social, and economic. It is mainly based on interpretations of the Quran and Sunna.

financial business according to *Shari'a* principles. There must, therefore, be CG mechanisms to assure them that the necessary safeguards to that effect are in place. The same stakeholders also need to be assured that the IIFS will nonetheless actively promote their financial interests, and will prove to be an efficient, stable, and trustworthy provider of financial services. In practice, depositors and borrowers need to be reassured that the types of liabilities and assets that IIFSs deal with are competitive and offer a risk-return trade-off acceptable to their clients. This combination of requirements of *Shari'a* compliance and business performance raises specific challenges and agency problems. It underlines the need for distinctive CG structures.

Risk Management

Enhancing risk management practices and their related skill and information requirements is another challenge facing IIFSs. Among risk categories, liquidity risks are substantial because of the inability to manage asset and liability maturity mismatches, due to the absence of *Shari'a*-compliant instruments such as treasury bills and lender of last resort facilities. IIFSs can use fewer risk-hedging instruments and techniques than conventional banks. Generally, they operate in an environment with underdeveloped or nonexistent interbank and money markets securities, and with limited availability of and access to lender of last resort facilities operated by central banks.

Diversification of Financial Services

Financial diversification and quality of services are primary objectives for IIFSs. Many explicitly specify them in their mission statements. However, beyond diversifying general financial services, IIFSs can play a major role in catering to a mostly overlooked segment of the poor—Muslims who demand *Shari'a*-compliant products. To achieve the scale necessary to meet this demand will take innovative approaches to the key challenges faced by conventional microfinance, namely, financial sustainability, political risk of disappointing results, and transparency.

Islamic microfinance has not yet really emerged in the region, though some initiatives may have been launched under the umbrella of conventional microfinance. The Yemen Hodeida microfinance project did provide scope to Islamic microfinance. Initiatives are ongoing in Syria and the West Bank and Gaza. The IsDB is also spearheading efforts to promote Islamic microfinance. A challenge in this area is the skepticism of conventional microfinance toward Islamic microfinance. It often stems from a sense that Islamic microfinance is bound to be more costly in an industry that already has to overcome a cost disadvantage due to the small nature of its operations. However, this view may be overlooking the fact that Islamic finance offers a bundle of services unlike those of conventional microfinance institutions. Indeed, the materiality of Islamic financial transactions entails that the provider of finance may be equally the provider of the equipment. In addition, that materiality condition may provide alternative risk mitigation that may not exist in straightforward financing. Market participants would need to explore systematically the potential of extending facilities to the bottom of the pyramid, a market with a huge growth potential.[17]

CONCLUSION

The foregoing primer on Islamic finance provides an overview of the development of the industry and the challenges it faces. Islamic finance has an uneven presence in terms of the size of the market, the services it offers, and the regulators' attention it attracts. However, Islamic finance offers serious opportunities for economic growth and poverty reduction. The potential of Islamic finance has not escaped international market players, whether sovereign or corporate entities. Regional authorities and market participants need to seize the opportunities. Knowledge and pragmatism can allow Islamic finance to deliver many development benefits.

Three aspects are of paramount importance: the development of knowledge and data on the sector, a clear legal and regulatory framework, and an enabling broad institutional infrastructure.

A major handicap in assessing the sector and guiding its development is the limited systemic quantitative knowledge on its size and performance. Such information needs to be developed, disclosed, and easily retrieved. The efforts of the General Council of Islamic Banks and Financial Institutions (CIBAFI), IsDB, AAOIFI, and IFSB in this area offer useful bases to build upon. But the case is now urgent, given the delays, the growing size of the industry, and increasing competitive pressures. It requires funding and pragmatic cooperation from all members of the Islamic finance community.

Related to information is knowledge and skills development. Islamic finance needs the same rigorous knowledge and skills that allow conventional finance to develop. In addition, it requires a practical knowledge of how *Shari'a* principles bear on Islamic finance. Pragmatism and knowledge are essential given the competitive pressures. However, opportunism in the design and offering of products is likely to be dangerous for the reputation risk it would engender. Knowledge and skills need to be developed at both

---

[17]Mobile banking and transfer services have the potential of reducing risks and costs.

the regulator and the market participant levels. Business associations and central banks' training institutes can usefully take the lead. Funding of their activities in this area is needed as well as IIFSs' funding for staff training.[18]

A technical assistance and training fund can provide support to individual IIFSs and regulators with limited resources, and can help them adopt best practices. It can also fund professional training. The resources required for such a fund are not beyond the financial industry's means but its impact would be significant.

A second pillar is the clarity of the legal and regulatory framework that should govern Islamic financial services. There is a need to develop a best practice benchmark in terms of regulatory approach. It is not a recommendation to pursue uniformity, but to develop benchmarks for best approaches to deal with Islamic finance. Such benchmarks would provide reference points to assessors, as well as guidance to regulators on the need to explain why their approach differs from the benchmark. The AAOIFI, IFSB, and IIFM could play significant roles in organizing the development of such benchmarks. These would not be substitutes for the standards they have or would develop; they would rather be benchmarks of what constitutes best practices. It could be similar to the role of the Basel Core Principles (BCPs) relative to the Basel II Accord. The BCPs provide a reference point that facilitate cross-jurisdictional assessments without imposing uniformity.

The legal and regulatory regime to govern Islamic finance needs to ensure a level playing field with conventional finance. It should foster financial stability as well as competition and market vibrancy. For example, a requirement to meet the same capital adequacy ratio for IIFSs and conventional banks may handicap the former vis-à-vis the latter. IIFS liabilities may be more akin to mutual fund shares than to conventional deposits. In principle, depositors in investment accounts in IIFSs would not benefit from the guarantee of the face value of the deposit, in contrast to depositors in conventional finance. In addition, IIFSs are required to associate all their asset-side financial transactions with real economic transactions. A real commodity or asset needs to underlie all financing undertaken by IIFSs. That requirement is not neutral to their transaction costs, or to the credit and liquidity risks they face. Bahrain has been at the forefront on these issues in the region. The IFSB has developed standards on capital adequacy and risk management, as well as other aspects of a prudential framework for IIFSs.

Whether with respect to prudential guidelines, financial reporting, or financial markets infrastructure, it is now time to take thorough stock of available experience. Market participants, regulators, and international standard setting bodies have developed approaches and solutions. All these

---

[18] AAOIFI's Certified Islamic Public Accountant (CIPA) program is a promising initiative.

efforts provide a useful base. They should be thoroughly collected and reviewed with an objective of drawing best practices, pointing out gaps, and designing strategy. An assignment should be given for a lead role of a depository of information on the industry and the provision of an annual report on its development. Given the growth of the industry, the diversity of its products, and its wide geographical presence, an international cooperative approach and regional focuses are likely to be required. Such an effort needs to be institutionalized, adequately funded, and sustained. Ad hoc efforts may at best provide interesting insights but cannot develop a thorough approach on which to build a governing framework for the industry.

The third pillar that deserves attention is the broader institutional infrastructure that enables market development. Of particular relevance are mechanisms for dispute resolution concerning Islamic finance contracts and legal certainty. Financial authorities need to convey clearly the laws that would govern Islamic finance and the available dispute resolution mechanisms. Another aspect is the legal framework that allows asset-based securitization. *Sukuk*s are a type of asset-based security that generally requires a special purpose vehicle in the form of a trust to hold the assets during the life of the transaction. Adequate legislation governing the establishment and functioning of trusts would streamline the issuance of *sukuk*s and improve their competitiveness relative to conventional bond issuance.

Islamic finance has grown tremendously in response to genuine market demand and has been fostered by liquidity made available by hydrocarbon resources and improving economic performance. It has the potential to further promote growth and reduce poverty. That potential can be realized provided that information and knowledge are built up, regulation ensures transparency and a level playing field with conventional finance, and the broader institutional infrastructure is conducive to legal certainty and allows for clear dispute resolution mechanisms. Ultimately, Islamic financial services will deliver on their promise if conducted with transparency and in a competitive environment.

CHAPTER 6

Toward an Enabling Framework

S *hari'a*-compliant financial services endeavor to have fair contracts, to mitigate the risks of speculation, and to avoid the hubris of human behavior. While *Shari'a*-compliant finance dates back to the early days of Islam, it has experienced a new life since the early 1970s and a tremendous explosion since the beginning of this new millennium.

In the mid-1990s, UK financial authorities had identified the emergence of Islamic finance on the world stage. As mentioned in Chapter 2, in a speech in 1995, Lord Edward George, then governor of the Bank of England, recognized the "growing importance of Islamic banking in the Muslim world and its emergence on the international stage," as well as the need to put Islamic banking in the context of London's tradition of "competitive innovation."[1]

The size of Islamic finance, its worldwide rapid development, and its appeal for both Muslims and non-Muslims all raise challenges to policy makers, regulators, and supervisors, as well as domestic and international standard setters and reviewers.

The following focuses mainly on the regulatory challenges that Islamic banking faces. It first considers the rationale for regulating Islamic banks. It then highlights important aspects of Islamic finance that can be inconsistent with prevailing banking practices and the challenges this represents. It then outlines organizational arrangements that would help overcome the challenges, facilitate the establishment of Islamic financial services, and foster their development while requiring marginal adjustments in existing laws, regulations, and supervision practices.

---

[1] September 1995, at a conference organized by the Islamic Foundation.

RATIONALE FOR REGULATING ISLAMIC FINANCE

On the supply side, financial intermediaries operate according to Islamic finance principles while others wish to enter the market and offer Islamic financial services. At the same time, the demand is there with consumers, businesses, and investors wishing to manage their financial transactions according to Islamic principles.[2]

The desire to practice banking in compliance with *Shari'a* principles has led to the development of financial instruments specific to Islamic finance. Maybe foremost among Islamic banking instruments are investment accounts that are essentially a middle ground between a conventional deposit and a share in a mutual fund. Consequently, a challenge is to square the regulatory treatment of Islamic investment deposits with that of conventional ones. This goes to the core nature of banking as intermediation between depositors and the rest of the economy.

So far, the response to the regulatory challenge has been along one of two tracks. One point of view is that all this is financial intermediation; Islamic financial intermediation adds to the menu of financial services and would be consistent with the process of financial innovation. Accordingly, the laws, regulations, and supervision arrangements applying to financial intermediation should extend to Islamic finance. Adjustments and additions may be necessary as they would be in the normal course of other financial innovations.[3]

Another point of view is that Islamic financial intermediation is intrinsically different from conventional finance. Accordingly, it would be difficult to extend to Islamic finance a conventional finance framework; Islamic finance requires specific laws, regulations, and supervision arrangements to allow Islamic banks to operate.

Policy makers, regulators, and supervisors cannot ignore the emergence or presence of Islamic finance, neither in their own jurisdictions nor elsewhere.[4]

---

[2]Islamic finance assets have crossed the US$1 trillion mark. There is growing interest around the world, including the renminbi *sukuk* offered in September 2011 by Khazanah Nasional, Malaysia's sovereign wealth fund; see the *Financial Times* Special Report on Islamic Finance, December 14, 2011.

[3]According to the Central Bank of Nigeria: "Islamic banking, as one of the models of non-interest banking, serves the same purpose of providing financial services as do conventional financial institutions save that it operates in accordance with principles and rules of Islamic commercial jurisprudence that generally recognizes profit and loss sharing and the prohibition of interest, as a model."

[4]Hence also the development of international bodies such as the Accounting and Auditing Organization for Islamic Financial Institutions (AAOIFI), the Islamic Financial Services Board (IFSB), the International Islamic Financial Market (IIFM), and others supported notably by the Islamic Development Bank (IsDB).

Their role is mainly to ensure systemic financial stability and consumer protection without sacrificing financial market vibrancy. Ignoring Islamic finance would preempt them from monitoring a segment of financial intermediation and hinder their ability to promote financial stability. After all, financial crises create havoc in markets, have high economic and social costs, and may spill over into political upheavals. Similarly, policy makers, regulators, and supervisors should not stifle a market development that may foster growth, development, and inclusiveness. Financial repression and poor access to financial services are known to hold back growth, stifle development, and sustain social exclusion. It is essential to provide an institutional framework that allows Islamic finance to respond to market demand and permit the inclusion in financial intermediation of the large number of people who refrain from accessing financial services to remain true to their beliefs.

Among others, Malaysia and Bahrain have chosen the approach of establishing separate arrangements for Islamic and conventional finance, based on the second point of view just outlined.[5] Other countries have adopted the first point of view; they opted for extending the prevailing conventional financial arrangements to Islamic finance, introducing specific regulations and procedures where those of conventional finance do not apply or are lacking.[6]

This chapter contends that there is an intrinsic difficulty in the desire to put Islamic financial intermediation in the straitjacket of banking regulation. Islamic financial intermediation overlaps with banking but has a number of nonbanking financial intermediation services. It can develop and flourish if its practitioners, supporters, and regulators accepted that the concept of a bank as understood, implemented, and regulated is not consistent with all the services Islamic finance can offer in compliance with *Shari'a* principles.

---

[5] Among other countries, for example, the Central Bank of Kuwait has prepared a comprehensive manual encompassing the rules and regulations for the supervision and oversight of Islamic banks. This manual is the counterpart of the Central Bank of Kuwait's supervisory manual for conventional bank supervision.

[6] International standard setting bodies such as the AAOIFI and the IFSB seem to have implicitly adopted the first point of view, introducing rules and standards where they think conventional rules and standards are lacking. Of course this is not the case where it concerns AAOIFI's *Shari'a* standards. Similarly, Nigerian regulators require Islamic finance institutions to comply with the generally accepted accounting principles (GAAP) codified in local standards issued by the Nigerian Accounting Standards Board (NASB) and the International Financial Reporting Standards (IFRS)/International Accounting Standards (IAS). For transactions, products, and activities not covered by these standards, Nigeria requires application of the relevant provisions of the financial accounting and auditing standards issued by the AAOIFI.

Islamic financial services can develop, grow in importance, and contribute to financial inclusion if the industry also considers intermediation organizational arrangements other than banking. Other arrangements can allow the industry to remain true to its foundational principles and flourish, leverage prevailing regulations, and overcome the perception that it is a niche activity.

ISLAMIC FINANCE PRINCIPLES AND CONVENTIONAL BANKING REGULATION

In essence, the practice of Islamic financial intermediation entails complying with the following five principles:

1. Risk sharing, reflecting a symmetrical risk/return distribution to each participant to a transaction.
2. Materiality, entailing that a financial transaction needs to have a "material finality" being directly or indirectly linked to a real economic transaction.
3. No exploitation—a financial transaction should not lead to the exploitation of any party to the transaction.[7]
4. No *riba*, generally understood as no interest and sometimes as no usury gain.[8]
5. No involvement in sinful activities such as alcoholic beverages or gambling.

The following reviews the challenges posed by the principles of risk sharing, materiality, and no *riba*. The two other principles are not discussed, as they are not inconsistent with prevailing banking regulations. The no-exploitation principle is generally dealt with in both conventional and Islamic finance by codes of transparency and disclosure; it does not entail the potential of regulatory conflict between both modes of financing. Similarly, the absence of involvement in sinful activities is naturally accommodated in conventional banking regulation.

---

[7] *No exploitation* entails no information asymmetry between the parties to the contract and requires full disclosure of information.
[8] This term literally means an increase or addition and is recognized in Islamic jurisprudence to encompass the notions of both usury and interest. Any risk-free or guaranteed rate of return on a loan or an investment is considered *riba* and is therefore prohibited.

Risk Sharing

The risk-sharing principle has carried through to the design of deposits in Islamic financial institutions. The main issues relate to the nature of a deposit, depositors' rights as creditors, depositors' voice in governance, and capital adequacy.

Reflecting the risk-sharing principle, the value of revenue-earning deposits in Islamic financial institutions is supposed to track the performance of the investments they finance. Generally, these deposits are called investment deposits.[9] Their face value is not certain. In contrast, a conventional deposit is a "contractual loan arrangement between a financial institution and a client where the client places funds with the institution for later withdrawal or use for making payments."[10] Thus a deposit in a conventional bank is retrievable by the depositor at its face value. Accordingly, in principle, a revenue-earning "deposit" in an Islamic financial institution does not fit the prevailing definition of a deposit in a conventional bank.

Another implication of the risk-sharing principle is that the depositor is not a priority senior creditor of the financial institution in case of its liquidation. Indeed, the depositor is assumed to share the risk and bear the loss. This is inconsistent with the prevailing conventional banking practice where depositors normally have priority over secured and unsecured creditors in case of liquidation of a licensed banking institution.

A holder of an investment account in an Islamic financial institution has no voice in the governing bodies of the institution, very much like her or his counterpart depositor in a conventional bank. However, the former bears a risk similar to that borne by shareholders, unlike the conventional bank depositor who enters a contract with the bank with assurance regarding the face value of the deposit. Accordingly, when carried through to the investment deposit design, the risk-sharing principle entails a mismatch between responsibility and accountability of the depositor and the financial institution.

Conventional banking regulation stipulates that a bank needs to have a sufficient *capital cushion* to face unanticipated risks that can adversely affect its revenue performance and asset quality and its ability to honor its liabilities when due. The point is to get some assurance that a bank can

---

[9]Investment deposits are generally based on a *mudaraba* contract where the depositor is *rab ul mal* (i.e., owner of asset) and the financial institution is a *mudarib* (i.e., asset manager for the account of the asset owner). In principle, the asset manager receives a management fee and shares in the upside gains of the investments undertaken, but does not bear any loss; any loss should be borne solely by the asset owner, unless there is misconduct on the part of the *mudarib*.

[10]Bollen (2006).

sustain shocks and remain solvent, thus mitigating risks to its creditors, foremost among them depositors. The latter are not supposed to see a loss of value in their deposits. With this rationale in mind, it can be argued that Islamic financial institutions do not face similar obligations in principle, as the investment account holders are supposed to share in the upside benefit and in the downside loss. Accordingly, it has been suggested that Islamic investment deposit-taking institutions should not be subject to the same capital requirements as conventional banks.

The Islamic Financial Services Board (IFSB) capital adequacy standard addresses this issue by proposing essentially to calibrate the capital requirement to an assessed risk of face value withdrawals of deposits in Islamic banks. Paragraph 18 of the IFSB 2005 capital adequacy standard states: "The liability of the IAH is exclusively limited to the provided capital and the potential loss of the IIFS is restricted solely to the value of its work. However, if negligence, mismanagement, fraud or breach of contract conditions can be proven, the IIFS will be financially liable for the capital of the IAH. Therefore, credit and market risks of the investment made by the IAH shall normally be borne by themselves, while the operational risk is borne solely by the IIFS."[11] Accordingly, the capital adequacy ratio excludes assets funded by investment accounts. However, in recognition of displaced commercial risk, the standard proposes to modulate the value of risk-weighted assets funded by investment accounts by a ratio α.[12]

Moreover, the new Basel III principles may compound the challenge for Islamic banks with respect to the requirements for additional cushions to deal with adverse portfolio developments and accumulate reserves during the up cycle. The Basel Committee on Banking Supervision has introduced new measurements to better enable conventional banks to absorb losses.[13] These measurements take two forms of capital buffers: (1) A capital conservation buffer of 2.5 percent to provide relief to banks during periods of stress and (2) a countercyclical capital buffer to allow regulatory authorities to require up to another 2.5 percent during periods of high credit growth.

---

[11]IFSB (2005; see paragraph 18 and Appendix A). IIFS and IAH are acronyms for institution offering Islamic financial services and investment account holder, respectively.

[12]IFSB (2011). Displaced commercial risk relates to the risk incurred by the Islamic financial institutions by smoothing the returns to investment account holders based on the perceived need to be competitive with conventional banks in attracting depositors. The Guidance Note on the capital adequacy ratio calculation further elaborates on the calculation of the α ratio. See later on revenue smoothing.

[13]The Basel III requirements were implemented at the beginning of 2013 to be completed by 2019.

Materiality

The materiality principle entails that a financial transaction needs to have a "material finality." Accordingly, the financial transaction has to be directly or indirectly linked to a real economic transaction.[14] In practice, materiality will mean that the financial contract will not cover a purely financial transaction between the parties, but it would include the real transaction underlying the financial deal. For example, an Islamic financier would not provide finance to a client desiring to purchase a house, but would enter into a contract that has provisions related to the sale and purchase of the house and its use by the client.[15]

Thus, the materiality principle for Islamic finance requires the bundling of the financial and real transactions. The rationale is not to disconnect financial transactions from real economic activity. The divergence between returns in the real economy and conventional financial activity may be perceived as a reflection of a weak materiality content of conventional financial transactions. One can find allegations that such a disconnect has led to the growth of opaque financial transactions understood by a privileged few that have resulted in crises such as the subprime mortgage financing crisis of 2008–2009.

However, the materiality principle would conflict with the prevailing prohibition for conventional commercial banks to enter into partnerships, joint ventures, or the ownership of real estate and common stock. Here, the rationale for unbundling real and financial transactions is to clearly separate real and financial sector activity and avoid risks of conflicts of interests. Financial intermediaries are entrusted with a fiduciary responsibility for management of others' financial resources. Accordingly, it is essential to avoid providing them opportunities to pursue private gains with their clients' resources.

No *Riba*

The prohibition of earning or charging interest is the prevailing view among Islamic scholars. It is a central tenet of Islamic finance.[16] Basically, it reflects

---

[14] El-Hawary, Grais, and Iqbal (2004).

[15] See Muhammad Imran Ashraf Usmani (2002) for an overview of Islamic contracts and modes of financing.

[16] There are different types of *riba*, generally understood as interest. The prohibition of *riba* has generally carried over to the prohibition of charging or receiving interest. A minority interpretation is that *riba* refers to usury rates and not to reasonable rates charged. See Mahmoud El-Gamal (2003). See also www.islamic-finance.com/item5_f.htm.

the view that it is unethical to earn from the simple ownership and placement of financial resources without a matching effort. The remuneration resulting from a placement should not be preset and linked to the value placed. It should rather be the result of the efforts made in the economical use of the resources and accordingly should not be set a priori.

However, interest is a core feature of conventional banking. It is a reflection of the time value of money (i.e., the opportunity cost of not consuming today for the opportunity to consume tomorrow, or its flip side, the opportunity of consuming today at the cost of less consumption tomorrow). Conventional banking, central banking, monetary policy, and liquidity management have been built on the premise of the possibility of holding and exchanging interest-rate-bearing assets.

The prohibition in Islamic finance against engaging in interest-bearing transactions or transacting in interest-bearing debt instruments sets constraints that limit the ability of: (1) deposit-taking institutions to compete in attracting deposits; (2) deposit-taking institutions to manage liquidity by placing their own excess resources or accessing resources when needed, notably on money markets; or (3) monetary authorities, in particular central banks, to conduct monetary policy by injecting or withdrawing resources from the financial system.[17]

Competition in attracting deposits has led Islamic banks to adopt return-smoothing practices or to introduce other incentives to attract clients. However, the practice of smoothing raises a number of issues related to displaced commercial risk, capital requirement, transparency, and corporate governance. One potential consequence of smoothing is the shifting of the outcome of poor performance results onto shareholders and the erosion of the bank's capital. The possibility of this displacement has implications for regulatory capital requirement. Moreover, the practice of smoothing obscures the actual performance of the investments made. It makes it more difficult for account holders and other stakeholders to assess the bank's investment performance. In addition, the use of a profit equalization reserve and an investment risk reserve to manage the smoothing raises issues as to who is entitled to these funds. These reserves are generally funded out of business results, shifting returns distribution across years. Accordingly, contributors to those funds and those who may benefit from them may not be the same.[18] The IFSB has issued a Guidance

---

[17] Davies (2011).
[18] See Cunningham (2010). The Basel III requirements in terms of liquidity coverage ratio (LCR) and net stable funding ratio (NSFR) may also pose a challenge to IIFSs and their supervisors.

Note on the practice of smoothing returns but clearly states, "To make any endorsement of Smoothing would in any case be outside the remit of the IFSB, and the issuance of this GN should not be considered as an endorsement of the practice."[19]

The no-*riba* requirement compounds the difficulty of liquidity management for Islamic financial institutions.[20] Markets should allow parties to place excess liquidity and access liquidity when needed on a short-term basis. In fact, systemic liquidity management needs liquid money markets offering a level playing field to Islamic and conventional financial institutions. In dual Islamic and conventional financial systems, a uniform framework for monetary operations covering both Islamic and conventional financial institutions would be preferable. This requires the "design and use of neutral instruments that can be widely held by both conventional and Islamic banks."[21] In this context, Bahrain's and Malaysia's experiences stand out. Both countries have developed *Shari'a*-compliant money instruments. Bahrain has developed short-term *sukuk*s that in principle should provide a basis to manage liquidity. However, there seems to be a limited secondary market for such instruments, as they are generally held to maturity. Malaysia has developed a vibrant Islamic Interbank Money Market. However, it seems that its yields remain highly correlated with conventional money market rates.[22]

Islamic financial institutions' lack of access to interest-bearing paper constrains the conduct of monetary policy. Monetary authorities generally do not have at their disposal *Shari'a*-compliant instruments to mop up liquidity and raise the cost of funds. The use of central bank certificates or treasury bills bearing interest can deal with liquidity only in the conventional segment. They present an opportunity for conventional banks to hold normally risk-free government paper, an opportunity that escapes Islamic financial institutions, notwithstanding the progress achieved. On the other side, *Shari'a*-compliant instruments may lead to market segmentation, limit liquidity, and complicate the efficient transmission of monetary policy.[23]

---

[19] IFSB (2010).
[20] IFSB (2008).
[21] See Sundarajan (2006).
[22] Bacha (2008). Bacha also observes: "Ironical as it may be, the operations of an IIMM in a dual banking system may serve to bring the Islamic banking sector into closer orbit with the conventional sector."
[23] See Sundarajan (2006) and Grais (2008).

OVERCOMING THE CONSTRAINTS: AN ORGANIZATIONAL FRAMEWORK BEYOND BANKS

The foregoing outlined the double challenge faced by Islamic banking: (1) to comply with principles of Islamic finance, and (2) to fit within the conceptual and implementation framework of prevailing banking business. Most notably, this challenge is in the choice of regulation of Islamic banking, licensing and operation of an Islamic bank, and conduct of monetary policy. Significant efforts have been made in tackling these issues, and progress has been achieved in the regulation and operation of Islamic banks as well as the conduct of monetary policy. The progress consists either in designing separate regulation for Islamic banks or extending and adapting to them existing regulation, as mentioned earlier.[24] The former approach permits the design of rules well calibrated to Islamic banking. However, it entails loss of transparency of transactions across segments of the financial system and may result in maintaining Islamic finance as a niche activity to the side of mainstream finance. On the other hand, the second approach, of extending conventional regulation to Islamic finance, remains awkward as it essentially seeks to have Islamic banking formally comply with conventional regulation. In practice, it would entail either loose regulation of Islamic banking or the stifling of its development.[25]

We suggest here an organizational framework for Islamic financial activity that would allow it to flourish with minimal constraints from existing regulations. It would require minor regulatory adaptations while avoiding the hurdles of seeking the adoption of new regulations or awkwardly extending ones ill-suited for its development. Consistency with Islamic finance principles will be essentially the responsibility of Islamic financial organizations. They would enshrine those principles in their business policies and codes of conduct. The proposed approach is based on a consideration of the services that Islamic finance offers and on observing the degree of their similarity with services found across conventional finance, especially beyond banking. It would still require further progress in developing an effective framework and performing instruments for systemic liquidity management and the conduct of monetary policy.

---

[24] See El Tiby (2011).

[25] It is interesting to note the view of Ben Bernanke, U.S. Federal Reserve chairman: "I will argue that central banks and other regulators should resist the temptation to devise ad hoc rules for each new type of financial instrument or institution. Rather, we should strive to develop common, principles-based policy responses that can be applied consistently across the financial sector to meet clearly defined objectives." See Bernanke (2007).

Currently Islamic banks offer depositors *amana* accounts, as well as unrestricted and restricted investment account deposits, the latter two mostly based on *mudaraba* contracts. They fund various activities mainly through *murabaha, ijara, musharaka,* or *istisna'a* types of contracts. To offer their services, Islamic banks request banking licenses and face the challenges outlined.

The same type of financial intermediation could be organized within the framework of financial entities where a *holding group* would have several subsidiaries, each one conducting intermediation activity according to Islamic finance principles.[26] The subsidiaries would conduct businesses such as (1) *amana* banking, (2) private banking, (3) leasing-*ijara*, (4) project financing, or (5) private equity. Other subsidiaries may be established in line with the holding group's business plans. In particular, the holding group may choose to set up an investment banking subsidiary or integrate the activity within the core of the management of the holding group. Investment banking can help structure and place funding instruments such as *sukuks* for some of the subsidiaries (project financing or leasing).

The holding group would seek the licensing of each subsidiary within its overall business strategy. In a natural way, each subsidiary's business would be consistent with existing regulations and the essence of Islamic finance. Internal policies would help achieve full compliance with Islamic finance principles. A *Shari'a* board at the level of the holding group would perform the roles that existing *Shari'a* advisory boards play. The regulatory challenges of launching new Islamic financial services would be much diminished.

The following briefly highlights the features of subsidiaries and how the framework of the holding group permits simultaneous compliance with prevailing regulation and Islamic finance principles.

Amana banking would take *amana* deposits that would be guaranteed and nonremunerated, complying with banking regulations and Islamic finance. It would offer deposit, payment, transfer, and similar services needed in the conduct of current transactions. It could finance short-term trade transactions according to *murabaha* contracts. The services of the *amana* bank would be clearly specified as well as their costs. If it is established as

---

[26] See also El Gamal (2005): "I propose mutuality as a solution to the corporate governance and regulatory problems currently unresolved due to the peculiar investment account structure. I show that mutual banking would be closer to the religious tenets enshrined in the prohibition of *riba*, and thus would strengthen the brand-name of Islamic banking by re focusing it on the nature of finance and its objectives, and away from formal-legalistic contract mechanics."

a cooperative or credit union with *amana* depositors being member share-holders, they would share returns realized within each period.[27] It would in essence be a so-called narrow bank.

Private banking would offer retail financial advisory services and wealth management. It would care for unrestricted and restricted invest-ment account holders. It would identify and offer them investment opportu-nities in mutual funds and other *Shari'a*-compliant investments. Investment account holders would own certificates in special vehicles or funds with the clear awareness that the certificates' value and returns are not guaran-teed. Unlike in the current structure of Islamic banks, unrestricted invest-ment account holders would be certificate holders in special investment vehicles with recognized rights. The private banking subsidiary would not need a deposit-taking commercial bank license. It would not be pressed to engage in smoothing of returns, as it would be competing with similar service suppliers. Given that there would be clear disclosure of the risk and returns prospects, there would be no displaced commercial risk and no need for related capital requirements. Competition in attracting funds would be based on the subsidiary's performance track record across all investment vehicles in the market.

The offered investment vehicles would be either proprietary of the hold-ing group or stemming from an open architecture approach. Debt-based funds or ones that invest in financial papers of entities dealing with sinful activities would be excluded from the menu of offered investments. This private banking subsidiary could be licensed within the framework of pre-vailing regulation and operate in compliance with it. Its internal policies and recourse to a *Shari'a* advisory board would ensure its full compliance with Islamic finance.

The holding group would have a *leasing-ijara* subsidiary that would also be regulated and licensed according to the rules in place. It would compete with other leasing companies in the market offering equipment for lease to business entities.[28] The holding group's investment banking services could support the leasing-*ijara* subsidiary in securing funding for its activities.

A *project finance* company can be part of the overall structure within the holding group. This subsidiary would be expected to have recourse to various types of contracts as required. One would expected it to rely to a large extent on *bai salam* and *istisna'a*.[29]

---

[27]These returns are not known *ex ante* and accordingly their distribution to members-shareholders-depositors would be compliant with the risk sharing and no guaranteed returns principles.

[28] Some *Shari'a* pronouncements may restrict the activity to operating leases.

[29] See Zarqa (1997) for how *istisna'a* can be used for project financing.

The holding group can have a *private equity* management company subsidiary. Private equity fund management is intrinsically consistent with Islamic finance. It uses *mudaraba* contracts on the funding side, extends financing with *musharaka* contracts, and complies with the materiality principle. It can naturally be established within the framework of existing regulation. It can be made fully consistent with Islamic finance when the established private equity fund's policy excludes funding of sinful activities. A management fee and a *mudarib*'s profit share are earned by the management company. The *rab ul mal* or limited partner gets a share of return. He or she is like a restricted account holder who elects to invest in a particular private equity fund. Clear regulations and practices followed by private equity management ventures can easily be drawn upon.

Whatever the organizational framework adopted, it is essential that stakeholders have confidence that the business complies with the code of conduct it pledges to follow. A well-established confidence can enhance financial performance, mitigate financial risks, and encourage financial inclusion, hence social equity. It is important that all Islamic financial institutions develop within a governance framework that promotes stakeholders' confidence that pledges of *Shari'a* compliance are being fulfilled. From an implementation perspective, a pledge to comply with *Shari'a* principles is similar to a pledge to abide by a code of corporate governance. Significant efforts have been made by the AAOIFI, the IFSB, and others to set up principles of sound corporate governance for Islamic financial institutions.[30]

CONCLUSION

The foregoing has reviewed the challenges of reconciling compliance with Islamic finance principles with prevailing banking regulation. Most notably, these challenges lie in the incompatibility of the implications of the principles of (1) risk sharing, (2) materiality, and (3) prohibition of *riba* with the notion of a conventional deposit, restrictions on conventional banks to hold real assets, and systemic liquidity management, respectively.

Significant efforts have been made to address these issues and find ways to reconcile the conflicting requirements. Significant progress has been achieved. As a result, the growth of Islamic financial assets has been phenomenal. However, to date the industry remains well below its potential size or that of conventional finance.

---

[30] See IFSB (2006), IFSB (2007a), Grais (2009), and Grais and Pellegrini (2006a).

This chapter suggests the potential benefit to tackle the challenges by considering an organizational arrangement that would avoid many of the hurdles of reconciling Islamic finance principles with prevailing banking regulation. Islamic financial institutions could expand and offer new services, leveraging existing regulations without compromising *Shari'a* principles. Islamic finance holding groups with subsidiaries offering the broad menu of services could expand without the straitjacket regulatory requirements governing banks.

Four

Corporate Governance

Good corporate governance (CG) is crucial to the ability of a business to protect the interests of its stakeholders. These interests may extend beyond the purely financial to the stakeholders' ethical, religious, or other beliefs. An institution offering Islamic financial services (IIFS) is required to carry out its operations in compliance with the principles of *Shari'a*. A corporate structure that enables a financial institution to implement good governance through *Shari'a*-compliant operations is therefore essential for the stability and efficiency of Islamic financial services.

The practices of IIFSs raise specific corporate governance challenges. While a number of problems are common to all financial institutions, two broad sets of CG issues are specific to IIFSs. The first arises from the need to reassure stakeholders that IIFS activities fully comply with the precepts of Islamic jurisprudence.[1] Ultimately, the core mission of such an institution is to meet its stakeholders' desire to conduct their financial business according to *Shari'a* principles. The same stakeholders also need to be assured that the firm will nonetheless actively promote their financial interests and prove to be an efficient, stable, and trustworthy provider of financial services. This combination of *Shari'a* compliance and business performance raises specific challenges and agency problems, and underlines the need for distinctive CG structures.

---

[1] Islamic jurisprudence is also known as *fiqh*. It covers all aspects of life: religious, political, social, and economic. It is mainly based on interpretations of the Quran and Sunna (sayings and deeds of the Prophet).

This part deals with CG issues and challenges facing the Islamic finance industry. It deals first in Chapter 7 with the financial fiduciary responsibility IIFSs need to deal with. It then focuses in Chapter 8 on arrangements to ensure *Shari'a* compliance and provide comfort to stakeholders that this is indeed the case. Finally, Chapter 9 outlines a systemic Islamic finance *Shari'a* governance framework that pulls together various facets bearing on the CG of IIFSs in a jurisdiction.

Financial Fiduciary Governance

This chapter focuses on the corporate governance (CG) arrangements of institutions offering Islamic financial services (IIFSs) aimed at protecting stakeholders' financial interests.[1] Many IIFS CG issues are in common with those of their conventional counterparts. Others are distinctive. In particular, IIFSs offer depositors unrestricted investment accounts entailing that they share risks with shareholders but without a voting right. The chapter first reviews internal and external arrangements put in place by IIFSs to protect stakeholders' financial interests. It discusses shortcomings notably in terms of potential conflict of interest between shareholders and holders of unrestricted investment accounts. It then suggests a CG framework that combines internal and external arrangements to provide safeguards to unrestricted investment account holders without overburdening an IIFS's financial performance. The chapter uses a review of 13 IIFSs and regulatory information from countries where IIFSs have developed the most.

The chapter first reviews prevailing internal and external CG arrangements to protect stakeholders' financial interests in an IIFS, and identifies shortcomings. It then suggests measures to overcome these shortcomings.

---

[1] For an overview paper of CG of IIFSs, see Grais and Pellegrini (2006c). Grais and Pellegrini (2006b) deals with the protection of shareholders' ethical interests. Given that an Islamic financial institution's core mission is to enable its stakeholders to pursue their financial interests without breaching their religious beliefs, the IIFS's CG arrangements cannot underestimate the importance of having a framework that credibly protects these financial interests. IIFS mission statements appear to identify four categories of stakeholders: shareholders, depositors, borrowers, and socially vulnerable groups. Internal CG mechanisms can be expected to ensure that the interests of all these stakeholders are looked after. Broader institutional arrangements, or external mechanisms, would complement internal arrangements and enhance their effectiveness.

PROTECTING STAKEHOLDERS' FINANCIAL INTERESTS: PRACTICE AND SHORTCOMINGS

Corporate governance arrangements are generally perceived as structures and procedures specific to the business organization. However, broader institutional arrangements do bear on the quality and effectiveness of CG. In the following, the former and the latter are referred to as internal and external arrangements, respectively.

Internal Arrangements

Institutions offering Islamic financial services (IIFSs) generally put in place CG structures and systems similar to those of businesses offering conventional financial standards (BCFSs) to handle traditional agency problems between *shareholders* and management. Although not specific to IIFSs, the protection of small shareholders may be equally important for them. Indeed, concentrated ownership and control may be more widespread in IIFSs than with BCFSs. Table 7.1 shows that out of a sample of 21 IIFSs for which shareholder information was exhaustive, nine appear to be family owned and controlled, about 43 percent of the sample.[2] This translates into a concentration of control of executive decisions and a monolithic board of directors that may be biased in favor of specific interests unless adequately checked. Small shareholders as well as other stakeholders may accordingly be at risk. For example, management may use discretion in the funds they commingle to finance specific investments and provide better yields to dominant shareholders.[3]

---

[2]Data were collected through IIFS websites as well as the Bankscope and Capital Intelligence databases. *Control* is defined as effective control power over the enterprise. Further researchers may want to analyze more rigorously ownership structure differences between IIFSs and BCFSs. In particular, researchers may want to explore the ratio of independent directors to all directors in IIFSs to verify whether family ownership effectively leads to episodes of board capture.

[3]Paradoxically, family ownership in nonfinancial firms may solve the problems deriving from Berle and Means's (1932) separation of ownership from control. However, in financial firms, where substantial funds are contributed by depositors and not equity holders, this type of ownership worsens the position of nonshareholder stakeholders. Given the importance attached by IIFSs to stakeholders, this represents a relevant problem for them.

TABLE 7.1 Ownership Structure of IIFSs

	Family Owned	State Owned	Dispersed Ownership	Total Sample
Number	9	5	7	21
Percentage	43%	24%	33%	100%

Source: W. Grais and M. Pellegrini, "Corporate Governance and Stakeholders' Financial Interests in Institutions Offering Islamic Financial Services," World Bank Policy Research Working Paper 4053, November 2006.

Public ownership is also a frequent feature of IIFSs (see Table 7.1).[4] This raises the issue of contingent liability for public finances and the protection of the ultimate shareholder, the public at large. It also points to the need to pay attention to CG features that would provide management with enough leeway to operate at arm's length from public authorities. Nonetheless, these CG issues are not specific to IIFSs, and conventional approaches can be helpful to IIFSs in addressing them.

Next to shareholders, *depositors* are a second category of IIFS stakeholders. Generally, IIFSs offer three broad categories of deposit accounts: current, restricted investment, and unrestricted investment.[5] Each category raises some CG issues, but those of unrestricted investment account holders (UIAHs) may be the most challenging. Current and restricted accounts are briefly considered before turning to UIAHs.

Current accounts (CAs) in Islamic finance may take three general forms depending on national jurisdictions. In *amana* deposits, the financial institution acts as a trustee and promises to pay back the deposit in full. An example is the Jordan Islamic bank that offers "trust deposits." As the bank's terms and conditions state that "the bank may use such deposits at its own risk and responsibility in respect of profit and loss as these accounts do not share in investment risks and consequently do not share in investment profit or losses." Likewise, in a *qard hassan* (goodwill loan), the bank receives a loan from depositors and owes them only the principal amount. Iran's Law for Usury (Interest) Free Banking stipulates that "banks are obliged to repay

---

[4]The survey shows that 24 percent of IIFSs are fully state controlled (i.e., the state is the ultimate controller through golden shares of majority ownership). However, state ownership rises to 57 percent when one includes partial state ownership (without ultimate control).

[5]Most IIFSs also offer savings accounts. However, they usually fall in either the category of term investments or that of current accounts. We therefore distinguish only between investment deposits and current account deposits.

the principals of '*gharz-al-hasaneh*' (saving and current) deposits."[6] Last, *wadiah* current accounts are also based on principal amount guarantees. For instance, Bank Muamalat states that "the bank guarantees the value of the deposit thus creating a *Wadiah Yad-Dhamanah* contract." In all cases, the financial institution obtains an implicit or explicit authorization to use the deposit money for whatever purpose permitted by *Shari'a*, but to pay no fixed interest or profit shares to the depositors, with the exception of gifts (*hibah*) distributed at the bank's discretion.[7] Given the similarities with conventional checking accounts, Islamic current accounts do not pose CG issues specific to IIFSs.

In the case of restricted investment accounts (RIAs), the bank acts only as fund manager—agent or nonparticipating *mudarib*—and is not authorized to mix its own funds with those of investors without their prior permission. The IIFSs operate these accounts under the principle of *mudaraba* and tailor modes of investment as well as profit distribution to the risk appetites and needs of the individual clients. Funds provided by restricted investment account holders are off the balance sheet. The relevant information about such accounts is provided in the statement of changes in restricted investments and their equivalent, or as a footnote to the statement of financial position, a treatment similar to that for funds' management in BCFSs. This treatment is confirmed by the Accounting and Auditing Organization for Islamic Financial Institutions (AAOIFI) standards, which prefer to consider restricted investment accounts as off-balance-sheet items, since the financial institution has no unconditional right to use or dispose of these funds. Investments for RIA depositors are not considered assets of the institution (under the assumption that the underlying *mudaraba* contract is nonparticipating).

Restricted investment account holders would want to be reassured that the financial institution conforms to their investment mandates. However, this should not be a major distinctive issue for IIFSs. First, RIA depositors are normally savvy high-net-worth investors, whose holdings are large enough to induce them to directly monitor the agent's behavior. Second, disclosure practices for RIA holders can be drawn from the ones in place for fund management in BCFSs, where AAOIFI standards do not apply. RIAs in IIFSs are similar to managed investments in BCFSs.

Unrestricted investment account (UIA) holders are the third and often most important category of IIFS depositors. They are a characteristic feature

---

[6] "Article 4, Iran's Law for Usury (Interest) Free Banking," www.cbi.ir/simplelist/1457 .aspx.
[7] In the case of *amana* deposits, the authorization must be obtained from the depositor while in *qard hassan*, this is not needed. For more, refer to Ahmad (1997).

of Islamic finance, raising a distinctive CG challenge. Essentially, it is the asymmetry between the extent of these depositors' participation in bearing the financial institution's risks and their ability to influence the institution's business conduct. Usually, UIA holders enter into a *mudaraba* contract with the institution.[8] The essence of the contract is that the financial institution manages their funds and shares with them returns according to a predetermined ratio. Funds provided by the UIA holders are placed in investment pools, and profits, if any, on investments are distributed at maturity according to the profit and loss sharing (PLS) ratio specified in the contract. The UIA holders, and not the financial institution, bear the risk of the performance of the investment pool, except for misconduct on the part of the institution.[9]

Thus, UIA holders are stakeholders akin to shareholders. They are principals entrusting their resources to an agent, in this case the management of the Islamic financial institution. A significant difference, however, is that the agent is appointed by another principal, the shareholder. Whereas the latter can influence business conduct through CG structures and processes in place, UIA holders do not have any similar channel to express their views. Their only option is the withdrawal of their funds (i.e., exit from the enterprise), when feasible. In short, UIA holders constitute a sui generis category of depositors with no *ex ante* guarantee, in principle, on either the capital value they have placed or the returns. They do not have an institutional voice on the conduct of the business, and they delegate the appointment of their agent to another principal whose interests may not always accord with theirs.

An IIFS's investment decisions are controlled by a board of directors that is accountable to shareholders, whose interests may be at odds with those of UIA holders. In particular, the larger the share of profits distributed to such investors, the lower will be the dividend payments to shareholders. In principle, this should not constitute a problem, given that the allocation of returns is governed by the ratio specified in the *mudaraba* contract. However, IIFSs commingle shareholders' and UIA holders' funds in common pools, which gives the management the leeway to direct resources of influential principals to projects with the likelihood of better returns. The incentive may be stronger in periods of high growth and profits on investment

---

[8] The case of *wikala* UIAs, which are based on an agency relationship with the IIFS earning a flat fee, rather than a share of profits, is not considered here.

[9] This risk-sharing feature has led some to argue that UIAs are not liabilities for the IIFS and accordingly they should not be required to meet the same capital requirements as BCFSs. In particular, the credit and market risk would fall on depositors, while the bank would only be subject to operational risk.

accounts when shareholder-controlled management and boards may favor shareholders' investments.[10] A high degree of concentrated ownership in the institution may exacerbate this issue. Commingling also impacts other stakeholders. Current account holders could be subsidizing other stakeholders with their safekeeping deposits. Likewise, RIA profits could be transferred to the corporate balance sheet.[11]

In addition, UIA holders do not have a say in the management and use of reserve funds to which they are implicitly required to contribute. IIFSs generally put in place reserve funds with the stated objective of providing a cushion of resources that can be used to weather adverse developments in the investment portfolio.[12] They are considered important to deal with competitive pressure from BCFSs and other IIFSs. Returns to UIA holders vary according to the performance of the financial institution. Therefore, UIA holders may be induced to transfer their funds to a better-performing IIFS. To mitigate such a risk, IIFSs set up profit equalization reserves (PERs) and use them in periods of poor performance to complement the returns that would be due to these depositors. The funds are fed by retaining earnings of UIA holders in periods of high returns on investment. Similar arrangements help the IIFS protect the principal of UIA holders. A special risk investment reserve is used for compensating a loss of principal resulting from poor investment results.

The use of profit equalization and risk investment funds raises issues pertaining to the governance of these funds and the protection of UIA holders' rights.[13] First and foremost, smoothing of returns to these depositors

---

[10]This is indeed what happened in the case of Ihlas Finance House, which used the impressive growth in the deposit base to mask transfers of funds to shareholders, as mentioned in the paper "Corporate Governance: Overview of Issues and Options" by Grais and Pellegrini (2006). It is to be noted that the expropriation process could also be inverse: In years of poor performance, losses borne by investment accounts may be shifted to other stakeholders, including shareholders, to prevent a flight of depositors. This practice, commonly known as displacement risk, was adopted by Kuwait Finance House when it was engulfed in the crash of the Souk al Manakh.

[11]The prohibition to transfer funds from an RIA to the IIFS's balance sheet is an established practice in some jurisdictions. In Bahrain, for instance, the Monetary Agency must give prior approval to such types of transfers.

[12]These reserves are generally known as profit equalization reserves (PERs) and investment risk reserves (IRRs). We follow AAOIFI's definition in Financial Accounting Standard (FAS) 11.

[13]We are not here concerned with the fact that the existence of such funds may be contrary to the theory of Islamic financial intermediation, in that it creates a de facto insurance against market risk.

as currently practiced is a significant obstacle to transparency. By maintaining a stable return to this category of depositors, managers automatically send the signal that the firm is healthy and profitable, while the reality may be otherwise. Smoothing of returns therefore introduces a veil of opacity between depositors and the firm. This problem is heightened by the limited transparency on the use, size, and allocation of these funds. An informal survey of 13 IIFSs shows that of the four IIFSs that admitted resorting to reserves, only two provide information in their financial statements and annual reports on the share of funds transferred from or to these reserves.[14] Limited disclosure does not provide comfort to UIA holders on their fair treatment. Second, these depositors lack the rights to influence the use of such resources and to verify the degree of risk of management's investments. Such reserves are considered retained earnings, at least in the AAOIFI definition, and reinvested in profit-bearing activities.[15] Third, individual UIA holders may not be able to opt out of their participation in the accumulation of these reserves. UIA holders with a long-term investment perspective may find it useful to delegate the intertemporal allocation of their income to a financial intermediary.[16] However, a UIA holder with a high discount rate may be negatively affected by the imposition of this practice. Finally, UIA holders who withdraw their deposits lose their claim on the accumulated reserves and would, in practice, be contributing to the future consumption of other UIA holders.[17]

IIFS stakeholders also include *borrowers* who need access to financial resources to pursue economic activities. IIFS mission statements often mention the special emphasis they place on contributing to the development of the communities they serve. Data on the comparative performance of IIFSs in this regard are not yet available. However, it is noticeable that many IIFSs attach a high importance to preferential policies for residents of their local communities. Several IIFSs offer vocational training for local residents in the form of awards or traineeships for local school or university students.

---

[14] For the sample used, the only two banks that disclose use of PERs are Bank Muamalat and Dubai Islamic Bank.

[15] AAOIFI FAS 16.

[16] According to a study by Allen and Gale (1997), financial intermediaries appear to be as efficient as markets in intertemporal consumption smoothing.

[17] In this regard, some banks require customers to waive their rights on these funds. For example, the terms and conditions of Islamic Bank of Britain state: "you (the UIAH) authorize us to deduct from net income your profit stabilization reserve contribution for payment into the profit stabilization reserve account. Upon such deduction you agree that you relinquish any right you may have to the monies in the profit stabilization reserve account" (www.islamic-bank.com, last visited April 18, 2005).

However, further research on the comparative treatment of borrowers by IIFSs and BCFSs is needed.

A last, but equally important, category of stakeholders is that of *socially vulnerable groups*. The emphasis by IIFSs on their social role is not uniform. However, there is a noticeable consistency in respecting the social obligations of Islamic finance. IIFSs usually take pride in social services provided, as signaled by the disclosure of their accomplishments in their annual reports. In our sample of 13 IIFSs, we found that all of them discharged their almsgiving duties (*zakat*) as required by *Shari'a* from all responsible corporate citizens. The majority also provided charitable loans (*qard hassan*) to help disadvantaged groups meet social obligations like marriage. Three IIFSs also conducted charitable activities in the form of competitions, prizes, and awards. Activities financed range from the implementation of development and humanitarian programs and the construction of hospitals and mosques to the financing of education, house refurbishments, and in-kind donations. In general, it appears that IIFSs live up to their social goals as claimed in their mission statements.

External Arrangements

Internal CG arrangements are generally reinforced by external ones that set the framework governing business activity and provide the information necessary for their official and private monitoring. These external arrangements relate to (1) the legal and regulatory prudential framework governing IIFS activities and (2) the financial information infrastructure that permits their monitoring. However, while their purpose is generally to strengthen CG, external arrangements may challenge efforts at *Shari'a* compliance or weaken transparency, notably of accounts. The development of external CG arrangements for IIFSs would seem to lag those for their BCFS counterparts.

Legal and Regulatory Arrangements

Legislative and regulatory issues that impact the profitability and stability of IIFSs may be broadly categorized under rules on taxation, rules on permissible activities, stakeholder protection rules, and capital adequacy regulations. With regard to taxation, the asset-based nature of Islamic finance requires that in a single transaction, property may change ownership several times. For instance, in a *Shari'a*-compliant mortgage, the property must change hands twice—from seller to bank and from bank to customer. Accordingly, a *Shari'a*-compliant mortgage involves the payment of two sets of stamp duty whereas a conventional mortgage is subject to a single stamp duty. This is tantamount to an additional fee levied on the IIFS. This issue has been tackled in several countries but has not attracted regulatory attention in others.[18]

Second, some *Shari'a*-compliant activities may be incompatible with conventional finance regulatory framework. By their nature, IIFSs utilize a series of transactions that may be prohibited by conventional regulations. For instance, an Islamic financial transaction may require that an Islamic financial institution owns property for short intervals of time. However, in some countries, deposit-taking institutions are explicitly prohibited from investing in movable or immovable assets for business purposes.[19] Similarly, no IIFS transaction may involve interest. However, conventional payment systems or reserve requirement rules may oblige them to do so.[20] Likewise, conventional lender-of-last-resort mechanisms may not be deemed to be *Shari'a* compliant.[21] The problem can be acute in the case of liquidity

---

[18] In the United States, double stamp duties on Islamic financial instruments may still apply. In the United Kingdom, on the contrary, the issue has been resolved by the gradual introduction of practical measures to tackle the issue of unfair taxation for Islamic financial products. These include relief from double stamp duty for Islamic property finance products, as well as the simplification of taxation procedures for profits earned by UIAHs. Until recently, no tax has been imposed on the profits disbursed to UIAHs. However, such profits were fully taxable in the hands of UIAHs. From now on, a small tax comparable to that levied on conventional savings accounts will be deducted at source. Accordingly, UIAHs won't have to include profits from their UIAs in their tax declarations. In countries with separate legislation the issue of taxation is generally addressed.

[19] In countries with established dual financial systems, derogations on ownership of property are usually granted to IIFSs. For instance, Article 54 of the Banking Law of Jordan (Law No. 28 of 2002) exempts IIFSs from rules that would otherwise constrain their investments in movable and immovable properties.

[20] For instance, in India a strict interpretation of reserve requirement rules that oblige banks to open interest-bearing accounts with the central bank prevents the licensing of IIFSs as full-fledged banks. Accordingly, IIFSs opt for nonbanking statuses that may impose operational limitations on their activities. This has repercussions on investors as underlined in an earlier section. In other jurisdictions where IIFSs must maintain statutory deposits with central regulators, IIFSs usually use interest earnings for charitable purposes. This is the case of Bahrain-based IIFSs. In Malaysia, on the contrary, the deposits with the central bank are *ex ante* non-interest-bearing as provided for by an amendment to the Central Bank Act, 1958 (Section 37 1c, revised 1994).

[21] In Indonesia, Malaysia, and Sudan, central banks have established *Shari'a*-compliant lending facilities. For instance, regulation 5/3/2002 on "Short-Term Financing Facility for *Shari'a* Banks" allows IIFSs licensed in Indonesia to overcome short-term liquidity shortages by borrowing in *Shari'a*-compliant *wadiah* certificates. However, in other countries, the issue has not been addressed.

management instruments, such as for satisfying short-term liquidity needs, because of the nonexistence of Islamic secondary markets. Some regulators and IIFSs have addressed the problem through the establishment of the Bahrain-based International Islamic Financial Market (IIFM) and Liquidity Management Center (LMC).[22] Nevertheless, it would appear that the majority of IIFSs still lack access to secondary markets and are forced to maintain unusually high levels of liquidity, thus curbing investment opportunities and profits.

Third, rules to protect stakeholders often imply principal amount guarantees in the form of deposit protection schemes. Indeed, in most countries, stakeholders may not be fully aware of the profit and risk sharing implications of *Shari'a*-compliant investment accounts.[23] Guided by concerns on depositor protection, regulators may refuse to treat UIAs as sui generis deposits and instead opt for regulating them as interest-bearing deposits, thus extending to them the provisions of deposit insurance legislation. Nonetheless, applying insurance schemes to what are essentially investment accounts may be unacceptable in terms of *Shari'a*-prescribed risk sharing and may altogether induce IIFSs to decline to mobilize savings with such an instrument. In practice, some IIFSs have addressed this issue by licensing UIAs as mutual funds. This solution brings UIAs under securities regulation that meshes with their profit and risk sharing nature. However, the mutual fund product may limit the scope of services IIFSs offer their clients. Alternatively, UIAs may be insured as conventional deposits. This option does nevertheless represent a second-best, if unacceptable, solution for Islamic jurists.[24]

---

[22] The IIFM is sponsored by several regulators, and its role is the creation of an active *Shari'a*-compliant secondary market. The LMC is a joint private-sector initiative (Dubai Islamic Bank, Bahrain Islamic Bank, and Kuwait Finance) with the same purpose.

[23] This does not simply apply to non-Islamic countries. In fact, the case of IFH underscored a general lack of awareness of the nonapplicability of conventional deposit insurance to IIFSs in Turkey. It also showed the risks that such lack of awareness may result in panic and systemic banking crises.

[24] In the United States, there is at least one UIA facility (University Bank, Ann Arbor, Michigan) that has been licensed as a deposit institution and insured along Federal Deposit Insurance Corporation (FDIC) provisions. The Bank's SSB has certified that the application of insurance was the best possible solution within regulatory constraints. In the United Kingdom, the FSA has adopted a solution that tries to reconcile depositor protection with risk and profit sharing. All UIAs are insured as prescribed by the EU Directive on Deposits (94/19/EC). However, if the IIFS incurs losses, the individual UIAH may waive deposit insurance and voluntarily decide to bear investment losses.

Finally, due to the distinctiveness of financial instruments used by IIFSs, conventional Basel risk weighting may not be suited to Islamic banks. For instance, in a profit and risk sharing account, credit and market risk would fall normally on the investor while operational risk would fall on the IIFS, solely responsible for losses deriving from failure to comply with *Shari'a*. Likewise, instruments on the assets side of an Islamic financial institution's balance sheet may be subject to risks that are different from those arising in conventional counterparts. To address this deficiency, some countries have adopted a capital adequacy calculation that accounts for IIFS-specific risks.[25] However, it appears that several countries have simply extended the Basel framework to IIFSs. This latter practice may be contrary to the trend toward risk-based regulation.

Generally, a regulatory framework that does not address specific IIFS issues may lead Islamic financial institutions to pursue a licensing status (e.g., nonbank) that may not correspond to the nature of their activities. It may weaken external arrangements bearing on CG and adversely affect market development and stability as well as the institutions' performance. A careful assessment of the impact of the regulatory arrangements governing IIFSs is warranted.

Financial Information Infrastructure

Widely available and affordable financial information supports official and private monitoring of financial businesses' performance. It promotes transparency and supports market discipline, two important ingredients of sound CG. Financial information may be particularly important for IIFSs due to the private equity nature of UIAs and the assumption that UIA holders have more at stake than conventional depositors. UIA holders should therefore be interested in directly monitoring the IIFS's performance. However, this requires an institutional infrastructure that facilitates the production of accurate financial information, the availability of agents that can interpret and disseminate it, as well as arrangements to protect its integrity. On all these counts, the Islamic financial industry faces challenges. Existing limited infrastructure reduces the role that information flows may play in

---

[25] Some national regulations are based on AAOIFI's "Statement on the Purpose & Calculation of the Capital Adequacy Ratio for Islamic Banks." AAOIFI recommends the inclusion of 50 percent risk-weighted assets of the UIA to cover "fiduciary risk" and "displaced commercial risk" that arise in UIA operations. However, it does not address the risk peculiarities of IIFSs on the assets side of the balance sheet. This problem will be resolved by the forthcoming IFSB capital adequacy standard, which will deal with UIAs and instruments on the assets side of the balance sheet.

promoting competition and market activities that would induce managers to adopt sound CG practices.

Issues such as the *protection of information integrity* concern both IIFSs and BCFSs. Other issues have a special connotation in the context of Islamic finance and are the focus here. For instance, a core component of *financial information infrastructure* is a chart of accounts that businesses would use to organize and produce credible financial statements. The accounting profession has gradually developed standards at the national and international levels, generally with official support. An increasing number of countries have adopted International Financial Reporting Standards (IFRS) in the wake of an apparent consensus to promote international convergence. However, IFRS is designed for conventional businesses, including BCFSs. The nature of IIFS products, their practice of setting up reserve funds to smooth profit distribution and protect the UIA holders' principal, and the commitment to distribute *zakat* are among IIFS features that may not directly fit into the IFRS framework. This realization has led to the establishment in the early 1990s of AAOIFI, which gradually developed standards dealing with IIFS specificities.[26]

While progress has been achieved with AAOIFI's work, the accounting pillar of the financial information infrastructure for IIFS continues to present two sets of weaknesses. Wherever IFRSs are the only rule, they may not induce the production of financial statements reflecting their genuine performance and may give a false sense of reliability. AAOIFI standards, in contrast, would be expected to deal adequately with IIFS specificities. However, they reduce cross-sector comparability. In addition, the direct references to religion may discourage application in secular countries. A review of 13 auditors' reports confirms that practices vary across countries. In particular, only seven of the 13 sampled IIFSs utilize some form of IIFS-specific standards. Table 7.2 shows which countries have issued standards based on, or inspired by, AAOIFI's work.

The *provision of financial information* on IIFSs remains constrained by a series of issues. First of all, providers and analysts may not be entirely familiar with the nature of IIFSs and with AAOIFI standards. However, market forces have already brought about substantial progress. For instance, leading international rating agencies now monitor and rate IIFSs and are acquainted with

---

[26] AAOIFI's standards are mandatory for the following markets: Bahrain, Jordan, Sudan, Qatar, and Dubai International Financial Center. Syria is considering their adoption. The standards are used as guidelines in Saudi Arabia, Kuwait, Malaysia, Lebanon, and Indonesia. Most Islamic banks' *Shari'a* supervisory committees use AAOIFI standards as guidelines.

TABLE 7.2   Country Approaches to Accounting and Auditing Standards for IIFSs

Country	AAOIFI Standards (Adopted/ Recommended/Adapted) or National IIFS-Specific Standards	Non-IIFS-Specific Standards
Bahrain	✓	
DIFC*	✓	
Egypt		✓
Indonesia	✓	
Jordan	✓	
Lebanon	✓	
Malaysia	✓	
Philippines		✓
Qatar	✓	
Saudi Arabia	✓**	
Sudan	✓	
Syria	✓	
Thailand		✓
Turkey		✓
United States		✓
United Kingdom		✓

*Dubai International Financial Center.
**The Saudi Arabian Monetary Agency recommended that IIFS seek guidance from AAOIFI FAS in compiling their statements, but officially requires IFRS.

AAOIFI prescriptions.[27] They have also tailored their rating mechanisms to the risk profile of Islamic banks.[28] However, the lack of internationally accepted and standardized accountancy practices for IIFSs derived from the still limited application of AAOIFI standards, as pointed out earlier, reduces comparability across markets and banks and may reduce consistency in ratings.

---

[27] These are Fitch Ratings, Capital Intelligence, and Moody's Investors Service. Capital Intelligence was the pioneer in rating and analyzing IIFSs. It now covers 21 IIFSs across eight countries.

[28] Capital Intelligence uses the same categories to rate IIFSs and BCFSs, falling namely into six areas: regulation and supervision, operating environment, franchise strength, management quality, financial fundamentals, and external support. However, given the nature of IIFSs, the analytical focus is adjusted. For instance, liquidity risk management may be more important in rating an IIFS than in a BCFS, given the lack of *Shari'a*-compliant secondary markets.

These financial information weaknesses do not serve to create a *competitive environment* for IIFSs. Instead, they limit the contribution that competition can bring to sound IIFS corporate governance.[29] The principal information weakness in IIFSs is the limited application of internationally accepted standards tailored to them. This has the effect of reducing the accuracy of information reported as well as of diminishing comparability across IIFSs. In addition, it reduces the scope for product competition and diminishes incentives to adopt corporate control mechanisms that would minimize costs. Weaknesses in producing and analyzing financial information do not provide the means for fluid mergers and acquisitions activity and hence shelter managers from the threat of takeover in the event of poor performance.

EMPOWERMENT AND ENABLING REGULATIONS

The following offers suggestions to strengthen internal and external CG arrangements that bear on stakeholders' financial interests.

Internal Governance: Stakeholders' Empowerment

The protection of IIFS stakeholders' financial interests requires the application of established CG principles, adapted to the framework of Islamic finance. In addition, regulators need to implement solutions that address problems specific to IIFSs. First, regulators need to focus on transparency requirements, given the limited disclosures that characterize IIFSs. Second, mechanisms to ensure protection of minority shareholders would seem to be at least as important in IIFSs as in BCFSs. Third, the practice of commingling would need attention, as it decreases investors' confidence in a fair and proper use of their funds. Fourth, UIA holders need to be empowered to look after their own interests; this may require, among other things, clear and harmonized rules on the use of reserves.

Islamic financial institutions generally appear less transparent than their conventional counterparts. It is therefore necessary for an Islamic financial institution to focus on creating a culture of transparency that protects all investors. Taking a cue from the Organisation for Economic Co-operation and Development (OECD) principles, "disseminating information should provide for equal, timely and cost-efficient access to relevant information by users."[30]

---

[29] Grosfeld and Tressel (2001) provide evidence that competition has an important complementary effect where good CG mechanisms are already in place.
[30] OECD (2004).

Thus, an Islamic financial institution would need to publish its corporate governance code or policy and the process by which it is implemented.

The particular need to protect the interests of minority shareholders in an Islamic financial institution arises out of the concentration of ownership frequently observed in such institutions. For instance, in an environment where the largest stockholders are also likely to occupy executive positions, CG mechanisms like executive stock options and registered shares may be counterproductive for the fair governance of the institution. Likewise, relying on the markets for corporate takeovers is not an option when managing families are solidly in control through super-voting shares or majority stakes.[31] In such a situation, the ownership structure needs to contain guarantees for minority shareholders, such as the attribution of a fixed number of minority directors, or independent safeguards in the nomination of outside directors. Alternatively, regulators could consider the introduction of remedies that would allow minority owners to sue the ultimate controlling shareholders rather than managers.[32]

Next, the widely prevalent practice of commingling funds in an Islamic financial institution can limit the transparency of the institution's compliance with its clients' investment objectives. Accordingly, regulatory authorities need to consider rules on firewalls and sanctions for breaches. This is of paramount importance in the case of UIA holders, whose funds are usually pooled with those of shareholders.

Finally, the regulatory framework needs to address UIA holders' rights and their protection. Three alternative options to empower and protect UIA holders could be considered. In the first one, rights that normally belong to equity holders can be extended to UIA holders. The second option goes in the opposite direction: UIA holders could be granted full debt-holding status and the protection it carries. In the third option, the sui generis status of UIA holders could be maintained, provided that specific governance structures for protecting their interests are in place. Each of these options is discussed in the following.

---

[31] This does not consider the already limited use of hostile takeovers in banking due to the opacity of the system and regulatory restrictions. In general, the disciplining power of competition is hindered in banking by limited product market competition as banks construct long-term relationships with customers. Even if product markets were fully competitive, capital markets would still function poorly due to waves of irrational optimism and pessimism that result in shareholders looking at immediate revenues rather than the long-term ability of firms to pay dividends. For more, see Levine (2004) and Prowse (1998).

[32] In Canada, for instance, shareholders have a right to apply to courts for relief if any act or omission by their corporation or its directors is oppressive, is unfairly prejudicial, or unfairly disregards the interests of any shareholder or if the business or affairs of the corporation are conducted in a manner that has this effect.

On the first option, of extending shareholders' rights and duties to UIA holders, it can be argued that, given the equity-like investment of these depositors, they should be on an equal footing with shareholders and thus have the right to elect board representatives. This would increase their ability to air their demands and concerns with management. It would also satisfy depositors' demand for greater involvement in the strategic management of the bank.[33]

However, the election of UIA holders' representatives may fragment the board of directors along conflicting demands of different groups. Operationally, this could lead to decisional deadlocks to the detriment of efficient management and profit performance. In addition, the extension of shareholders' rights to UIA holders raises a legal issue. This category of depositors and shareholders is subject to two very different types of legal liabilities. The liability of investment account holders is limited to losses occurring on their investments. The liability of shareholders, in contrast, covers *all* losses that the bank may incur in the course of its business, including losses from funds provided by current account holders. In this light, the power to elect board representatives would give UIA holders a role in the strategic management of the entire institution that might not be commensurate with their risks.

If extending shareholders' rights to UIA holders is deemed impractical, depositors' protection could be another option. In most financial systems, regulators act on behalf of debt holders by requiring insurance on all deposits and taking control away from equity holders in case of distress. The PLS nature of investment accounts prevents, however, the application of deposit insurance as it is. Accordingly, a *Shari'a*-compliant version of deposit insurance could be put in place. It would cover current account holders under all circumstances of bank insolvency and UIA holders only in cases of insolvency resulting from proven fraudulent mismanagement.[34] Such a measure may reduce systemic risk associated with bank panic behavior and permit redress for UIA holders affected by the failure of an Islamic financial institution.[35]

---

[33] In a survey of IIFS consumers' preferences, Chapra and Ahmed (2002) record an interest by depositors to be involved in the strategic management of the bank.

[34] In case of bank liquidation, the Central Bank of Jordan distinguishes between investment accounts and deposit accounts. While the latter can be covered by deposit insurance, the former are charged with the expenses and disbursements of the liquidator and only subsequently their entitlements are distributed according to PLS ratios. See Banking Law Art 56.

[35] This is the system that is currently in place in Turkey. As outlined in the paper "Corporate Governance: Overview of Issues and Options" by Grais and Pelligrini (2006), it was introduced following the runs on special finance houses' deposits following the collapse of IFH.

The objections to deposit protection schemes are well documented in a vast body of literature that stresses the moral hazard of deposit insurance as well as the collective action implications.[36] The latter point may be especially relevant in the case of IIFSs. In theory, UIA holders could be considered to have a higher degree of sophistication than conventional bank depositors, and therefore be less inclined to leave the monitoring of the institution's performance to others. Thus, deposit protection schemes may prove to be a more significant disincentive to oversight of managers' decisions. More importantly, the establishment of protection mechanisms does not guarantee per se an impartial conduct of business, because it leaves unchanged those governance structures that would permit a shareholder-controlled management to be biased against UIA holders in determining investment policies.

A third option would be to put in place new governance structures that cater to the specific needs of UIA holders. One possibility is the election of a special representative or a body that would act as intermediary and, if necessary, whistle-blower. The main rationale for such a mechanism would be the creation of a permanent institutional channel to facilitate information flows from and to this category of depositors. While theoretically feasible, this policy presents drawbacks. In particular, the creation of a new agent would bring with it additional agency problems and the risk of multiplying, rather than diffusing, the asymmetries of information to which these depositors are subject. There is no guarantee that UIA holders would effectively monitor the conduct of their representative or that the representative would be immune from opportunistic behavior, such as collusion with the units of the institution in charge of appointments and remuneration. The creation of a composite body, made up of representatives from several parts of the firm, would perhaps reduce the tendency to collusion, on the assumption that the different members would check each other's behavior.

It appears, therefore, that the creation of governance bodies for the protection of UIA holders may be a reasonable solution to the immediate problem. Nonetheless, it does not resolve the tension between the debt-holding status of these depositors and the equity nature of their investments. Ultimately, it would be necessary to find organizational solutions that resolve this conflict.[37]

In conjunction with mitigating conflicts of interest, regulatory efforts would need to emphasize a transparent conduct of business. In this regard,

---

[36] For an empirical treatment of this issue, refer to Demirgüç-Kunt and Detragiache (2002).

[37] One option is the licensing of UIAs as collective investment schemes.

the smoothing of returns to UIA holders as currently practiced appears to be a significant obstacle to transparency. By maintaining a stable return to this category of depositors, managers could mislead them on the institution's true performance and introduce a veil of opacity between these depositors and the institution. In addition, the accumulation of a profit equalization reserve (PER) may be an appropriation of resources by the bank, unless the choice to smooth returns is left to the investor instead of the institution's management. Accordingly, where practiced, smoothing of returns should be subject to strict requirements. Waivers on resources contributed to the PER should be eliminated.

Another option is to issue profit equalization certificates against PER to UIA holders that they could redeem on leaving the financial institution.[38] In all circumstances, however, the financial institution should be fully transparent in the use of such funds. AAOIFI FAS 11 provides clear principles and guidelines on this issue. In particular, it guides IIFSs to disclose the shares of actual profits and use of the PER in the returns they receive.[39] In addition, each Islamic financial institution would need to adopt clear provisions regulating contributions to the PER and their disclosure in financial statements and annual reports.[40]

Strengthening the External Environment

An external environment that takes account of IIFS specificities would enhance the soundness of CG at the broader institutional level. Public-sector and private-sector activities can converge to provide a sound framework for the protection of the financial interests of IIFS stakeholders.

---

[38]This would imply acceptance by UIAHs that they may lose part of their principal if the IIFS has had negative profits during the term of their investments. The problem with such a scheme is that UIAHs would probably extend financing in the hope of future returns. This would be tantamount to a restriction of their exit options.

[39]Some IIFSs have already established the practice of distinguishing between profit distribution and reserve distributed.

[40]Decisions pertaining to PER and IIR should ideally be left to the business. However, concerns over maintaining the UIAH principal and the systemic consequences that losses may provoke have led some regulators to intervene. For instance, the Banking Law of Jordan as amended in 2003 establishes a minimum deduction of 10 percent on earnings to be invested in an investment risk fund in order to cover losses in mutual investment accounts. Such minimum deduction may be increased by the central bank (Art. 55).

FLEXIBLE REGULATORY APPROACH AND PRIVATE INITIATIVES

As observed earlier, IIFSs would require regulatory and legislative solutions that differ in certain respects from those governing BCFSs. Regulators would therefore need to adapt the underlying institutional and regulatory infrastructure, as well as encourage private-sector self-regulatory initiatives. Likewise, IIFSs should consider applying for licenses that best suit their needs. Supervisors need to be conversant with the arrangements put in place to ensure effective supervision without overburdening IIFS operations.

There is no single ideal model of regulation for IIFSs. In practice, though, Islamic finance is the most developed in countries that have separate arrangements for Islamic financial institutions. This would suggest that application of CG principles in a manner that recognizes IIFS specificities and results in an IIFS-specific regulatory infrastructure may support sounder CG. A rationale for separate arrangements can also be found in the enacting of Islamic finance laws in countries that had previously opted for a homogeneous regulatory framework, as well as by the creation of specialized Islamic finance regulatory divisions in the regulatory bodies. Nevertheless, establishing separate laws or institutions for the regulation of IIFSs could be an issue in non-Islamic countries. Also, IIFSs seem to flourish even in some countries that have not addressed the specificities of IIFSs through specific legislation. This is the case, for instance, in the United Kingdom, Saudi Arabia, or Bahrain, where the lack of an IIFS-specific legal framework does not equate with a neglect of the industry. In particular, regulators in these countries have shown willingness to adapt regulatory arrangements whenever needed, guided by the imperatives of fair competition, systemic stability, and investor protection.

In some situations, *private initiatives* may play a role when IIFSs and regulators cannot find workable solutions to address regulatory concerns. For instance, the issue of last-resort lending may be addressed by setting up a *takaful*-like arrangement. Each Islamic financial institution would contribute a fixed amount to a *Shari'a*-compliant mutual insurance pool and tap from its profits in times of distress.[41] Creating a lending facility of this type outside central banks may be desirable in those countries where central banks are reluctant to establish separate lending instruments for IIFSs.

---

[41] This idea echoes Chapra and Ahmed (2002) who propose the setup of a common pool at central banks where banks could deposit a percentage of their deposits and borrow interest-free in case of need provided that the net use of this facility is zero. While the ideas are essentially equivalent, creating a private *takaful*-like structure outside central banks may be a more workable solution for non-Muslim jurisdictions.

Likewise, in the case of liquidity risk, an Islamic financial institution may replicate or reinforce private liquidity risk management arrangements along the lines of the LMC.

In those countries where regulators would not consider adapting their arrangements to IIFSs, the latter may wish to seek an alternative *licensing status* that does not conflict with the nature of Islamic finance. For example, licensing IIFSs as financial cooperatives would present CG advantages.[42] However, it would raise other CG issues. Furthermore, it may place the IIFSs on a nonlevel playing field with BCFSs in those countries where legislation restricts the scope of activities by nonbanking institutions.

ENHANCING FINANCIAL INFORMATION FLOWS

A comprehensive flow of quality financial information requires the standardization and harmonization of accounting and auditing practices for IIFSs. Accounting standards that permit clear financial reporting by an IIFS would enhance stakeholders' confidence, while lowering the costs of information collection would induce reputable private agents to extend their operations to the IIFS market. This would enable synergies among supervisors, market monitors, and rating agencies, thereby encouraging sound CG.

A chart of accounts that permits IIFSs to provide clear and reliable financial reporting is a priority to improve their CG. Significant progress has been achieved by AAOIFI in this respect. Adoption of AAOIFI standards, creation of AAOIFI-inspired national standards, or recommendation of selected AAOIFI standards to integrate existing accounting and auditing standards needs to be considered in countries with a significant IIFS presence. AAOIFI's standards present advantages. First, they are the only existing comprehensive source of accounting standards for IIFSs. Their periodical review process should ensure that up-to-date accounting and auditing practices are retained. Second, they allow comparability across Islamic banks in different countries, although they may limit comparability across IIFSs and BCFSs.[43] Third, it may be easier for various stakeholders involved in Islamic finance to gain familiarity with a single accounting framework

---

[42] For instance, to better manage their liquidity, IIFSs could emulate the financial cooperatives' practice of organizing in conglomerates or networks and commit to satisfying each other's liquidity needs.

[43] One criticism of AAOIFI standards is that they depart too significantly from the format of IFRS. However, thanks to the ongoing review process, one may envisage a progressive adaptation of AAOIFI standards to the general IFRS format.

instead of a multiplicity of national ones. In spite of increased comparability across sectors, the simple extension of IFRS or national conventional standards is not likely to bring the same clarity, because it may not fully disclose all relevant information.[44]

Information reported in a consistent and accurate manner would provide the needed inputs to rating agencies, financial media, investment advisers, and CG analysts. Current progress by rating agencies on covering IIFSs augurs well for the future. In the short term, public authorities may also play an active role in supplying the infrastructure for information sharing, by creating, for instance, public rating agencies, without the intention of usurping the private-sector role and exclusively where such markets are missing. Adequate provision of information also requires authorities to put in place enabling norms that allow reputable private agents to access the necessary information and respect its integrity.

CONCLUSION

Overall, the introduction of new internal and external corporate governance (CG) structures, together with the reinforcement of existing ones, can provide stakeholders with sufficient comfort on the actions of management and other organs of the financial institution. Internally, this requires procedures for the protection of minority shareholders and provisions for increased disclosure. In addition, concrete approaches to addressing the problems of commingling, UIA holders' rights, and the utilization of reserves would complete the internal CG of IIFSs. Externally, recognizing the specificity of IIFSs will contribute to the stability of the industry and the protection of its stakeholders. Regulators need to be flexible and to work with the Islamic financial institutions to understand fully the needs of the industry and thereby develop an appropriate regulatory framework. Also, recourse to private self-regulatory initiatives may be more important in Islamic finance than in BCFSs. In those countries where regulations present constraints on Islamic finance, IIFSs need to evaluate the available options to determine which licensing status is best tailored to their needs and those of their stakeholders. Also, in order to be able to meaningfully oversee the institution's operations, the regulatory and other authorities,

---

[44]When AAOIFI standards were issued, Moody's observed the following to convey the scope of the problem: ". . . [W]hen reading these standards, the most striking realization is how little is disclosed in the current financial statements (i.e., not based on IIFS specific standards)."

as well as market participants, would need to have a full understanding of the various nuances of the legal and regulatory framework in which the institution operates. The role of public authorities should be further complemented and supported by reputable agents that would send signals to market players. This requires the existence of an IIFS-specific accounting and auditing infrastructure that would facilitate timely and reliable financial information.

CHAPTER 8

Corporate Governance and *Shari'a* Compliance

The structures and processes established within an institution offering Islamic financial services (IIFS) for monitoring and evaluating *Shari'a* compliance rely essentially on arrangements internal to the firm. By being incorporated into the institutional structure, a *Shari'a* supervisory board (SSB) has the advantage of being close to the market. Competent, independent, and empowered to approve new *Shari'a*-conforming instruments, an SSB can enable innovation likely to emerge within the institution.

This chapter reviews the issues and options facing current arrangements for ensuring *Shari'a* compliance by IIFSs. It considers a framework that draws on internal and external arrangements to the firm and emphasizes market discipline. In issuing its *fatwas*, an SSB could be guided by standardized contracts and practices that could be harmonized by self-regulatory professional associations. Such a framework could ensure adequate consistency of interpretation and enhance the enforceability of contracts before civil courts. The review of transactions would be entrusted mainly to internal review units, which would collaborate with external auditors responsible for issuing an annual opinion on whether the institution's activities have met its *Shari'a* requirements. This process would be sustained by reputable entities such as rating agencies, stock markets, financial media, and researchers who would channel signals to market players. This framework would enhance public understanding of the requirements of *Shari'a* and lead to a more effective utilization of options available to stakeholders to achieve continuing improvements in Islamic financial services.

INTRODUCTION[1]

Enhancing stakeholders' value is a central purpose for any business, including financial services, whether conventional or Islamic. Their stability, financial performance, and ability to intermediate resources will depend on stakeholders' confidence in individual institutions and the industry. A particular confidence feature with respect to Islamic financial services is the requirement of conveying to stakeholders that their financial business is conducted in conformity with their religious beliefs. Corporate governance (CG) arrangements, internal and external to the corporate entity, include structures and procedures that should provide sufficient assurance that the business is conducted in accordance with stated objectives, in particular compliance with *Shari'a*.[2]

A widely adopted approach is to have independent bodies certify *Shari'a* compliance by the IIFS. The reliance on independent bodies reflects the currently limited role that market discipline can play in ensuring such compliance. Hirschman contended that stakeholders generally have two ways of reacting to performance deterioration in business organizations.[3] The first is for the stakeholder to quit the organization. The other is for the stakeholder to agitate and exert influence for change from within the organization. The potential role that these two mechanisms can play in upholding conformity with *Shari'a* is constrained by the perceived complexity of Islamic financial instruments and their limited commoditization. The diversity of jurisprudence on permissible transactions and the limited disclosure of relevant and reliable financial information compound the difficulty. In addition, market participants and other stakeholders are likely to lack sufficient knowledge of *Shari'a* or of financial principles, or of both, to judge the transactions of an IIFS. In line with the foregoing, compliance with *Shari'a* is primarily ensured through organs internal to the IIFS. At the same time, a broader enabling institutional environment, sometime referred to as external corporate governance, is being put in place.

---

[1] The chapter is adapted from Grais and Pellegrini (2006a). The authors of the present book would like to thank Matteo Pellegrini for his contribution to the content of the chapter as well as Arun Adarkar, Stijn Claessens, Dahlia El-Hawary, Zamir Iqbal, Luigi Passamonti, Leila Triki, and participants to meetings of the Islamic Financial Services Board and the Accounting and Auditing Organization for Islamic Institutions Services for helpful comments. All remaining errors are the authors' own.

[2] This chapter deals with CG arrangements that address issues of *Shari'a* compliance. Grais and Pellegrini (2006c) provide an overview of the issues and challenges of CG for IIFSs. Grais and Pellegrini (2006b) deal with IIFS CG that address stakeholders' financial interests.

[3] Hirschman (1970).

This chapter reviews prevailing internal arrangements that deal with *Shari'a* compliance in individual IIFSs; it examines the CG issues involved, and proposes measures to strengthen their effectiveness. It then considers external arrangements that complement the ones adopted by individual institutions to promote compliance with *Shari'a*. The concluding section summarizes the overall strengths and weaknesses of existing arrangements.

INTERNAL CORPORATE GOVERNANCE ARRANGEMENTS FOR *SHARI'A* COMPLIANCE

Currently, the most widely adopted approach is to establish independent bodies of knowledgeable agents. These bodies are usually *internal* to the institution and part of its governance structure. They include *Shari'a* supervisory boards and *Shari'a* review units. The following first analyzes existing arrangements and then considers options to strengthen them.

Internal Arrangements

Each institution offering Islamic financial services has in-house religious advisers, who are collectively known as the *Shari'a* supervisory board (SSB).[4] In principle, the role of the SSB covers five main areas: certifying permissible financial instruments through *fatwas* (*ex ante Shari'a* audit), verifying that transactions comply with issued *fatwas* (*ex post Shari'a* audit), calculating and paying *zakat*, disposing of non-*Shari'a*-compliant earnings, and advising on the distribution of income or expenses among shareholders and investment account holders.[5] The SSB issues a report to certify that all financial transactions comply with the aforementioned principles. This report is often an integral part of the annual report of the Islamic financial institution.

---

[4]They exist in all Islamic countries with the exception of Iran, where compliance of the whole banking system with *Shari'a* is guaranteed and monitored by the central bank.

[5]A *fatwa* is a religious edict or proclamation. It is a legal opinion issued by a qualified Muslim scholar on matters of religious belief and practice. The social nature of Islamic finance emerges most clearly in the practices of *zakat* and *qard hassan*. *Zakat* is a tax on wealth, while *qard hassan* refers to zero-return beneficence loans made to the needy. The objective, according to the Meezan Bank of Pakistan, is the "implementation of an equitable economic system, providing a strong foundation for establishing a fair and just society for mankind." See also Briston and El-Ashker (1986) and Abdel Karim (1990).

In practice, an SSB's tasks may vary according to provisions stipulated in the articles of association of the financial institution or those stipulated by national regulators. A review of 13 IIFSs shows that all SSBs were entrusted with *ex ante* monitoring and the calculation of *zakat*.[6] However, *ex post* monitoring was within the exclusive competence of *Shari'a* review units in at least two cases.[7] In another case, the SSB could issue recommendations on how the institution could best fulfill its social role as well as promote Islamic finance.[8] In addition to internal corporate arrangements, national regulators and international standard setters implement guidelines for SSBs. These often refer to SSBs' general duty to ensure *Shari'a* compliance of transactions and, less frequently, indicate areas of competence, composition, and decision making. Table 8.1 provides an overview of practices in selected countries that have introduced guidelines or legislative references on the functioning of SSBs.[9]

The functioning of SSBs raises five main corporate governance issues: independence, confidentiality, competence, consistency, and disclosure. The first concerns the *independence* of the SSB from management. Generally, members of the SSB are appointed by the bank's shareholders, represented by the board of directors. As such, they are employed by the financial institution and report to the board of directors. Their remuneration is proposed by the management and approved by the board. The SSB members' dual relationship with the institution as providers of remunerated services and as assessors of the nature of operations could be seen as creating a possible conflict of interest.

---

[6] The sample reflects the accessibility of relevant information in these IIFSs. Sources are annual reports, articles of association, and all information posted on the websites of the following IIFSs: Bahrain Islamic Bank, Al Rajhi Banking Corporation, Bank Islam Malaysia Berhad, Jordan Islamic Bank, Kuwait Finance House, Bank Muamalat Malaysia, Shamil Bank Bahrain, Islamic Bank of Britain, Emirates Islamic Bank, Dubai Islamic Bank, Islamic Bank Bangladesh Limited, First Islamic Investment Bank, and Bank Rakyat Malaysia. Iranian IIFSs were not considered.

[7] This is the case of Al Rajhi Banking Corporation of Saudi Arabia and Dubai Islamic Bank. Such decisions may reflect the difficulties that SSBs may encounter in assessing volumes of transactions in large IIFSs.

[8] The 2002 Annual SSB report of Islamic Bank Bangladesh Ltd contains suggestions on investment strategies, such as housing schemes to help the poor, and on research policy, such as the publication and translation of Islamic banking books (www.islamibankbd.com, last visited April 18, 2005).

[9] Only those countries are included where authorities have implemented laws or acts or issued circulars and regulations on internal *Shari'a* supervisory boards. Appendix 8B details the legal bases and the provisions of these regulations.

TABLE 8.1 Regulations on Internal *Shari'a* Advisory*

Country	SSB Terms of Reference	SSB Composition	SSB Decision Making	SSB Appointment and Dismissal	SSB Fit and Proper Criteria
Bahrain	✓	✓	Unspecified	✓	✓
DIFC**	✓	✓	Unspecified	✓	✓
Indonesia	✓	Unspecified	Unspecified	✓	✓
Jordan	✓	✓	✓	✓	Unspecified
Kuwait	✓	✓	✓	Unspecified	Unspecified
Lebanon	✓	✓	Unspecified	✓	Unspecified
Malaysia	✓	Unspecified	Unspecified	Unspecified	✓
Pakistan	✓	✓	Unspecified	✓	✓
Philippines	✓	✓	Unspecified	Unspecified	✓
Thailand	✓	✓	Unspecified	✓	✓
UAE	✓	✓	Unspecified	✓	Unspecified

*See Appendix 8B for details of the legal bases and the provisions of these regulations.
**Dubai International Financial Centre.
Source: Official government websites and central banks' annual reports.

In principle, SSB members are required to submit an unbiased opinion in all matters pertaining to their assignment. However, their employment status generates an economic stake in the financial institution, which can negatively impact their independence. The opinions of the SSB may, for example, prohibit the bank from engaging in certain profitable transactions or impose a reallocation of illicit income to charity, resulting in a poorer overall financial performance. Under these circumstances, the bank managers may be tempted to use their leverage to influence SSB members, producing what is commonly referred to as "*fatwa* shopping" or "*Shari'a* advisory à la carte."

In practice, the risk of such conflict of interest is mitigated by the ethical standards of the SSB members, and the high cost that a stained reputation would inflict on them and on the financial institution. Generally, members of SSBs are highly regarded *Shari'a* scholars and guardians of its principles. Therefore, a less than truthful assessment and disclosure of *Shari'a* compliance by an SSB would seem to be highly unlikely. In the event that it does occur and comes to light, it would seriously damage the concerned scholars' reputations and the prospect for further recourse to their services. Similarly, managerial interference in compliance assessments can lead to a loss of shareholders' and stakeholders' confidence. Management may be penalized and face dismissal. All that being said, and the heavy costs of untruthful assessments notwithstanding, a potential conflict of interest is inherent in existing corporate arrangements regarding SSBs.[10]

The issue of *confidentiality* is intertwined with that of independence. Often, some *Shari'a* scholars sit on the SSBs of more than one financial institution. This association with multiple IIFSs may be seen as a strength inasmuch as it could enhance an SSB's independence vis-à-vis a particular institution. However, it does give the particular individual access to proprietary information of other, possibly competing institutions. Thus SSB members may find themselves in another type of potential conflict of interest. In current practice, Malaysia has attempted to deal with the issue by discouraging jurists from sitting on the SSB of more than one IIFS. While this eliminates confidentiality concerns, the practice poses other potential problems. First, it would exacerbate lack of competence where there is a scarcity of *Fiqh al-Muamalat* jurists.[11] Second, it may prevent the formation of an efficient labor market for *Shari'a* audit, by decreasing the economic appeal of the profession. Last, it may create a symbiotic relationship between the auditor and the financial institution that could undermine impartiality.

---

[10]This is akin to the situation of company auditors, though not identical.
[11]*Fiqh al-Muamalat* literally translates into Islamic commercial jurisprudence.

The third issue relates to the nature of the *competence* required of SSB members. Due to the unique role that they are called upon to fulfill, SSB members should ideally be knowledgeable in both Islamic law and commercial and accounting practices (*Fiqh al-Muamalat*). In practice, it would appear that few scholars are well-versed in both disciplines. The issue has been addressed by including members from different backgrounds in most SSBs.[12] However, the combination of experts rather than expertise creates the challenge of overcoming different perspectives as well as the risk of potential failure of communication. Over time, the demand gap for combined *Shari'a* and financial skills is likely to be reduced through public policy and normal labor market operations. Progress in this direction is already noticeable in countries where the Islamic financial industry is well established. For instance, by 2005, the Securities Commission of Malaysia had certified a total of 27 individuals and three companies eligible for *Shari'a* advisory on unit trust funds, for a total of 24 companies offering such funds.[13] However, in countries where Islamic finance is less developed, other transitional arrangements may be needed.

The fourth issue concerns *consistency* of judgment across banks over time, or across jurisdictions within the same bank. In essence the activities of SSBs are in the nature of creating jurisprudence by the interpretation of legal sources. It should therefore not be surprising to find conflicting opinions on the admissibility of specific financial instruments or transactions.[14] In reality, however, the diversity of opinions is less widespread than might be expected. The General Council of Islamic Banks and Financial Institutions (CIBAFI) sampled about 6,000 *fatwa*s, and found that 90 percent were consistent across banks. The fact that over 100 *Shari'a* scholars around the world issued these *fatwa*s would suggest an overall consistency in the interpretation of the sources.[15] Further, this high degree of consistency between

---

[12] AAOIFI (Governance Standard 1) recommends including jurists of *Fiqh al-Muamalat*.
[13] The proportion of advisers to companies seems to be quite large. Every management company must appoint at least three *Shari'a* advisers for each company. This means that every adviser would serve on the SSBs of two or more fund management companies. Data on *Shari'a* advisers and approved instruments are available at www.sc.com.my (March 14, 2005).
[14] A typical example is the financing of leisure activities, which is frowned upon as *haram* by some *fiqh* scholars. Moreover, Islamic jurisprudence is based on different schools of thought that may vary from country to country (the Shiah branch and the Sunni branch, which in turn includes the Madhahib: Shafie, Hanafi, Hanbali, and Maliki traditions).
[15] As quoted in the proceedings of the Fourth Harvard University Forum on Islamic Finance, available at www.hifip.harvard.edu/MoreInfo.asp?news_id=34 (visited March 14, 2005).

the *fatwa*s would also point to a substantial independence of SSBs. Nevertheless, as the industry expands, the number of conflicting *fatwa*s on the permissibility of an instrument is likely to increase. This could undermine customer confidence in the industry and have repercussions on the enforceability of contracts.[16]

The last and overarching issue relates to *disclosure* of all information relating to *Shari'a* advisories. In addition to the positive aspects of thus empowering stakeholders, disclosure could be the means to address some of the issues discussed in the preceding paragraphs. A transparent financial institution would ideally disclose the duties, the decision-making process, areas of competence, and the composition of its SSB, as well as publish all *fatwa*s issued by the SSB. This would strengthen stakeholders' confidence in the credibility of SSB assessments. In addition, public disclosure of such information would provide a forum for educating the public, thus paving the way for a larger role for market discipline in regard to *Shari'a* compliance. Finally, it would decrease the costs that external agents may face in assessing the quality of internal *Shari'a* supervision.

Despite all these potential benefits, transparency does not currently seem to be widely prevalent. Out of 13 banks reviewed, all declared the existence of an SSB within the organization and disclosed information on its composition.[17] However, only seven made the annual report of the SSB easily accessible, and seven did not provide detailed information on the professional backgrounds of SSB members.[18] Moreover, only two banks disclosed the *fatwa*s authorizing the provision of financial services and products. Only one disclosed provisions for decision making and interaction with other bodies of the firm. Finally, only one institution disclosed on its website the

---

[16]It may be hard to invalidate contracts on grounds of a breach of *Shari'a* law if *Shari'a* has no legal force in the country and there are no widely acceptable codified standards or contract specimens.

[17]Sources are annual reports, articles of association, and information posted on the websites of the following IIFSs: Bahrain Islamic Bank, Al Rajhi Banking Corporation, Bank Islam Malaysia Berhad, Jordan Islamic Bank, Kuwait Finance House, Bank Muamalat Malaysia, Shamil Bank, Bahrain, Islamic Bank of Britain, Emirates Islamic Bank, Dubai Islamic Bank, Islamic Bank Bangladesh Limited, First Islamic Investment Bank, and Bank Rakyat Malaysia. Iranian IIFSs were not considered. Appendix 8C provides an index of *Shari'a* advisory disclosure for 13 IIFSs and compares desirable with effective *Shari'a*-related disclosure.

[18]This means that the SSB report was available either on the website or in the annual report. The proportion is 7 out of 11, because the SSBs of two recently established IIFSs had not yet issued a report. In Appendix 8C, both are counted as disclosed items.

duties and obligations of the SSB.[19] The practice of limited disclosure by banks would not support building confidence in *Shari'a* compliance.[20]

Besides *Shari'a* boards, most IIFSs, particularly those complying with Accounting and Auditing Organization for Islamic Financial Institutions (AAOIFI) standards, have established another internal *Shari'a* review structure, generally in the form of review units.[21] These internal *Shari'a* review units are independent from other departments or are an integral part of the internal audit and control department. The array of tasks that they perform is parallel to those of audit departments—reviewers generally use all necessary powers to ascertain that all financial transactions implemented by management comply with SSB rulings.[22] In some instances *Shari'a* review units have exclusive competence on *ex post* monitoring.[23]

These review units and SSBs face similar challenges, relating, in particular, to independence and competence. First, like SSBs and internal auditors, internal *Shari'a* reviewers may be subject to a conflict of interest stemming from their employment status, with their appointment and remuneration determined by management while their role is as assessors of managerial processes and decisions. The scarcity of professionals with combined *Shari'a* knowledge and financial skills also affects internal *Shari'a* review departments. Like SSB members, internal *Shari'a* reviewers should be knowledgeable in *Fiqh al-Muamalat*. Yet, as already observed, the scarcity of such experts is likely to bear on the quality of *Shari'a* reviews in IIFSs. The issue may have greater implications in this case, because *Shari'a* reviewers would also be assigned to the training of other employees on the principles of

---

[19] While most of this information is usually available through the Articles of Association, the SSB letter of appointment, or individual *fatwas*, these documents are not easily available to customers. This is in stark contrast with businesses offering conventional financial services (BCFSs), which generally have on their websites thorough information on their CG practices.

[20] See Appendix 8C.

[21] AAOIFI recommends internal *Shari'a* review in its Governance Guidance 3. In Pakistan, for example, this is dealt with in Annexure III to Islamic Banking Department (IBD) Circular No. 02 of 2004, Central Bank of Pakistan

[22] In this respect, the role of the internal review unit is limited to a complementary *ex post* monitoring. This makes its task secondary, if more focused and defined, to that of the SSB, which is the ultimate arbiter in matters of *Shari'a* compliance.

[23] This is the case for large Islamic banks where the SSB may not be able to assess large volumes of transactions. Therefore, separate *Shari'a* control departments are operational. This seems to be the case in Al Rajhi Banking and Investment Corporation and Dubai Islamic Bank.

Fiqh al-Muamalat.[24] Thus, their pronouncements and counsel could have pervasive effects throughout their respective IIFSs.

Strengthening Internal Arrangements for *Shari'a* Compliance

The actions of SSBs and *Shari'a* reviewers at the individual institutional level have so far been relied upon to provide some degree of comfort in assuring IIFS compliance with *Shari'a*. However, in line with the foregoing discussions, IIFSs, national regulators, and international standard setters could further address the issues of: (1) independence of the SSB, (2) confidentiality of its activities, (3) competence of its members, (4) consistency of pronouncements, and (5) disclosure of *Shari'a* decisions and audit.

The issue of *independence* is common to *Shari'a* review bodies. Prevailing approaches to the regulation of internal audit departments and external audit firms can provide guidance on how to ensure integrity of pronouncements on *Shari'a* compliance. The literature on internal audit independence pinpoints three factors that significantly contribute to the degree of auditor independence: (1) clarity of definition of the auditor's responsibilities, (2) the position of the auditor within the organizational structure of the institution, and (3) the reporting authority for audit results. This would suggest that the independence of both *Shari'a* advisers and reviewers could be enhanced by clearly defining their responsibilities and powers in the articles of association of the company or in a charter of independence. Their powers would include the authority to access all records and staff necessary to conduct the audit and to require management to respond formally, and in a timely manner, to significant adverse audit findings by taking appropriate corrective action. Such powers should not include operational tasks that could impair their independence.[25]

Second, the organizational status of internal *Shari'a* bodies should be sufficiently articulated to permit the accomplishment of audit responsibilities. This appears to be fundamental in the case of *Shari'a* review units that have to deal with large volumes of transactions in conducting *ex post* assessments. Third, the independence of action of SSBs and *Shari'a* reviewers and their ability to withstand pressures from management can be assured only as long as *Shari'a* bodies functionally report, and are accountable, to an individual or entity with sufficient authority to: (1) safeguard their independence,

---

[24] According to AAOIFI Standard 3. In some cases educational activities are delegated to separate units, as, for instance, in the Al Rajhi Corporation (www.alrajhibank .com.sa, April 2005).

[25] These may include preparing reports or records, developing procedures, or performing other operational duties normally reviewed by auditors.

(2) achieve a broad audit coverage, (3) ensure adequate consideration of audit reports, and (4) generate appropriate action on audit recommendations. This role is generally performed by independent directors involved in the audit committee. In the case of those IIFSs with concentrated shareholding, this role may be assumed by minority shareholders' directors.[26] However, following the practice of external auditors in some jurisdictions, *Shari'a* reviewers may be required to report fraud or unexplained breaches of rules directly to supervisory authorities. The latter option could be difficult to implement in countries where supervisors may regard matters of *Shari'a* compliance to be outside their competence.

The foregoing would require carrying existing international norms into national ones and enforcement of monitoring mechanisms. The Basel Committee on Banking Supervision (BCBS) and Organisation for Economic Co-operation and Development (OECD) codes contain clear provisions on directors' independence designed to curb collusion opportunities between management and other internal bodies. Likewise, AAOIFI's "governance standards on the definition, appointment, composition and report of SSBs" and "Codes of Ethics" contain clear provisions on the duties and powers of SSBs that would limit a bank's discretion in the definition of SSB prerogatives and thereby deprive managers of one instrument of control.[27] In addition, they contain provisions on fixing remuneration, selection and dismissal of SSB members, as well as incompatibility clauses to diffuse conflicts of interest.[28] A number of national regulators have already included such prohibitions in circulars or legislative acts, mostly

---

[26] Outside directors in concentrated ownership corporations are generally appointed by the majority shareholders themselves and may not be truly independent.

[27] The codes are the Code of Ethics for Accountants and Auditors of Islamic Financial Institutions and the Code of Ethics for the Employees of Islamic Financial Institutions. The SSBs' prerogatives include *ex ante* and *ex post* evaluation, calculation of *zakat*, and allocation of profits or charging of losses to unrestricted investment account holders.

[28] For instance, dismissal of SSBs may be prompted only by a request of the board of directors approved by the general assembly of shareholders. This will prevent so-called *fatwa* shopping. Further, the standards provisions prohibit the appointment of "directors or significant stakeholders" as SSB members and the prohibition for *Shari'a* review units to carry out operational activities (for instance, a division in the internal audit department). Depending on local circumstances, such provisions may be strengthened by introducing severe sanctions for accepting loans from the audited company, having a family relationship with the audit client, or having any form of direct or indirect material interest in the business. For instance, in Malaysia, the approval and dismissal of SSBs must be communicated to the central bank.

in the form of fit criteria and prohibited interests for the appointment of SSB members or advisers.[29]

Following the practice of periodically rotating external auditing companies, mandatory rotation of SSBs would seem to be desirable. Proponents of this measure argue that a long-term client relationship can impair the auditor's objectivity. Therefore, by periodically interrupting such a relationship through mandatory rotation, the bank's management would be deprived of its ability to influence the auditors with the threat of terminating their mandate. In Italy, where mandatory rotation of external auditors is implemented, a review of the practice by the Galgano Committee, instituted following the U.S. corporate governance scandals, recommended that "in order to safeguard an auditor's independence the audit engagement should not be immediately renewed. The exclusion of an immediate renewal of the engagement avoids any influence on the judgment of the auditors driven by a hope for renewal."[30]

Opponents of this measure abound. Summer (1998) argues that "by destroying rents from an ongoing relation, the rotation rule undermines incentives for building up a reputation of honesty." He therefore suggests that competition in the auditor market may be a better safeguard for auditors' independence. An independent review of the practice by the Bocconi University concluded that rotation compromises audit quality, which strictly depends on a good knowledge of the business and its management.[31]

Transposing such arguments into a *Shari'a* framework, rotation of SSBs may lead to greater independence, but could also produce similar inefficiencies and failures in *Shari'a* compliance verification in the transitional phase. Mandatory rotation of SSBs may also exacerbate inconsistency in the

---

[29] Examples include Annexure IV to the Islamic Banking Department (IBD) Circular No. 2 of 2004 of the State Bank of Pakistan on "Fit & proper criteria for appointment of *Shari'a* advisors"; Chapter 5 of Islamic Bank of Thailand Act B.E. 2545 on "Advisory Council of the Islamic Bank of Thailand," and Bank Negara Malaysia's 2004 "Guidelines on the Governance of *Shari'a* Committee for Islamic Financial Institutions."

[30] The report grants the possibility of renewal six years after the end of the engagement. Quoted in English in FEE (2004).

[31] This report quantified the quality of audit services by the number of suspensions of partners imposed by the Consob (the Italian national commission for the 20 audit firms of listed companies). Cases of suspension normally arise when auditors do not pinpoint material misstatements. As the report states: "The number of partner suspensions in Italy, imposed during the period between 1992 and 2001 amounted to 40. The analysis of the distribution of suspensions shows how they are mainly concentrated in the first year of an appointment with a total number of 13. The number of suspensions imposed over the following years drops dramatically, from one to three a year." For more, see FEE (2004).

application of *Shari'a* within the same bank. An alternative may be found in the practice of periodically rotating SSB members rather than entire boards. This would infuse fresh approaches in the SSB and may increase independence through peer review; it would not necessarily compromise the audit quality, as the continuing members would assure continuity.

Preserving *confidentiality* of information may require solutions that echo those applied to the auditing profession. For instance, *Shari'a* auditors may be required to abide by codes of professional conduct. AAOIFI's Code of Ethics for Accountants and Auditors for Islamic Banks and Financial Institutions provides conduct guidelines tailored to *Fiqh al-Muamalat* professionals. Nevertheless, the applicability of such code in non-Islamic countries may be constrained by direct references to Islamic morals and *Shari'a* law. A viable alternative might be for regulators to extend standard auditing profession requirements to *Shari'a* auditors.

Ensuring the *competence* of SSB members and *Shari'a* reviewers requires a multipronged approach. Short-term policies to increase the number of qualified *Shari'a* advisers would include training activities in *Fiqh al-Muamalat* at the bank level, in specialized training institutes, and in other government-recognized or government-related organizations such as central banks.[32] *Fiqh al-Muamalat* degrees could be created and promoted by providing grants and certifying universities. Concurrently, the abilities of *Shari'a* advisers and reviewers would be certified. The process of certification would begin at the IIFS level where managing bodies would appoint SSB members according to established criteria on expertise, education, and track record that would be spelled out in the articles of association. The background of SSB members would also be disclosed in accessible information venues, such as websites and annual reports. This process may be complemented by self-regulatory professional associations or national authorities who would enforce nationwide mandatory criteria.[33] Similarly, a national registration process might be established along the lines of the certification of *Shari'a* advisers implemented by the Securities Commission of Malaysia. This would have the additional advantage of a centralized and therefore standardized assessment of *Shari'a* experts' skills. Besides safeguarding competence, this option may increase independence in *Shari'a* audits.

Disclosure of the processes leading to *Shari'a* pronouncements and related information needs to be the cornerstone of *Shari'a* governance. These issues may not have received sufficient attention from either IIFSs

---

[32] Some examples include the Islamic Banking and Finance Institute of Malaysia, the Bahrain Institute of Banking and Finance, the Bangladesh Bank Training Academy, and Iran's Training and Human Resource Studies Department.

[33] This is the case of Pakistan's "Fit & proper criteria for appointment of *Shari'a* advisors" that explicitly require "minimum qualification and experience."

themselves or their regulators and supervisors. Therefore, policies need to be put in place that would ensure adequate disclosure in terms of both quality and ease of retrieval, such as through IIFS websites and annual reports. Of particular importance would be, inter alia, the SSB annual report and its *fatwa*s. Informing IIFS stakeholders on the composition, powers, competence, and decision making of SSBs would also enhance the transparency of the processes leading to *Shari'a* pronouncements.

EXTERNAL ARRANGEMENTS FOR *SHARI'A* COMPLIANCE

Under the prevailing current decentralized system of *Shari'a* advisory, the flexibility in *fiqh* opinions has encouraged innovation in Islamic financial products, contributing significantly to the dynamism of the industry. Nevertheless, because of the very nature of jurisprudence, interpretation of *Shari'a* by a large number of independent scholars, notably in the various SSBs, gives rise to inconsistencies in the *fatwa*s across SSBs, or even over time in the same SSB. Internal systems and procedures could be developed in IIFSs to limit inconsistencies and explain different pronouncements. External arrangements, including mechanisms of market discipline, can provide complementary channels, inducing compliance with rulings and their harmonization. The following first analyzes existing external arrangements and then considers options to strengthen them.

Existing External Arrangements

The broad *Shari'a* governance framework may feature (1) arrangements put in place by regulators, and (2) the presence of providers of financial information services external to the firms. Among regulatory arrangements, *centralized SSBs* are the most noteworthy. While there are significant differences across countries, centralized SSBs are usually concerned with *ex ante* monitoring, mostly understood as standardization of *Shari'a* interpretation, and *ex post* monitoring of *Shari'a* compliance. They also offer arbitration to settle *Shari'a* disputes arising between members of the same SSB. In addition, a few countries have set up public rating agencies that assess financial instruments and institutions. These are meant to create a positive climate for *Shari'a*-compliant investments. Table 8.2 offers an overview of such regulatory institutions in key jurisdictions where Islamic finance services are offered.

One of the distinctive goals of these bodies is the standardization of *Shari'a* practices within their jurisdictions. Countries such as Kuwait, Malaysia, and Pakistan have taken significant actions in this respect, while others have not followed this route. The standardization of Islamic instruments may be a major determinant in ensuring the enforceability of

TABLE 8.2 External *Shari'a* Corporate Governance Institutions by Country*

Country	Centralized SSB or High *Shari'a* Authority or *Fatwa* Board	Islamic Rating Agency
Jordan	No	No
Malaysia	✓	✓
Sudan	✓	No
Bahrain	No[†]	No[†]
Kuwait	✓	No
Pakistan	✓	No
UAE	✓	No
Indonesia	✓	No

* See Appendix 8D for the names and powers of these departments/authorities.
[†] Bahrain is the seat of the International Islamic Financial Market (IIFM) and the Islamic International Rating Agency (IIRA) that, respectively, set standards for Islamic jurisprudence and rate Islamic instruments on an international scale.
Source: Official government websites and central banks' annual reports.

Islamic financial contracts in disputes brought before civil courts that are not legally bound by the *Shari'a*. Accordingly, standardization of practices would support property rights of involved stakeholders as well as sustain the development of IIFSs in non-Islamic countries. However, the practice of centralized SSBs creates the possibility that one IIFS group operating in different jurisdictions may have products deemed *Shari'a* compliant in one place and not in another. In addition, regulators in non-Islamic jurisdictions would consider that matters relating to *Shari'a* are not in their purview (e.g., the UK Financial Services Authority).[34]

Private mechanisms for the external governance of *Shari'a* compliance are equally limited. In particular, private rating agencies have not yet developed the necessary skills or found enough incentives to monitor the IIFSs' *Shari'a* compliance. "Islamic rating" has so far been the exclusive domain of government-sponsored organizations such as the Islamic International Rating Agency (IIRA) or the Malaysian Rating Corporation. Likewise, other external entities with an interest in Islamic finance, such as the financial

---

[34] In Malaysia, for instance, the judicial system has agreed to resort to the central bank's *Shari'a* Council for opinions on the permissibility of Islamic financial instruments, whenever a court case brought before it may require it. It would be hard to replicate such a scheme in other countries, where regulators may not want to get involved in *Shari'a* issues.

media and external auditors, are still generally less concerned with assessments of *Shari'a* compliance.

A notable exception is the multiplication of Islamic stock market indexes whose major contribution is the identification of *halal* investments.[35] Islamic stock market indexes, like the FTSE Global Islamic Index, the Dow Jones Islamic Market Indexes, and the Indonesian *Shari'a* Index, may contribute to better *Shari'a* governance for publicly traded IIFSs. By filtering out companies with activities that are incompatible with *Shari'a*, as well as firms with unacceptable levels of debt or interest income, they contribute to reducing adverse selection in investments by IIFSs and give additional comfort on the *halal* nature of IIFS activities.[36] However, current practice is not likely to meet with a full consensus of *Shari'a* scholars. Usually, these indexes include companies that deal in interest because of the lack of a fully interest-free international market. While some Islamic finance scholars may find this approach acceptable, others will not, thus limiting the role of these indexes in enhancing *Shari'a* governance.

Strengthening External Arrangements for *Shari'a* Compliance

Literature and practice have focused on establishing external CG structures to ensure effective *Shari'a* audit. In proposing the externalization of *Shari'a* advisory, Chapra and Ahmed (2002) suggest that chartered audit firms should acquire the necessary knowledge to undertake *Shari'a* audit. This process is already under way as evidenced by the increasing number of independent consulting companies and law firms offering *Shari'a* advisory services.[37] In addition to reducing internal audit costs in the Islamic financial institution, the use of such services would possibly give the institution access to a broader range of expertise. In addition, the public may perceive chartered *Shari'a* audit companies as more independent from the institution's management. It is not certain, however, that switching to external *Shari'a* audit would bring tangible guarantees of *Shari'a* compliance. Potential for so-called *Shari'a* advisory à la carte would not end with the externalization of services. In addition,

---

[35] *Halal* conveys goodness and by extension has taken on the meaning of permissible.
[36] In the case of Dow Jones Islamic Market Indexes, excluded businesses include: alcohol; conventional financial services (banking, insurance, etc.); entertainment (casinos/gambling, cinema, pornography, hotels, etc.); tobacco manufacturers; pork-related products; and defense and weapons companies. Companies classified in other industry groups may also be excluded if they are deemed to have material ownership of or revenues from the businesses mentioned.
[37] For example: www.yasaar.org/rationale.htm and www.islamic-banking.com/shariah/index.php.

externalization will not improve, and may in fact worsen, the accuracy of *Shari'a* audit. Internal auditors are generally familiar with the records systems, policies, and procedures of the institution and can provide quick responses to managers. The result could be a more detailed and exhaustive internal audit.

The idea of external firms undertaking *Shari'a* audit presents some advantages if it is viewed as complementing internal *Shari'a* audit. *Shari'a* audit firms would perform a role similar to that of their counterparts in conventional finance, thus introducing an additional layer in the *Shari'a* verification process. Such a system would obviously entail a clear separation of preaudit and postaudit functions. Complementary internal and external audit would apply only to the postaudit function, while the internal preaudit unit, the SSB, would have the sole authority to issue *fatwa*s. Internal audit by the SSB would have an independent appraisal function, including the review of *Shari'a* verification systems and controls, while external *Shari'a* auditors would have a statutory responsibility to express an independent opinion on *Shari'a* compliance. To avoid duplication, the latter function could be performed by *Shari'a* departments set up by existing chartered auditors. (Table 8.3 shows how internal and external *Shari'a* review may be differentiated and illustrates the merit of specialization.)

A framework of coexisting internal and external *Shari'a* audits as described does not help to resolve the difficulties caused by inconsistencies in the body of *fatwa*s. In an effort to alleviate this problem, some jurisdictions have moved toward a system of centralized SSBs. The latter carry the expectation of harmonization of permissible financial instruments through adjudicating disputes between *Shari'a* advisers and by standardizing existing practices. However, the ongoing globalization of Islamic finance as well as constraints on its applicability in secular countries limits the feasibility of this approach. To circumvent these limitations, Khan and Feddad (2004) recommend the gradual international codification and standardization of *fatwa*s. This duty may be delegated to an existing international organization whose mission already involves the promotion of harmonization and convergence of *Shari'a* interpretations.[38] Alternatively, a new self-regulating

---

[38] AAOIFI's mission statements declare that "the powers of (AAOIFI's) *Shari'a* Board include, among others, the following: achieving harmonization and convergence in the concepts and application among the *Shari'a* supervisory boards of Islamic financial institutions to avoid contradiction or inconsistency between the *fatwa*s and applications by these institutions, thereby providing a proactive role for the *Shari'a* supervisory boards of Islamic financial institutions and central banks. . . ." Likewise, IIFM's "role includes the promotion of harmonization and convergence of Shariah interpretations in developing Islamic banking products and practices that are universally acceptable." Sources: www.aaoifi.com and www.iifm.net.

TABLE 8.3 Comparison of Internal and External *Shari'a* Review

	Internal *Shari'a* Review Unit	External *Shari'a* Auditing Firm
Focus	Provides exhaustive internal review, and trains employees on *Shari'a*-related matters. Responds to managerial concerns over upholding *Shari'a* conformance of all transactions.	Primarily provides an independent certification as to the reasonableness of financial information provided to shareholders and stakeholders. Responds to regulators' and stakeholders' desire for an independent appraisal of *Shari'a* compliance.
Activities	Assesses compliance of all transactions with the *fatuas* issued by the SSB. To this effect, it creates systems of control and assessment.	Assesses the information provided by the managers and presents statements according to relevant *Shari'a* accounting standards. Uses samples of transactions to evaluate truthfulness of compliance and expresses an opinion on financial statements.
Management	Reports to management administratively. Builds relationships throughout the organization to ensure concerns are identified and resolved in a timely manner.	Primarily reports to the audit committee on financials and internal control.
Board of Directors/Audit Committee	Reports directly to the audit committee. Provides opinions on the organization's business risks, financial statements, system of internal control, and level of compliance with laws, regulations, and policies.	Attests to the audit committee the accuracy of the financial reports and attests on management's assessment on internal controls over financial reporting. Provides updates on pending accounting pronouncements and their potential impact on the organization.

Independence	Should demonstrate organizational independence and objectivity in work approach, but is not independent of the organization. (Is independent of the activity audited, but is integral to the organization.)	Is organizationally and managerially independent of the organization.
Results	Identifies problems, makes recommendations, and helps facilitate resolutions.	Meets statutory requirements and provides necessary adjustments to meet financial accuracy.
Risk	Identifies and qualifies key business risks to estimate probability of occurrence and impact on business. Makes appropriate recommendations as a result of the risk assessment.	Identifies key transactions and exposures for financial statements.
Fraud	Includes fraud detection steps in audit programs. Investigates allegations of fraud. Reviews fraud prevention controls and detection processes put in place by management and makes recommendations for improvement.	Includes fraud-detection steps in audit plan. Gathers information necessary to identify risks of material misstatement due to fraud, by inquiring of management and others within the entity about the risks of fraud. Considers the results of the analytical procedures performed in planning the audit and fraud risk factors.
Recommendations	Communicates to management in the audit reports recommendations for corrective action.	Communicates recommendations for corrective action.

Source: Adapted from table in Richards (2002).

nonprofit association of *Fiqh al-Muamalat* experts may be created. However, despite its apparent advantages, the creation of a global *Shari'a* regulator is likely to meet with resistance, specifically from jurists who regard Islamic *fiqh* as a pluralist body of knowledge. Also, the centralization of competences in a global regulator may undermine product innovation and financial engineering.[39]

Overreliance on the public sector for regulating *Shari'a* matters may also present other difficulties, such as the reluctance of authorities in a large number of jurisdictions to be involved in what they would consider private religious matters. In such situations, the private sector could fill the gap and play a more decisive role in the *Shari'a* compliance process. The focus would be on consolidating the *Shari'a*-related information infrastructure by creating new processes or strengthening the existing infrastructure. Next to external *Shari'a* audit firms, representational agents that normally channel financial information to the public may acquire new skills and assess IIFS compliance with Islamic finance rules.

In the future, key players in this field may be the private rating agencies. One may anticipate that they would gradually develop skills to evaluate *Shari'a* compliance and make this information readily available to investors using their existing dissemination infrastructure. Their coverage may also include companies in which IIFSs have a stake. This would create a positive climate for *Shari'a*-compliant investments, particularly for partnership and venture capital transactions. It is noteworthy that some leading rating companies have included "religious supervision" as an item in their reports on IIFSs.[40] However, this is often limited to a summary statement on the existence of an SSB and the conclusions of the SSB annual reports. Eventually, one may envisage a more articulate contribution through the adoption of *Shari'a* compliance indicators that would quantify *Shari'a* disclosure, profit sharing, and *zakat*.[41] In addition, Islamic market indexes may prove important. One may expect that current criticisms about their use will diminish with the development of

---

[39]This would obviously depend on the degree of powers transferred to such an organization. For instance, the State Bank of Pakistan has issued "Essentials of Islamic Modes of Financing" to ensure compliance with minimum *Shari'a* standards, which do not present an obstacle to innovation and yet contribute to harmonizing permissible contracts. For more, see www.sbp.org.pk.

[40]This is notably the case for Capital Intelligence bank reports.

[41]Shahul et al. (2004) propose the creation of two (disclosure and performance) "Islamicity Indices." They quantify, among other things, *Shari'a* compliance, corporate governance practices, social and environmental impact, profit-sharing performance, and *zakat* performance.

the industry. With the progressive increase of *halal* products, filters may be tightened to meet with greater scholarly approval.

CONCLUSION

Overall, current practice to ensure *Shari'a* compliance relies essentially on internal corporate structures, in particular SSBs. These certainly offer stakeholders a level of comfort. Nevertheless, they face a number of challenges relating to their independence, the confidentiality of institution-specific proprietary information, the limited availability of professionals with both *Shari'a* scholarship and financial skills, and the need for consistency in pronouncements between the various SSBs. A few jurisdictions have tried to address some of these issues by introducing an external institutional infrastructure. This, however, creates potential difficulties arising out of inconsistent pronouncements for IIFS groups operating in different jurisdictions, and may be problematic for regulators in non-Islamic countries. Market solutions to offer services that would promote *Shari'a* compliance are still minimal.

Figure 8.1 summarizes structures and processes internal and external to an IIFS that can jointly provide an effective framework to monitor and assess *Shari'a* compliance. Such a framework can be instrumental in

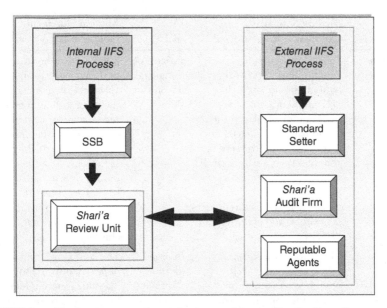

FIGURE 8.1   Effective Framework to Monitor and Assess *Shari'a* Compliance

enhancing stakeholders' confidence. It would enable innovation that can generally be expected to emerge mainly within the firm, where a sufficiently competent and independent SSB would be empowered to approve new *Shari'a*-conforming instruments. In issuing its *fatwas*, the SSB can be guided by standardized contracts and practices consistent with principles emerging from external arrangements, notably from international standard setting official or self-regulatory bodies. The review of transactions would mainly be entrusted to internal review units, which would collaborate with external auditors, responsible for issuing an annual opinion on whether the IIFS activities meet *Shari'a* requirements. This process would be sustained by reputable agents like rating agencies, stock markets, financial media, and researchers that would channel signals to market players. Such a framework, including structures and processes internal and external to the IIFS, can be expected to enhance public understanding of the requirements of *Shari'a*. It would be conducive to the development of market discipline, as it would permit an effective utilization of exit and participatory actions.

APPENDIX 8A: MISSION STATEMENTS OF INSTITUTIONS OFFERING ISLAMIC FINANCIAL SERVICES AND INSTITUTIONS OFFERING CONVENTIONAL FINANCIAL SERVICES

IIFS	Mission Statement, Objectives, or Vision	ICFS	Mission Statement, Objectives, or Vision
Jordan Islamic Bank, Jordan	[The bank's goals are] commitment to providing banking services based on compliance with the rules and principles of the glorious Islamic *Shari'a* in all our activities to serve our community as a whole, and commitment to equally serve the interests of all related parties including shareholders, depositors, and employees. (Website)	Mizuho Financial Group, Japan	[Our] . . . basic principles of the consolidation are: (1) offer a wide range of the highest-quality financial services to our customers; (2) maximize shareholders' value, and, as the leader of Japan's financial services industry, earn the trust of society at large; (3) offer attractive and rewarding job opportunities for employees. . . .
Bank Islam Malaysia Berhad	The Corporate Mission of the Bank is to seek to operate as a commercial bank functioning on the basis of Islamic	Norges Bank, Norway	The company's primary objective must be to maximize shareholders' long-term returns. There must be a clearly defined

IIFS	Mission Statement, Objectives, or Vision	ICFS	Mission Statement, Objectives, or Vision
	principles, providing banking facilities and services to Muslims and the whole population of this country, with viability and capability to sustain itself and grow in the process.		business strategy that is anchored in the board of directors. The company must present accurate, adequate, and timely information concerning its financial position and other relevant information.
	[The Bank's] Corporate Objective is to provide its customers with Islamic Banking facilities and services of the highest possible quality; to attain viability and sufficient level of profitability to sustain growth; to develop and foster a competent and innovative management imbibed with high standards of integrity and Islamic banking professionalism; to develop a motivated workforce inculcated with appropriate work ethics fully committed to the Bank and to offer efficient and courteous service to customers; to constantly strive to protect its shareholders' interest; to be always conscious of its responsibilities and duties as an Islamic corporate citizen.		The company's board of directors shall protect the interests of all shareholders and shall be accountable for the decisions made by the board. The board of directors shall supervise the day-to-day management and company activities, and shall ensure a proper organization of these activities, including adequate internal control systems.
Kuwait Finance House, Kuwait	In accordance with the Islamic principles, KFH ensures that while working with the public professionally, the company guarantees an honorable relationship with its client base and the Muslim community as a whole.	Coastal Federal Bank, United States	Our basic corporate objective [is] maximizing the value of our shareholders' investment.

(continued)

IIFS	Mission Statement, Objectives, or Vision	ICFS	Mission Statement, Objectives, or Vision
Faisal Islamic Bank of Egypt	The ultimate goal being to eventually institute an elaborate and comprehensive banking system based on the rules of Islamic *Shari'ah* which meets the needs of all those concerned . . . shareholders-clients-employees.	Deutsche Bank, Germany	Mission: We compete to be the leading global provider of financial solutions for demanding clients creating exceptional value for our shareholders and people.
Bank Muamalat Berhad, Malaysia	To build the bank into a modern, dynamic, and strong Islamic Bank that would play a role in providing a viable alternative to the conventional system, that will contribute to the development of Modern Malaysia.	Common-wealth Bank, Australia	The key financial objective of the Bank is to have Total Shareholder Return in the top quartile of our Australian listed peers over each rolling five-year period.
Badr-Forte Bank, Russia	To contribute to the globalization of Islamic Banking as the principal institution within the Russian Federation implementing Islamic financial and economic concepts, which offer a unique solution for social justice and harmony in our contemporary society.	BBVA Group, Spain	The seven corporate principles are as follows: Focus on the customer as the center of business; creation of shareholder value through business activity; teamwork as the engine in the creation of value; a management style that generates enthusiasm; ethical behavior and personal integrity as a way of understanding and conducting business; innovation as the engine of progress; and corporate social responsibility as an intrinsic part of development.
Al Baraka Islamic Bank, (Bahrain and Pakistan)	We strive to be a premier regional Islamic bank, dedicated to the economic and social development of our target markets, maximizing our clients and shareholders' value, and focusing on the	BNP Paribas, France	BNP Paribas founds its corporate project on three commitments: (1) toward its customers, BNP Paribas undertakes to give first priority to their satisfaction and to

IIFS	Mission Statement, Objectives, or Vision	ICFS	Mission Statement, Objectives, or Vision
	human resource development in an environment of creativity and innovation. Al Baraka is committed to develop and promote an integrated Islamic Financial System. Compliance with the rules and principles of Islamic *Shari'a* is the core of the banking and financial activities of the Bank. To this end, the Bank has successfully sought the advice and expertise of Islamic scholars acclaimed for their knowledge and piety from all over the Islamic world to guide its path and monitor its performance. (Website)		constantly improve the quality of their welcome and of the services offered; (2) toward its shareholders, BNP Paribas undertakes to put value creation at the very heart of its options; (3) toward its employees, BNP Paribas undertakes to ensure a dynamic and stimulating management of careers and remuneration by developing employee share-ownership and promoting social dialogue. The respect of these commitments is guaranteed by the team spirit of all the bank's employees and their adherence to a code of ethics founded on transparency, professionalism, and quality.
Dubai Islamic Bank, UAE	Objectives of the Bank: (1) Providing banking services of the highest standards according to Islamic *Shari'a* without dealing in *riba* (interest on money) and by using the state-of-the-art technology in computer, telecommunication, and information system. (2) Investing funds prudently to achieve optimum and not maximum profits, for the mutual benefit of customers and the bank. (3) Coordination, cooperation, and integration with	Jyske Bank A/S, Denmark	. . . The Jyske Bank Group is managed and operated as a business. At the same time, we attach great importance to treating the three groups of stakeholders— shareholders, customers, and employees—with equal respect. . . . Our objective is to provide our shareholders with a satisfactory long-term return on their investment. Thus, the aim is for Jyske Bank every year to be one

(*continued*)

IIFS	Mission Statement, Objectives, or Vision	ICFS	Mission Statement, Objectives, or Vision
	other financial bodies that apply Islamic *Shari'a* in their dealings, in order to support creating a base and regulations for an Islamic financial system. (4) Development of the Islamic society in all fields of the economy by investing in industries, agriculture, commerce, and real estate in order provide job opportunities. (5) Promotion of social benevolence through its Islamic methods, particularly through *zakat*. (6) Contributing to the welfare of society in line with the five main tenets of Islam, namely protection of life, purity of mind, property, honor, and social justice. (7) Promoting the savings habit and encouraging people to invest wisely within the parameters of Islamic *Shari'a* through investment and finance instruments to suit individual requirements. (8) Making available the necessary capital for entrepreneurs for the establishment of economic projects and creation of alternative instruments for finance according to Islamic *Shari'a*.		of the top-performing Danish banks based on the level of our earnings. Jyske Bank is thus an excellent choice for shareholders who want to make a long-term investment and who do not attach great importance to decisions which generate only short-term price increases.
Islamic Bank of Thailand, Thailand	[The bank's goals are]: to maintain the role of a bank that is not tied up with interest; to strengthen the business; to carry out social and organizational stability;	RHB Group, Malaysia	Mission: To become the most admired Malaysian financial services company by providing excellent customer services, enhancing shareholder

IIFS	Mission Statement, Objectives, or Vision	ICFS	Mission Statement, Objectives, or Vision
	to provide an excellent service; and to direct and supervise well the community development.		value, providing challenging career and learning opportunities for employees, and demonstrating responsibility for society.
ABC Islamic Bank (E.C.)	Our mission is to uphold our carefully formulated Islamic principles in the quest for mutual prosperity for our clients and the Bank. In pursuit of our mission, we commit the Bank to the purest forms of Islamic banking products and services from a *Shari'a* perspective. We remain demonstrably independent from the conventional sector and recognize the importance of Islam's social objectives in conducting business. We are committed to delivering a level of service that matches, or exceeds, the market practice internationally. To do so, we seek to employ the best available human resources and the technology to apply the highest professional, moral, and ethical standards.	HSBC Canada, Canada	HSBC in Canada is committed to being Canada's leading international financial services organization, a leader in chosen markets, and recognized by its clients as proactive, responsive, competitive, and secure. To achieve a superior long-term return for our shareholder we will efficiently deliver a differentiated client experience which reflects our commitment to excellence in sales, service, and products, and which is delivered by highly motivated and well-qualified employees, working as a team. Through managing for value, HSBC in Canada is committed to making a world of difference to its clients, employees, communities, and shareholders.
Meezan Bank Limited, Pakistan	Establish Islamic banking as banking of first choice to facilitate the implementation of an equitable economic system, providing a strong foundation for establishing a fair and just society for mankind. To be a premier	Barclays Group, UK	Barclays aims to be one of the most admired financial services organizations in the world, in the eyes of our shareholders, our customers, our colleagues, and the communities in which we work.

(continued)

IIFS	Mission Statement, Objectives, or Vision	ICFS	Mission Statement, Objectives, or Vision
	Islamic bank, offering a one-stop shop for innovative value-added products and services to our customers within the bounds of *Shari'a*, while optimizing the stakeholders' value through an organizational culture based on learning, fairness, respect for individual enterprise, and performance. (Website)		The best measure of our long-term performance is the total return we give to our shareholders—the increase in the price of our shares, assuming that any dividends are used to buy more shares, known as "Total Shareholder Return."

Source: Official country websites and central bank annual reports. Extracts of corporate mission and goals obtained from websites and annual reports.

APPENDIX 8B: LEGAL BASIS AND NATURE OF REGULATIONS ON INTERNAL *SHARI'A* SUPERVISORY BOARDS IN SELECTED COUNTRIES

Country	Legal Base for SSB	SSB Competences as Spelled Out by Existing Laws	SSB Composition	SSB Decision Making	SSB Appointment and Dismissal Rules	Fit and Proper Criteria for SSB Members
Bahrain	*BMA Rulebook*, Vol. 2: *Islamic Banks—The BMA* (2005) and *all* AAOIFI standards.	General duty to verify *Shari'a* compliance and issue an annual report. Binding advice. The shareholders shall decide how SSB will discharge this duty.	Al least three members (according to AAOIFI).	Unspecified (to be decided by shareholders).	Appointed by shareholders. Dismissal is proposed by Board and approved by shareholders (according to AAOIFI standards).	Conflict of interest and competence clauses (according to AAOIFI governance standards).
DIFC*	Law regulating Islamic financial business, DIFC Law No. 13 of 2004 and the Islamic Financial Business Module of the DFSA Rulebook.	Oversees and advises on *Shari'a* compliance. Specific duties to be established and documented by the business offering Islamic financial services (BIFS).	No less than three members.	Unspecified.	Appointed and dismissed by the bank's governing body.	They must be competent (based on previous experience and qualifications) and are not directors or controllers of the BIFS.
Indonesia	Act No. 7 of 1992 as amended by Act 10 of 1998, Regulation 4/1/PBI/2002.	General obligation to verify *Shari'a* compliance (duties as stipulated by National *Shari'a* Board and established in bank's articles of association).	Unspecified.	Unspecified.	Any appointment or replacement of SSB members must be reported to Bank Indonesia and approved by the National *Shari'a* Board.	Documentary evidence on SSB members' previous experience to be submitted to Bank Indonesia's Board of Governors.

(continued)

Country	Legal Base for SSB	SSB Competences as Spelled Out by Existing Laws	SSB Composition	SSB Decision Making	SSB Appointment and Dismissal Rules	Fit and Proper Criteria for SSB Members
Jordan	Art. 58 of Law 28 of 2000 as amended by temporary Law No. 46 of 2003.	*Ex ante* audit (*fatwas*), *ex post* audit, opinions on *Shari'a* matters referred to it.	No less than three members.	By unanimous or majority vote. Its votes are valid only if a majority of members is present.	Appointed by the general assembly of shareholders. Discharged only through a reasoned decision taken by two-thirds of the board of directors and endorsed by the general assembly. Changes have to be notified to the Central Bank.	Unspecified.
Kuwait	Art. 93 of Law No. 32 of 1968.	General obligation to verify *Shari'a* compliance of banking operations.	No less than three members.	By unanimity. In case of conflict the matter is referred to the Fatwa Board.	Unspecified.	Unspecified.
Lebanon	Law No. 575 on "Establishing Islamic Banks in Lebanon."	Certification of *Shari'a* compliance and proposals for properly achieving bank's objectives pursuant to *Shari'a*.	Three members.	Unspecified.	Appointment for a renewable three-year period.	Unspecified (experts' background must be in Islamic law, doctrine, and banking and financial operations).
Malaysia	Islamic Banking Act of 1983 and Central Bank of Malaysia Act 1958 (revised 1994) and Guidelines on the Governance of *Shari'a* Committees (2004).	Binding advice on *Shari'a* compliance of banking operations for Islamic banks. The Central *Shari'a* Advisory Council is the ultimate arbiter.	Unspecified.	Unspecified.	Unspecified.	There are several incompatibility clauses.

Pakistan	IBD Circular No. 02 of 2004.	General obligation to verify *Shari'a* compliance of banking operations. The SSB must submit an annual report to shareholders.	Only one adviser required. A board may be set up at the bank's discretion.	Unspecified.	Appointment must be approved by State Bank of Pakistan.	They are compulsory and relate to minimum qualification and experience, track record, solvency, financial integrity, honesty and reputation, and no conflicts of interest.
Philippines	Republic Act No. 6848 and Manual of Regulations for Banks-Implementing Rules and Regulations of Republic Act No. 6848.	Offers advice and undertakes reviews on matters relating to *Shari'a* compliance.	At least three but no more than five members.	Unspecified.	Unspecified.	SSB members must be Islamic scholars and jurists of comparative law.
Thailand	Islamic Bank of Thailand Act B.E. 2545.	It has "the authority and duty to give advice and recommendations to the Board of Directors concerning Islamic principles related to the operation of the bank."	Not more than four members.	At least half of the SSB members form a quorum and decisions are taken by majority vote.	SSB members have a two-year tenure and may be reappointed. They are appointed and removed by the board of directors.	Financial integrity, competence, honesty, and no conflicts of interest.
UAE	Federal Law No. 6 of 1985.	General obligation to verify *Shari'a* compliance of banking operations. Detailed competences to be established by the bank.	No less than three members.	To be decided in the articles of association of the bank.	SSB members must be approved by the Higher *Shari'a* Authority.	Unspecified.

*Dubai International Financial Center.

APPENDIX 8C: *SHARI'A* GOVERNANCE DISCLOSURE INDEXES IN 13 IIFSS

IIFS*	SSB Composition	Background of SSB	SSB Annual Report†	Fatwas	Decision Making	Duties and Powers
A	1	1	1	0	0	0
B	1	0	1	0	0	0
C	1	0	1	0	0	0
D	1	0	1	1	0	0
E	1	0	0	0	0	0
F	1	0	0	0	0	0
G	1	0	1	0	1	0
H	1	1	1	1	0	0
I	1	1	0	0	0	1
L	1	1	1	0	0	0
M	1	1	1	0	0	0
N	1	1	1	0	0	0
O	1	0	0	0	0	0
Effective disclosure	1.00	0.46	0.69	0.15	0.08	0.08
Desirable disclosure	1.00	1.00	1.00	1.00	1.00	1.00

*The six indexes are calculated by attributing a 1 to every item that is disclosed and a 0 to items that are not disclosed in information venues such as annual reports and websites by selected 13 IIFSs. The average across IIFSs for every item is then taken to calculate the effective disclosure index. The desirable disclosure index is 1, assuming that ideally every IIFS in the sample ought to disclose information on *Shari'a* governance processes and structures.

†Two IIFSs had not issued an SSB report due to their recent establishment. Nevertheless, the items are counted as disclosed due to the IIFSs' overall high level of disclosure.

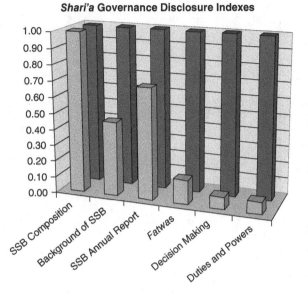

	SSB Composition	Background of SSB	SSB Annual Report	*Fatwas*	Decision Making	Duties and Powers
Effective Disclosure Index	1.00	0.46	0.69	0.15	0.08	0.08
Desirable Disclosure	1.00	1.00	1.00	1.00	1.00	1.00

FIGURE 8C.1   *Shari'a* Governance Disclosure Indexes

APPENDIX 8D: EXTERNAL *SHARI'A* CORPORATE GOVERNANCE INSTITUTIONS BY COUNTRY

Country	*Separate* Islamic Banking and *Takaful* Department at Central Bank	Centralized SSB or High *Shari'a* Authority or *Fatwa* Board	Islamic Rating Agency	Separate Islamic Capital Market Department within Securities Regulator
Bahrain	Yes, Islamic Financial Institutions Supervision Directorate	No, but the International Islamic Financial Market is to promote the harmonization and convergence of *Shari'a* interpretations in developing Islamic banking products and practices that are universally acceptable.	No, but Islamic International Rating Agency operates in Bahrain.	No
Indonesia	Yes, the Directorate of *Shari'a* Banking	Yes, the National *Shari'a* Board is authorized to issue *fatwas* concerning products, services, and operations of banks offering Islamic financial services (BIFSs). It also recommends *Shari'a* advisers to BIFSs.	No	
Jordan	No	No	No	No
Kuwait	No	The Fatwa Board in the Ministry of Awqaf and Islamic Affairs is the final authority on *Shari'a* disputes. Its advice is binding when it arbitrates on disputes between members of the same SSB.	No	No

Malaysia	Yes, Regulation Department–Islamic Banking and Takaful	Yes. The *Shari'a* Council advises central bank on *Shari'a* matters and is the ultimate arbiter in *Shari'a* interpretation disputes. The directives issued by Bank Negara Malaysia (BNM) in consultation with the *Shari'a* Council have binding authority over banks with Islamic windows.	Yes, Malaysian Rating Corporation–Islamic Capital Market Department.	Yes, Malaysian SEC-Islamic Capital Market Department. The SEC also has its own *Shari'a* Advisory Board.
Sudan	N/A, the whole financial regulatory system is Islamic.	Yes, the *Shari'a* High Supervisory Board is responsible for *fatwas*, contract specimen, arbitrage, consultations relating to Islamic legal aspects, training, research, lectures, and seminars.	No	N/A, the whole financial regulatory system is Islamic.
Pakistan	Yes, Islamic Banking Department	Yes, the *Shari'a* board of the State Bank is to advise the central banks on matters of *Shari'a*. It also produces specimen of permissible Islamic financial contract to ensure compliance with minimum *Shari'a* standards.	No	No, but several departments share Islamic finance portfolio.
UAE	No	Yes, the Higher *Shari'a* Authority, attached to the Ministry of Justice and Islamic Affairs, is the final arbiter on *Shari'a* matters. It is also responsible for *Shari'a* supervision.	No	No

Source: Official country websites and central bank annual reports.

CHAPTER 9

Toward a Systemic *Shari'a* Governance Framework

This chapter deals with systemic *Shari'a* governance for Islamic financial services (IFS).[1] By contrast to the two preceding chapters that focus on governance at the level of a corporation, this chapter looks at the broad *Shari'a* governance framework within a jurisdiction. Its focus is not *Shari'a* governance arrangements within a financial organization but *Shari'a* governance arrangements from a systemic perspective.[2]

Confidence that institutions offering Islamic financial services (IIFSs) abide by the code of conduct they pledge to follow enhances their financial performance. Sound corporate governance (CG) helps mitigate financial risks and encourages financial inclusion, hence social equity. Accordingly, it is important that these institutions develop within a governance framework that promotes stakeholders' confidence that pledges of *Shari'a* compliance are being fulfilled. A pledge to abide by *Shari'a* is a pledge to conduct socially responsible financial intermediation. The elected code of business conduct is derived from *Shari'a* principles. Thus, from an implementation perspective, a pledge to comply with *Shari'a* principles is similar to a pledge to abide by a code of corporate governance. As with other pledges of business conduct, public confidence is critical for performance. A credible systemic *Shari'a* governance framework (SSGF) can help develop confidence.

Implementing an SSGF raises three sets of questions, namely: (1) what should be complied with, or what rules need to be respected; (2) who should

---

[1] It does not deal with general corporate governance issues as identified in the Organisation for Economic Co-operation and Development (OECD) or Bank for International Settlements (BIS) principles of corporate governance.

[2] See, for example, Grais and Pellegrini (2006c) and the references therein. See also Abdel Ba'ri Mashaal, "Strategy for External *Shariah* Supervision," paper presented at the 4th AAOIFI *Shari'a* conference, Bahrain, October 2004.

be complying, or alternatively to whom do these rules apply; and (3) how to ensure that the rules are observed, or how to assess that they are actually complied with. Thus the development and implementation of an SSGF can be expected to reflect the weights given to each of these perspectives. An SSGF may be considered from the perspective of the *Shari'a* rules that should be complied with. But compliance may also be considered from the perspective of the organization, product, service, or process that needs to be compliant. In addition, compliance may be considered from the perspective of how a financial organization pledging to comply or an agency assessing or sanctioning compliance are ensuring compliance. An effective SSGF would balance the three perspectives.

The following provides, first, reasons underlying the need for a sound SSGF for IFS. It then considers various features an SSGF can be expected to have and identifies agents with different perspectives that would be involved in an SSGF. Selected SSGF experiences are reviewed and their major features highlighted. The chapter then suggests an outline of an SSGF that may be adapted to various jurisdictions.

BUSINESS RATIONALE FOR AN EFFECTIVE SYSTEMIC *SHARI'A* GOVERNANCE FRAMEWORK

Enhancing stakeholders' value is a central purpose for any business, whether conventional or *Shari'a* compliant. IFS's stability, financial performance, and ability to intermediate resources will depend on stakeholders' confidence in individual institutions and the industry. A particular confidence feature with respect to IFS is the requirement of conveying to stakeholders that their financial business is conducted in conformity with their religious beliefs.[3] Governance arrangements, internal and external to corporate entities, include structures and procedures that should provide sufficient confidence that the business is conducted in accordance with stated objectives, in particular compliance with *Shari'a*.

Empirical evidence points to positive effects of good CG on the performance of firms in four areas. First, it facilitates access to external finance. Investors and fund providers are more likely to extend financing to a business if they are comfortable with its CG arrangements, including the clarity and enforceability of stakeholders' rights. Second, good CG tends to lower the cost of resources, by conveying a sense of reduced risk that translates

---

[3] For an Islamic financial services entity, stakeholders' comfort that the entity is actually complying with *Shari'a* enhances for them the value of that entity beyond financial aspects.

into notably stakeholders' readiness to accept lower returns. Third, good CG is proven to lead to better operational performance. Finally, it reduces the risks of contagion from financial distress. In addition to reducing the internal risk through raising investors' risk awareness and willingness to invest, it increases the robustness and resilience of firms to external shocks.[4] As a result, CG risks have an impact on a company's valuation.[5] A 2002 McKinsey survey showed that institutional investors would pay a premium to own well-governed companies; such premiums would average 30 percent in Eastern Europe and Africa, and 22 percent in Asia and Latin America.

Companies with good governance perform better. A 2004 study of Standard & Poor's S&P 500 firms by Deutsche Bank showed that companies with strong or improving corporate governance outperformed those with poor or deteriorating practices by about 19 percent over a two-year period. Good governance improves client credit risk. A report by Fitch Ratings found a statistically significant relationship between a firm's corporate governance and its credit quality, with stronger and weaker governance practices resulting in higher and lower credit ratings, respectively. Good governance improves a bank's credit ratings: Romania's Banca Comerciala Romana (BCR) improved its corporate governance and brought it into line with European Union standards. In 2005, these corporate governance improvements were specifically mentioned by Fitch Ratings and S&P as an important reason to upgrade BCR's ratings in 2005.[6]

Sound and efficient *Shari'a* governance can expand IIFSs' access to financial resources as well as reduce the cost of their funding. Indeed, depositors and investors that want to abide by *Shari'a* principles are more likely to channel their resources to competitive IIFSs with sound and efficient governance, including systems and processes that ensure *Shari'a* compliance. In addition, those depositors and investors may be inclined to trade risk and returns, accepting lower return promises from institutions that are more transparent and convey a higher sense of trust to their stakeholders. Reliable *Shari'a* governance can also reduce IIFSs' operational risks and consequently enhance their financial performance. Indeed, *Shari'a* noncompliance would be sanctioned with nonrecognition of income and reduced returns. Given

---

[4] S. Claessens, "Corporate Governance and Development," October 2003, http://ssrn.com/abstract=642721

[5] R. Grandmont, G. Grant, and F. Silva, "Beyond the Numbers—Corporate Governance: Implications for Investors," Deutsche Bank, April 1, 2004.

[6] See International Finance Corporation: "Corporate Governance Finance, Sustaining Sustainable Finance," Viewpoint, www.ifc.org.

evidence from Malaysia on Muslim depositors' behavior, reduced returns would be damaging to IIFS performance.[7] Furthermore, clear and transparent systemic *Shari'a* governance reduces uncertainty risks as to rulings in cases of dispute, supporting improved ratings of IIFSs. Finally, the risk to the reputation of the industry of a loss of credibility of its pledges to conduct business according to *Shari'a* may have dangerous contagion effects.

Thus the effectiveness of an SSGF is essential for IIFS's credibility, market performance, and financial stability. But its framework and implementation should not stifle IFS's market initiative and dynamism.

DIMENSIONS OF *SHARI'A* GOVERNANCE: TOWARD AN ANALYTICAL FRAMEWORK

Designing corporate governance arrangements that incorporate incentives that would induce IIFS managers to internalize stakeholders' interests is a challenge. IIFS mission statements emphasize the primacy of serving stakeholders' interests without ignoring shareholders' value. However, pursuing stakeholders' value entails multidimensional business objectives, likely to be more difficult to capture in measurable and easy-to-monitor indicators. In contrast, conventional shareholding corporations emphasize shareholders' value. Though they do not ignore stakeholders' interests, they are likely to perceive them more as constraints to their overarching objective. As observable indicators to monitor shareholders' value may be more readily available, the design of managers' incentives for conventional businesses has appeared more tractable than for those emphasizing less easily measurable stakeholders' value.

Another corporate governance challenge for IIFSs relates to the mobilization of deposits through risk sharing, profit and loss sharing, and investment accounts.[8] Unrestricted investment account holders are stakeholders sharing risks and benefits with shareholders and among themselves. They do not, however, have a voting right or exercise control on management. Compounding the issue, a large number of IIFSs have concentrated

---

[7] "The existence of the utility maximization theory among the Muslim customers is further confirmed by the negative relationship between the interest rate of conventional banks and the amount deposited in interest-free deposit facilities." In S. Haron and N. Ahmad, "The Effects of Conventional Interest Rates and Rate of Profit on Funds Deposited with Islamic Banking System in Malaysia," *International Journal of Islamic Financial Services* 1, no. 4 (2000).

[8] This aspect is mentioned in previous chapters on corporate governance in this book. It is brought in here as a reminder as it is critical in shaping an SSGF.

ownership or are state-owned. Such concentration is susceptible to producing biased decisions.[9] As a result, investment account holders find themselves in the situation of principals who delegate to other principals that may have conflicting interests the responsibility of selecting and monitoring their agent.

Given the challenge of measuring stakeholders' value, the ambiguous position of unrestricted investment account holders, and the broad nature of *Shari'a* governance, the following identifies elements of an analytical framework that should help structure, organize, and assess an SSGF. The analytical framework would be based on (1) criteria to guide choices, (2) relevant perspectives to understand the rationales of certain choices, and (3) assumptions on the potential impact of the perspectives on the criteria. These three aspects are considered next.

Criteria for a *Shari'a* Governance Framework

In considering an SSGF, effectiveness of design can usefully be assessed against a set of criteria. Such criteria can also help assess changes aimed at adapting the framework to *Shari'a* trends and market developments. Of course there is no universally relevant set of criteria. However, one can identify some criteria that apply to similar situations and on which consensus may develop. These are bound to evolve with the deepening of knowledge and experience.

One can think of the following six criteria as a guide to consider a *Shari'a* governance framework. They can help assess the framework as a whole and its specific elements. The identified criteria are: (1) the degree of their legitimacy and acceptability, (2) the extent they support market dynamism, (3) their encouragement of clarity and transparency, (4) their comprehensiveness, (5) the cost of implementation, and (6) the ease of monitoring and calibration of remedial action to deviations.

The first criterion is the *legitimacy* of the governance framework and its *acceptability* to its stakeholders.[10] A top priority is that the framework leads to acceptable and credible *Shari'a* pronouncements. For that purpose, stakeholders need to believe in the independence, confidentiality, competence, consistency, and disclosure of pronouncements and the bodies that emit them. Acceptability would also have two other main dimensions. First is the framework's adequacy to the culture and market practices of the place

---

[9]J. Tirole, "Corporate Governance," Centre for Economic Policy Research, Discussion Paper no. 2086, 1999.

[10]For stakeholders' versus shareholders' governance in IFS, see Grais and Pellegrini (2006b).

where it is supposed to be implemented. A second dimension is the presence of adequate incentives and enforceable penalties to induce acceptability and to penalize breaches. The broader the acceptability of an SSGF, the broader IFS markets can be. Followers of the broadest accepted *Shari'a* framework would have the most widely accepted *Shari'a* passport and be enabled to access larger markets.

The second criterion is the extent to which the framework fosters or hinders *market dynamism*. Most regulations face the challenge of balancing different objectives. In conventional finance, regulators are faced with the challenge of balancing the requirements of stability with those of market initiative. These issues have led to the distinction between principle-based and rule-based regulation and supervision. They have also encouraged regulatory reform, promoting risk self-assessments and risk-based supervision. Indeed, such views stem from the belief that financial innovation is best fostered by proximity to markets. A dynamic process of financial innovation is stimulated by closeness to markets and nimble adaptation to their needs.[11] An effective *Shari'a* framework should ensure compliance without stifling markets with too rigid rules.

The third criterion is the *clarity and transparency* of the framework. The clearer and more transparent the framework, the more credible it can be and accordingly can secure better acceptability. In addition, clarity and transparency are essential for market dynamism, as they provide visibility of market rules to market participants. One particular aspect deserving attention is the degree of certainty associated with the framework. A notable issue is the clarity and transparency of dispute resolution mechanisms and the degree of uncertainty as to their outcome. An aspect of certainty is reduced costs for new initiatives and new products, and a better environment for innovation.

The fourth criterion is that of *comprehensiveness*. An SSGF may be comprehensive and addressing *Shari'a* compliance issues at all levels. It may also be specific to certain levels of *Shari'a* compliance. In certain jurisdictions, such as those where the regulator does not possess competency and/or

---

[11] An example of the trade-off between market vibrancy and compliance is illustrated by a recommendation of the *Shari'a* committee of AAOIFI. The meeting held in Bahrain in February 2008 issued "new recommendations regarding *Sukuk* structures and issuance, especially relating to the ownership of underlying assets in a *Sukuk* transaction and the guarantee of the principal investment to *Sukuk* certificate holders. The immediate reaction of some bankers has been that the recommendations may put a dampener on the issuance of future *Sukuk* because of these extra 'constraints' and thus affect their future tradability." See www.islamicfinancenews .wordpress.com.

authority in *Shari'a* compliance issues, the framework will be specific to organizations and products. In other jurisdictions where *Shari'a* compliance is a systemic issue, the framework is bound to be more comprehensive. There may be some trade-off between comprehensiveness and breadth of acceptability, as acceptability may be more difficult over a broader than a smaller set of issues.

The fifth criterion is the *ease of implementation*. Any governance framework need to be assessed against the ease and cost of its implementation. The implementation of any regulation as well as code of conduct will entail costs for the monitors and the monitored. The expected benefit from general principles may be lost without further specifics on the actual steps of their implementation. However, rules that are overly constraining could be difficult and costly to implement. The balance between these two aspects will bear on the effectiveness of an SSGF and on market vibrancy. It has been alleged that the requirements of the Sarbanes-Oxley framework introduced in the United States following the Enron debacle has had perverse effects due to overly stringent rules. Some publicly listed companies have opted to become private, while others have preferred listing in other jurisdictions, affecting the competitiveness of U.S. stock markets.[12]

Finally, the effectiveness of an SSGF can be enhanced if implementation is *easy to monitor* and *credible remedial actions* can be introduced in case of deviation. Monitoring requires stakeholders' access to the monitored as well as information, including data collection. The IIFS's supervisor may have an important role in an SSGF. However, the coverage of its supervision is likely to vary across jurisdictions depending on the responsibilities and accountabilities the legislation assigns to it. Market monitors such as rating agencies may be an instrument in developing market discipline. An SSGF that is too complex to monitor would induce a supervisor's forbearance and discourage market monitors' engagement. In addition, it would accommodate opacity and facilitate deviation. An SSGF needs to envisage remedial actions wherever deviations are observed. However, the remedial actions need be calibrated to the gravity of the deviation.

Components of *Shari'a* Governance

A main objective of *Shari'a* governance is that structures and systems enable IIFSs to comply with *Shari'a*. The structures and systems can be specific to a particular organization, to products and services, or to the jurisdiction where an IIFS operates. The foregoing criteria can provide guidance at each

---

[12]The "implement or explain" principle provides flexibility with accountability. It addresses to a certain extent the trade-off between too much generality and specificity.

of these levels. Progress toward specificity can be provided by addressing these four questions:

1. What should *Shari'a* governance ensure? In particular, what are the principles that need to be complied with?
2. What product and institution should be assessed by the governance framework for their *Shari'a* compliance?
3. What should be the role of different organizations in *Shari'a* governance?
4. When is a *Shari'a* compliance pronouncement needed?

Regarding the question of what should be complied with, the market faces the existence of different and evolving pronouncements on compliance. These differences may stem from the existence of separate broad *Shari'a* schools . Though *fatwa* convergence may be more widespread than is apparent, *Shari'a* assessments may rely in various degrees on one or another body of interpretations, leading to variations in views on compliance requirements. From the preceding criteria of clarity and transparency, a disclosure of the *Shari'a* foundations of a *Shari'a* governance framework and its component elements may be beneficial. It could also contribute to market dynamism and increased legal certainty. While the disclosure of notably the Dow Jones Islamic Market Index, Moody's, and FTSE Islamic Index does contribute to the transparency of their screening criteria, the reason for the differences may remain puzzling for the external observer. Indeed, what underlies the alternative use of total assets or market capitalization? Is this an idiosyncratic difference between *Shari'a* boards or a systemic difference between schools of thought? An SSGF may gain in breadth of acceptability if the reasons for those differences were more widely shared.

An expanding body of *Shari'a* pronouncements goes in parallel with IIFS's continuous diversification of offerings of products and services. Each new offering needs to be assessed for both its market potential and its *Shari'a* compliance. *Shari'a* governance needs to be able to be nimble to promptly assess potential compliance issues of a new offering. It also needs to be able to factor in market developments, as well as competition. Thus, the ability of *Shari'a* governance to process promptly and effectively market innovation in the form of products and services—including investment portfolios or funds—or institutional processes does matter. One can refer to the February 2008 recommendations on *sukuk*s, their timing and impact on market development, issued by the *Shari'a* committee of the Accounting and Auditing Organization for Islamic Financial Institutions (AAOIFI).

Table 9.1 provides a summary of the organizations and institutions that may be involved in a *Shari'a* governance framework. They include

TABLE 9.1   Five Components of an SSGF

Category of Agents	Pledge/Mandate
– Market Participant: *Shari'a*-Compliant Financial Institution	
Commercial bank Investment bank Asset/portfolio manager Brokerage	Pledge to comply with *Shari'a* principles in all their operations, and offer *Shari'a*-compliant products according to disclosed *Shari'a* principles
– Official Market Regulator, Supervisor	
Banking regulator/supervisor Capital market regulator/sup Non-bank financial reg/sup Payments systems manager	• Enable a regulatory environment that ensures market vibrancy, financial stability, on a level playing field for *Shari'a* and non-*Shari'a* abiding financial institutions • May or may not have a role in *Shari'a* compliance—practices differ
– Associative Standard Setters Like	
Accounting Auditing Governance *Shari'a* standard setters	• Develop standards and codes compatible with, and adapted to *Shari'a* principles • Develop standards on *Shari'a* principles, processes and products that gather market consensus
– Private Market Monitors, Assessors	
Data, info, and analysis provider Rating agency Financial advisory services Financial media	• Collect and develop information and analysis on markets and financial institutions • Assess market, product, and institutional performance and compliance with *Shari'a* and other standards
– International	
Multinational Financial Institutions Peer regulators and supervisors Standard setters	• Pledge compliance with *Shari'a* and harmonize *Shari'a* practices across jurisdictions where they operate • Compare, coordinate, harmonize practices and regulations
Multilateral public institutions and International assessors	• Set international standards • Strategically assess international developments and impact on growth and stability • Review standards and codes and promote international consultations, feedback, and reform
International market monitors	• International data providers, analysts, and media • International rating agencies provide insights and creditworthiness assessments

market participants such as *Shari'a*-compliant banks, investment banks, or finance houses; they may also include regulators and supervisors, business associations, and market monitors, as well as international bodies. Their role can be expected to depend on their mandate and the jurisdiction in which they operate, as well as business requirements.[13] Market participants such as banks would be expected to pledge in their mission statements to abide with *Shari'a* principles. Accordingly, they need to put in place structures and mechanisms to ensure the fulfillment of that pledge as well as disclose to external stakeholders their compliance mechanism and record.

The role of regulators and supervisors may be less clear-cut. Depending on constitutional arrangements, their role beyond business enablers and promoters of financial stability may be limited.[14] Religious and professional associations can self-regulate and issue codes of conduct that their members would be expected to abide by. Self-regulating organizations (SROs) may be a convenient element of an SSGF. An SRO would involve several organizations without centralized organizations' possible drawbacks. Moreover, the public authority may rely on the work of such associations as a source of guidelines or even an enforcer. Risk-rating agencies can play an important role in an SSGF as market monitors, informing depositors and investors of compliance and risks associated with noncompliance.

Furthermore, in the context of globally competitive economies and financial systems, an SSGF needs to envisage cross-border transactions as well as multinational IIFS. A relevant perspective in this context is the implication of *Shari'a* governance arrangements on external investors' and market analysts' perceptions of the soundness (riskiness/stability), efficiency, and inclusiveness of particular IIFS jurisdictions. International agencies and associations, including the AAOIFI, Islamic Financial Services Board (IFSB), International Islamic Financial Market (IIFM), and of course the Islamic Development Bank (IsDB) have a particular role in promoting coordination at the international level.

Furthermore, an SSGF is expected to consider compliance before an activity takes place or a product is introduced in the market, as well as after the fact. The former and latter assessments are referred to as *ex ante* and *ex post* audits in conventional finance. The assessors' independence from management

---

[13] International bodies and multinational organizations operate across jurisdictions, compounding their role.

[14] See for further analysis on this issue: D. El-Hawary, W. Grais, and Z. Iqbal, "Regulating Islamic Financial Institutions: The Nature of the Regulated," World Bank Policy Research Working Paper 3227, March 2004.

is critical. Such assessments can help avoid deviations before they are introduced as well as draw lessons from those that have taken place.[15]

Sources of Governance and SSGF's Criteria

Shari'a governance may be at the initiative of one of the identified components of an SSGF that pledge to comply with *Shari'a* principles. Table 9.2 provides a framework to discuss possible impacts of the source of initiative on the selected criteria; it is in no way a definite statement on these impacts. The five sources of governance initiative correspond to the components identified in the table, namely: (1) the concerned agent or self, (2) regulator/supervisor, (3) business associations, (4) market agents, and (5) the international community. A useful exercise in assessing an SSGF is to discuss specific initiatives that would fit in each cell of the table. Consider, for example, the "self" column. Each agent can provide itself with structures and processes for its own governance, based or not on an explicit governance code. Self-selected governance is likely to be accepted and considered legitimate. It is also likely to be designed to not inhibit market dynamism. However, it may be less concerned with comprehensiveness, clarity, and transparency, though this is not necessarily so. Self-governance would be concerned with the cost of implementation and would seek to make it easier. It may not focus too much on ease of review and remedial action.

TABLE 9.2 Suggested Impact of the Source of Governance on Selected SSGF Criteria

Impact On	Self	Regulator/ Supervisor	Association	Market	International
Legitimacy and acceptability	++	−−	++	++	−−
Market dynamism	++	~~	~~	++	~~
Clarity and transparency	~~	++	++	+	++
Comprehensiveness	~~	++	+	~~	++
Ease of implementation	++	~~	+	~~	~~
Ease of review and remedial action	~~	~~	+	~~	~~

++ positive, ~~ neutral, −− negative

---

[15]The current international financial architecture builds on 12 standards and codes that include the Basel Core Principles for Banking Supervision (BCP) as well as the OECD Corporate Governance Principles. The assessment of implementation of these codes helps countries compare their practices, peer review other countries, and identify remedial actions.

A discussion of Table 9.2 cells can provide a framework to assess the design of an SSGF. It can also help assess an existing SSGF in terms of objectives sought as reflected in the identified criteria or other ones. For example, in Malaysia, the *Shari'a* Advisory Council (SAC) is a body for recourse by the courts and arbitrators in the matter of *Shari'a*-compliant finance. Its decisions are advisory to courts but binding to arbitrators. However, the UAE Higher *Shari'a* Board provides binding pronouncements. Whereas both approaches are consistent with clarity and transparency, their implications in terms of market dynamism, cost of implementation, and remedial action are likely to differ.

PREVAILING *SHARI'A* GOVERNANCE FRAMEWORKS

SSGFs are increasingly multidimensional. The most common feature is the presence of a *Shari'a* board or committee for each organization offering IFS.[16] In many cases, IIFSs also have internal *Shari'a* audit departments that follow up on the compliance of day-to-day operations. Some jurisdictions have a central *Shari'a* body based either with the banking regulator or with a ministry. Whether centrally or IFS-based, *Shari'a* boards' decisions are either binding or advisory. Similarly, certain countries have adopted a code of *Shari'a* governance. Market monitors are developing services in *Shari'a* assessments providing advisory services and features of market discipline. In a few cases memorandums of understanding (MOUs) between jurisdictions have been developed.[17] International institutions have developed guidelines and standards. They have also taken a lead role in organizing international consultations and harmonization efforts.[18]

The following highlights systemic arrangements, contribution of external bodies, and market monitors' and analysts' roles. It then draws a synthetic picture of the impact of sources of governance on the identified criteria for an SSGF.

---

[16] This feature is less common in Iran, where only one bank had a *Shari'a* board. Bank Sepah is the only bank in Iran to have a *Shari'a* board and *Shari'a* advisers, but most of its financing is for real estate. In contrast, Bank Melli is mostly involved in trade and industrial financing, but although its assets exceed $20 billion (twice the size of the largest Arab Islamic bank, the Al Rajhi Banking and Investment Corporation), many observers outside Iran have doubts about its Islamic banking credentials. See Rodney Wilson (2002) "The evolution of the Islamic financial system" in Abdel Karim, Rifaat Ahmed, and Simon Archer: *Islamic Finance: Innovation and Growth*, London, Euromoney Books.

[17] For example, it is reported that Malaysia's SEC and the DIFC signed an MOU on mutually accepting *Shari'a* pronouncements.

[18] For a review of the features and roles of SGF components, see Grais and Pelligrini (2006a).

Systemic Arrangements

National regulators and supervisors are involved in different degrees in *Shari'a* governance. Non-Islamic jurisdictions such as the United Kingdom or Singapore will generally consider the issue to be outside their oversight. Their main concern is the stability and vibrancy of the financial system they oversee, and they leave to individual institutions the concern of putting in place structures and systems that allow them to comply with *Shari'a* principles. Regulators and supervisors in Islamic jurisdictions need to balance the requirements of ensuring that their systemic arrangements accommodate IIFSs and are adapted to their operations while at the same time they comply with international requirements applying to financial systems in general.

The Central Bank of Bahrain established a National *Shari'a* Board to verify *Shari'a* compliance of its own operations and products only. In Bahrain, all IIFSs are required to establish a "*Shari'a* Supervisory Committee" and comply with the AAOIFI's Governance Standards for Islamic Financial Institutions. There is no restriction on the right of a member of the National *Shari'a* Board to join the *Shari'a* committee of one or several institutions offering IFS.

Bank Negara Malaysia has a *Shari'a* Advisory Council (SAC) in compliance with the central bank's law. The SAC is competent to decide on all Islamic finance business, including *takaful*, regulated and supervised by the central bank, which issued "Guidelines for the Governance of *Shari'a* Committees for Islamic Financial Institutions." Members of SAC of the central bank may not serve in the *Shari'a* committee of a financial institution. A *Shari'a* adviser may be a member of the *Shari'a* committee of only one financial institution in the same industry.[19]

The State Bank of Pakistan (SBP) established a three-tiered SSGF. It includes a central *Shari'a* board at the SBP, a *Shari'a* compliance inspection, and *Shari'a* advisers at each financial institution. In contrast with Malaysia, an SBP *Shari'a* board member may be an IIFS's *Shari'a* adviser. Fit and proper rules require that a *Shari'a* board member have the required professional competency and may not have been involved with an illegal activity. (See Box 9.1.)[20]

---

[19] Aznan Bin Hasan, "Optimal *Shariah* Governance in Islamic Finance," Islamic Law Department, International Islamic University of Malaysia, undated.

[20] Aurangzeb (2002) suggests the creation of a *Shari'a* board at the SBP for the overall supervision and guidance of IFS in the country. The board would advise the central bank in matters of regulation and supervision and give its opinion and clearance on financial instruments issued by the SBP or IFS.

BOX 9.1 PAKISTAN: *SHARI'A* GOVERNANCE FRAMEWORK

Pakistan has adopted a three-tiered *Shari'a* Compliance Mechanism (SCM) to enable *Shari'a* compliance supervision on an ongoing basis: *Shari'a* advisers for banks, a *Shari'a* compliance inspection (SCI), and a centralized *Shari'a* board for the country at the State Bank of Pakistan (SBP).

The fit and proper criteria of each bank's *Shari'a* adviser are determined by the SBP. Apart from the usual criteria, an important one is the person's qualifications and experience in issuing *fatwa*s relating to financial transactions. The SBP's criteria are inclusive of all schools of thought and emphasize international qualifications and experience. These *Shari'a* scholars are nominated by the bank and appointed by it to oversee its operations after the SBP's approval.

The second element is an SCI, based on a comprehensive inspection manual. The SCI ensures that specific terms of Islamic contracts, *fatwa* on the transaction, and the sequence of execution of the agreement are conducted according to *Shari'a* principles. The SCI would audit transactions according to AAOIFI standards.

The third SCM element is SBP's *Shari'a* board. It has the unique feature of also including a chartered accountant, lawyer, and central banker. The rationale is that other disciplines are critical to successfully complying with *Shari'a* standards and ensuring that the *Shari'a* board's rulings are also compatible with the legal and financial infrastructure available to Islamic banks. The board is responsible to arbitrate conflicts arising out of the SCI, provide guidelines to the SBP for *Shari'a* aspects of regulations, help in product development, and assist in the approval of products developed by commercial banks.

To date, both the industry and the SBP have positive assessments of the system in place.

Source: Adapted from "*Shari'a* Compliant Corporate Governance," keynote address by Dr. Shamshad Akhtar, Governor of the State Bank of Pakistan, at the Annual Corporate Governance Conference, Dubai, November 27, 2006.

International Governance

A significant step was taken with the creation of the Accounting and Auditing Organization for Islamic Financial Institutions (AAOIFI) in the early 1990s. The pioneering work of the AAOIFI, supported by the Islamic

Development Bank (IsDB) and national regulators of member countries, led to the development of accounting as well as *Shari'a* standards. Whether adopted wholesale or used as guidance, these standards have contributed to more focused analysis in promoting financial reporting, disclosure, and transparency. Their existence provided a reference for all involved, whether agreeing or not. A first and big step had thus been taken toward a broad *Shari'a* governance framework. The AAOIFI early on issued two pronouncements on governance standards for Islamic financial institutions. They contain clear provisions on the duties and powers of *Shari'a* boards that would limit a bank's discretion in the definition of the board's prerogatives and thereby deprive managers of one instrument of control.[21] In addition, they contain provisions on fixing remuneration, selection, and dismissal of *Shari'a* boards' members, as well as incompatibility clauses to diffuse conflicts of interest.[22] A number of national regulators have included such prohibitions in circulars or legislative acts, mostly in the form of fit criteria and prohibited interests for the appointment of *Shari'a* boards' members or advisers.[23] The AAOIFI's self-regulatory organizational structure renders it an associative body at the international level. It gives it a channel to build consensus and legitimacy among members. Its performance can be viewed as significant and positive when checked against the criteria outlined earlier.[24]

---

[21] The codes are the Code of Ethics for Accountants and Auditors of Islamic Financial Institutions and the Code of Ethics for the Employees of Islamic Financial Institutions. The *Shari'a* board's prerogatives include *ex ante* and *ex post* evaluation, calculation of *zakat*, and allocation of profits or charging of losses to unrestricted investment account holders. The AAOIFI standard requires at least three individuals on each board.

[22] For instance, dismissal of a *Shari'a* board may only be prompted by a request of the board of directors approved by the general assembly of shareholders. This will prevent so-called *fatwa* shopping. Further, the standards provisions prohibit the appointment of "directors or significant stakeholders" as board members and prohibit *Shari'a* review units from carrying out operational activities (for instance, a division in the internal audit department). Depending on local circumstances, such provisions may be strengthened by introducing severe sanctions for accepting loans from the audited company, having family relationship with the audit client, or having any form of direct or indirect material interest in the business. For instance, in Malaysia, the approval and dismissal must be communicated to the central bank.

[23] Bank Negara Malaysia's 2004 "Guidelines on the Governance of *Shari'a* Committee for Islamic Financial Institutions."

[24] AAOIFI's standards are mandatory for the following markets: Bahrain, Jordan, Sudan, Qatar, and Dubai International Financial Center. Syria is considering their adoption. The standards are used as guidelines in Saudi Arabia, Kuwait, Malaysia, Lebanon, and Indonesia. Most IIFS *Shari'a* supervisory committees use AAOIFI standards as guidelines.

BOX 9.2 IFSB GUIDING PRINCIPLES ON CORPORATE GOVERNANCE FOR INSTITUTIONS OFFERING ISLAMIC FINANCIAL SERVICES

Principle 1.1: IIFS shall establish a comprehensive governance policy framework which sets out the strategic roles and functions of each organ of governance and mechanisms for balancing the IIFS's accountabilities to various stakeholders.

Principle 1.2: IIFS shall ensure that the reporting of their financial and nonfinancial information meets the requirements of internationally recognized accounting standards which are in compliance with *Shari'a* rules and principles and are applicable to the Islamic financial services industry as recognized by the supervisory authorities of the country.

Principle 2.1: IIFS shall acknowledge IAHs' right to monitor the performance of their investments and the associated risks, and put into place adequate means to ensure that these rights are observed and exercised.

Principle 2.2: IIFS shall adopt a sound investment strategy which is appropriately aligned to the risk and return expectations of IAH (bearing in mind the distinction between restricted and unrestricted IAH), and be transparent in smoothing any returns.

Principle 3.1: IIFS shall have in place an appropriate mechanism for obtaining rulings from *Shari'a* scholars, applying *fatwa*, and monitoring *Shari'a* compliance in all aspects of their products, operations, and activities.

Principle 3.2: IIFS shall comply with the *Shari'a* rules and principles as expressed in the rulings of the IIFS's *Shari'a* scholars. The IIFS shall make these rulings available to the public.

Principle 4: IIFS shall make adequate and timely disclosure to IAH and the public of material and relevant information on the investment accounts that they manage.

Source: The IFSB Guiding Principles.

Another significant step toward an SSGF was taken with the establishment of the Islamic Financial Services Board (IFSB) in 2002. A number of central banks and the IsDB joined efforts to provide IIFSs with a prudential regulation standard setting body. The IFSB's first initiatives led to the formulation of capital adequacy, risk management, and corporate governance principles that complement those of the Basel Committee and the Organisation for Economic Co-operation and Development (OECD) for IFS. Box 9.2 reports the IFSB's corporate governance principles for institutions offering IFS, specifically for full-fledged *Shari'a*-compliant banks that are not engaged in *takaful* and are not collective investment schemes. While the various guidelines the IFSB is developing are building blocks of a comprehensive *Shari'a* governance framework, the corporate governance principles focus on one particular element, a category of market participants. Checking them against the criteria, they emphasize comprehensiveness (1.1), transparency (1.2, 2.1, 2.2, 3.2, and 4), and legitimacy (3.1 and 3.2). The IFSB's principles have provided a core reference to *Shari'a* governance that is consistent with international guidelines in the area. Together with its contributions in other areas of IFS, the IFSB is providing a set of complementary components that can strengthen an SSGF.

Market Governance

From another perspective, market-active organizations contribute to IIFS corporate governance. They include international market indexes and advisory and legal firms, as well as rating agencies.

In developing *Shari'a*-compliant equity market indexes and funds, companies have developed specific compliance criteria that apply to companies to be included in the index or portfolio. These generally include sector criteria as well as financial ratios. The concerned sectors are typically the same across organizations, as they refer to non-*halal* activities. However, there may be some variations as to the degree of involvement in those sectors.[25] In parallel, a set of financial ratios is not to be exceeded for investing in a company. In conventional parlance, such criteria would represent *screens*. A significant contribution of these initiatives is the disclosure and dissemination of the criteria they use. Table 9.3 provides an illustration of financial ratios used. They relate mostly to limiting interest as a source of income and sometimes the share of nonpermissible income. Variations across the sets do exist. However, without disclosure, those variations could hardly have been observed. In addition,

---

[25] But even if a certain limited level of involvement in certain nonpermissible activity may be accepted, objections should be made by shareholders and a share of income corresponding to the share of nonpermissible activity would be given to charity.

TABLE 9.3 Financial Ratios of Alternative *Shari'a* Screens

Screens Ratios	DJIM	FTSE*	S&P	MSCI†	HSBC	Meezan Bank
Liquidity Ratios						
Account receivables, cash, and short-term investments over total assets					50%	
Account receivables and cash over total assets		50%				
Account receivables over total assets			49%	70%		
Account receivables over market cap	33%					
Interest Income Ratios						
Total interest Income over total revenue‡	33%	5%	3%		5%	5%
Cash and short-term investments over market cap	33%					
Cash and short-term investments over total assets		33%		33.33%		
Indebtedness Ratios						
Total debt over total assets		33%	33%	33.33%		
Total debt over total market cap	33%	33%	33%		30%	30%
Permissible Income						
Noninterest, nonpermissible income		5%	5%			
Total investments in nonpermissible income over market cap						30%

Source: U. Derigs and S. Marzban, "New Strategies and a New Paradigm for *Shari'a*-Compliant Portfolio Optimization," *Journal of Banking & Finance* 33 (2009): 1166–1176, http://tcnh.ntt.edu.vn/images/tapchiqt/48.pdf.
* www.ftse.com/Indices/FTSE_Shari'a_Global_Equity_Index_Series/index.jsp.
† www.mscibarra.com/products/indices/islamic/.
‡ For Meezan Bank, the limit of 5 percent applies to interest and nonpermissible income; see M. I. A. Usmani, *Meezan Bank's Guide to Islamic Banking* (Karachi: Darul Ishaat, 2002).

variations can legitimately underlie market-related differences in offered products. A challenge of an SSGF is to pronounce about legitimacy and compliance with enough flexibility to allow for acceptable variations. Indeed, the latter are at the core of businesses' ability to compete and adapt to market demand.[26]

Unlike the Dow Jones Islamic Market Index (DJIM), which has its own in-house *Shari'a* board, the Financial Times Stock Exchange Index (FTSE) outsources its *Shari'a* advisory and screening to a specialized *Shari'a* advisory firm, Yasaar Limited, which has offices in the United Kingdom, Dubai, and Pakistan. FTSE's business is modeled on partnerships with stock exchanges, other associations, and commercial entities. It is more confident working with partners because it does not have in-house expertise on *Shari'a* screening and compliance.[27]

An increasing number of law firms and consulting companies are now offering *Shari'a* advisory services.[28] Lawyers have focused on issues of what law is applicable, jurisdiction of competence, arbitration, or legal certainty in *Shari'a* contracts.[29] Independent audit firms can reduce audit costs and give access to a broader range of expertise. If chartered, *Shari'a* audit companies may convey a greater sense of professionalism and independence from the IIFS management.[30] External firms undertaking *Shari'a* audit can usefully complement internal *Shari'a* audit.

Already, private rating agencies are engaged in the assessment of *Shari'a*-compliant institutions and products. Fitch, Standard & Poor's, and Moody's have developed competence in the sector. They regularly produce assessments of the industry, specific segments, risk assessment methodologies, and ratings of *Shari'a*-compliant institutions and products. *Shari'a*-compliant organizations such as Al Rajhi, Dubai Islamic Bank, and the Jordan Islamic Bank are being reviewed by one or more of those institutions. Similarly,

---

[26] For an interesting approach to review and integrate different sets of criteria, see Derigs and Marzban (2009).

[27] "We are an index provider—design, calculate, manage, disseminate, that is our specialty. We are not specialists in *Shariah* and any aspects of Islamic investment. To try to create this expertise in-house there has a number of shortcomings. It would be relatively narrow base and interpretation; by doing it this way we get far greater breadth of expertise; access to people who really know what they are doing. But, we have to be confident that our partner is good, professional, and experienced" (Donald Keith, Deputy Chief Executive of FTSE).

[28] For example: www.yasaar.org/rationale.htm and www.islamic-banking.com/shariah/index.php.

[29] See, for example, McMillen (2007) regarding securities laws, trusts, enforceability, and *sukuk*s.

[30] Possibility of "*Shari'a* advisory *à la carte*" would remain, however.

*sukuk*s have been rated before issuance to give confidence to investors. In addition, several institutions gathered to form the International Islamic Rating Agency (IIRA) to develop alternative specialization in rating services and access to them. Furthermore, national rating agencies such as the Malaysian Rating Corporation (MARC) have developed competence in the rating of IIFSs. Even if these agencies are under pressure following failure to unveil risks that led to the recent global financial crisis, they are bound to remain important monitors of developments in IFS.

TOWARD A SYSTEMIC *SHARI'A* FRAMEWORK

A configuration of a systemic SSGF is presented in Table 9.4. It includes elements such as an institution-specific *Shari'a* board, a code of ethics, and international standard setters. Domestic standard setting can be left to the regulator or emanate from business associations. For *Shari'a* governance, one can imagine an association of *Shari'a* scholars or of certified *Shari'a* audit firms. It could become a source of *Shari'a* standards alternative to the regulator. This approach would have the advantage of more immediate legitimacy and acceptability. In addition, it locates standard setting at proximity to the market, permitting a better calibration to the requirements of market dynamism, clarity, and transparency, as well as ease of implementation. An association of *Shari'a* specialists can be self-regulated. Its members could be certified and its activities supported by the authorities. The approach would leave more initiative with market-engaged individuals and institutions.

Thus one can envisage an SSGF that is centered on the five pillars identified in the table, but providing a prominent role to business associations and individual institutions under the overall oversight of the financial system supervisor. The latter three agents can together strengthen the role of markets in promoting an SSGF's effectiveness. Business associations can also provide a cost-efficient interface with the international financial community.

However, an SSGF needs to be adapted to domestic market development and cultural conditions. Depending on the latter, it may evolve from a large reliance on regulation to one that emphasizes self-governance and the role of business associations. Irrespective of the stage of its development, an SSGF needs to stress clarity and transparency. Accordingly, information organization, disclosure, and dissemination are always critical.

The following outlines an SSGF for a jurisdiction where financial regulators' and supervisors' primary objectives are the stability of the financial system and its vibrancy. Authorities' involvement with *Shari'a* compliance is therefore to encourage transparency and disclosure of the conduct of financial *Shari'a* intermediation and holding market participants accountable

TABLE 9.4 *Shari'a* Governance Framework

Shari'a Self-Governance	Regulator-Induced *Shari'a* Governance	Association-Induced *Shari'a* Governance	Market-Induced *Shari'a* Governance	Internationally Induced *Shari'a* Governance
Shari'a board	Central *Shari'a* board	Monitor and assess domestic and international SSGF	Certified *Shari'a* audit firms	International standard setters (e.g., IFSB, AAOIFI)
Shari'a review unit	Domestic standard setter	Resource for lessons of experience	Reputable agents (e.g., rating agencies)	International assessors and peer review
Shari'a-adapted management information system (MIS)	Organize *Shari'a*-adapted data reporting	Governance training	*Shari'a* legal and advisory services firms	International ratings of sovereign and IFS
Code of ethics	Regulator-issued code of governance	Business association's code of conduct	Information providers, reputable media	International forums and exchanges of experiences

for following on their pledges of *Shari'a* compliance and implementing the codes of conduct they have issued. Accordingly, in such an SSGF, financial regulators and supervisors would not issue or give pronouncements on *Shari'a* financial principles.

Regulators' and supervisors' roles are highlighted in column 2 of Table 9.4. The central bank and capital markets authority (CMA) would issue rules on transparency and disclosure to be followed by IIFSs. Together with the National Accounting Board and with reference to IFSB and AAOIFI guidelines, they would require IIFSs to provide them with periodically published financial and governance reports. The latter would include opinions on the observance of the pledged codes of conduct by each IIFS. The central bank and CMA would use these reports to assess operational risks and potential conflicts of interest. The central bank and the CMA would not necessarily have separate units dedicated to IFS, but would develop staff skills so that they can perform the foregoing functions. Given the regulators' primary objectives, they need not establish central *Shari'a* advisory boards that would settle disputes between *Shari'a* pronouncement or issue general *Shari'a* guidelines for the country's IIFSs.

The core source of financial *Shari'a* principles would be national professional associations. These would include associations of financial *Shari'a* professionals in the various areas of IFS activities. In particular, one can think of the following associations: (1) financial *Shari'a* scholars, (2) financial *Shari'a* legal advisers, (3) financial *Shari'a* accountants, (4) financial *Shari'a* auditors, and (5) financial *Shari'a* portfolio managers. It is preferable if such associations emerge on their prospective members' initiatives. However, public authorities need to encourage their development and develop a policy for their certification as professional associations. Associations' major functions are outlined in column 3 of the Table 9.4. They include the issuance of principles members should follow in the practice of the profession, the certification of members as fit and proper to practice, members' training activities and organization of a depository of professional resources, and the setting up of arbitration committees that would receive disputes between members and provide an opinion on their settlement. The associations would also be counterparts of international associations in the same activities. National associations would conclude memorandums of understanding providing the framework for their cooperation.

The associations could jointly issue a *Shari'a* governance code. It would be expected to include the principle that each IIFS would have a *Shari'a* advisory board (SAB). Safeguards would protect SAB's independence from management and the executive board. Its opinions would inform management's and the executive board's decisions but not direct them. Each SAB would provide the IIFS with its governing *Shari'a* principles that it would abide by. These principles would be the IIFS's governing code.[31] Management and the SAB would be supported by an internal *Shari'a* review unit that would help mainstream the IIFS's core principles that the SAB would have issued. Each IIFS would periodically disseminate a review of its activities, including an assessment of its compliance with the principles issued by its own SAB (see column 1 of Table 9.4). The associations' *Shari'a* governance code would be expected to recommend that SABs would have a membership of three to seven and identify eligibility fit and proper criteria. Each IIFS would be guided by the associations-issued *Shari'a* governance code in setting up its own *Shari'a* governance structures and processes.

The National Accounting Board, an association of accountants and the financial authorities, would develop financial reporting standards. The associations-issued *Shari'a* governance code would also point out the governance-related information to be reported. IIFSs would periodically report their performance according to those standards. The reports would be used by professional financial system monitors to provide data and analysis to the public. Similarly, rating agencies would draw on reported information and other standardized reports to develop their assessments. With the help of reliable and credible media, IIFSs would be subject to peer pressure and market discipline, encouraging them to abide by their adopted code of *Shari'a* governance.

National associations and regulators would actively participate in international governmental and business associations. They would play a role in the development of the international governance framework as it bears on IFS and *Shari'a* governance, and would also benefit from international developments in shaping national principles. In addition, they would undertake self-assessments of observance of international standards periodically, as well as invite independent external assessors through internationally accepted assessment mechanisms. They would also develop the skills of national professionals and have them participate in the peer reviews of other jurisdictions. National professionals would thereby be in direct contact with other experiences and practices, expanding skill resources available to the country.

CONCLUSION

At the core of the opportunity offered by IFS is the confidence stakeholders can have that the best effort is being made to comply with *Shari'a*

---

[31] See Box 9.2 for examples of guiding principles used by different IFS-engaged institutions.

principles. For that purpose a credible, robust, and non-market-stifling SSGF is essential.

This chapter addresses the question of *Shari'a* governance from a systemic perspective: namely, what is an effective framework for *Shari'a* governance in a jurisdiction. For that purpose, it identifies five criteria that may be deemed conducive to effective *Shari'a* governance. These are that an SSGF needs to be perceived as legitimate by those implementing it so that it receives broad acceptance; it needs to be perceived as not stifling markets, but encouraging their vibrancy; it needs to be viewed as sufficiently comprehensive so that it limits governance arbitrage such as so-called *fatwa* shopping; it needs to promote clarity and transparency to enable stakeholders to monitor their IFS agent's behavior; it needs to be easy and not too costly to implement in order not to encourage avoidance; and it needs to be easy to monitor and permit nonnuclear remedial action to correct deviations.

The chapter also identifies categories of organizations and institutions that may be subject to *Shari'a* governance or engaged in it as standard setters, reviewers, or otherwise. These are highlighted as self, regulators, associations, markets, and international bodies. Together those five groups can mutually reinforce the effectiveness of an SSGF while providing sufficient leeway in governance initiatives and implementation. The chapter also sketches a scenario of what each pillar's drivers' preferences would entail in terms of the criteria for an effective SSGF.

The five identified pillars are used as an organizing framework to review progress achieved in establishing an SSGF across the main jurisdictions involved in IFS. The emphasis remains on reliance on institution-specific *Shari'a* boards across jurisdictions. In certain jurisdictions regulators have put in place higher-level *Shari'a* boards mainly to resolve disputes at the level of lower boards or across them. They sometimes contribute opinions on *Shari'a*-compliant new market offerings. Thus it seems that in most jurisdictions the first two categories play a prominent role. Business associations, markets, and international bodies have a smaller role. However, organizations like the AAOIFI or the IFSB have contributed enormously to the industry and have a role to play in SSGF developments.

Islamic Finance: The International Landscape

Islamic finance is a significant part of the financial landscape of numerous countries. Iran, Gulf Cooperation Council (GCC) countries, Malaysia, and Sudan have been at the forefront of its development. This appendix provides an overview of the international landscape of Islamic finance.

While Islamic finance dates back to the early days of Islam, it has experienced a new life since the early 1970s and a tremendous explosion since the beginning of this new millennium. That explosion is manifest in the spectacular growth of the number and size of institutions offering Islamic financial services (IIFSs), their geographical spread across numerous countries, the diversity of their activities, and the growing body and quality of regulations attending to the sector.[1]

The present overview is also a statement that Islamic finance should be considered on the basis of facts and analysis and not ideology. Islamic financial services (IFS) are a fact on the ground. Institutions offering IFS pledge to respect a code of behavior based on values. The code's principles are enshrined in the contracts and product offerings. It happens to use the word *Islamic* as an umbrella qualification of its observance of the code. Possibly for that reason, in the current international context it gathers champions and advocates; it attracts many who see in it merely a business opportunity; it raises open (sometimes vehement) as well as silent opposition; and it often leaves many puzzled about its nature and value added. This leads to unnecessary mystification and often poorly based judgments on a financial market's reality, the opportunities it offers, and the risks associated with its practice.[2]

---

[1] See Part Three of this book for regulatory issues.
[2] The constitutions of Iran, Pakistan, and Sudan prescribe that the entire banking industry should follow Islamic principles.

A definite view on the size and spread of Islamic finance is still difficult to reach. Islamic financial services vary in their financial reporting and definitions, limiting the scope for aggregation. Efforts are being made by General Council of Islamic Banks and Financial Institutions (CIBAFI), the Islamic Development Bank (IsDB), the Accounting and Auditing Organization for Islamic Financial Institutions (AAOIFI), the Islamic Financial Services Board (IFSB), and others to organize the systematic recording and collection of data on Islamic finance.[3] However, these efforts have not yet led to the development of a reliable set of information produced periodically to provide a comprehensive overview of the industry and track its development.[4] Accordingly, this appendix uses information from various sources in its attempt to grasp the depth and breadth of Islamic finance's international presence.

After a brief summary of Islamic financial assets, this appendix introduces various main segments of Islamic finance. Data on these segments, collected from various data sources, is presented in subsequent sections: Islamic banking assets, the significant and growing *sukuk* markets, Islamic funds, and *takaful*.

OVERVIEW OF ISLAMIC FINANCIAL ASSETS

Based on the CIBAFI's Islamic finance directory and other sources, a joint effort of the IsDB, the IFSB, and the Islamic Research and Training Institute (IRTI) offers the most comprehensive estimates of worldwide Islamic financial assets for 2012. This work puts the size of Islamic financial assets at more than $1.6 trillion in 2012 and estimates that it could reach $1.8 trillion by the end of 2013.[5] Annual *sukuk* issues have grown from zero before 1996 to reach $49 billion by 2013. Moreover, investments and commercial banking activity have definitely expanded the assets managed by Islamic financial services in particular funds. Though caution with the numbers is advised, it is a best-effort estimate and gives a reference point to the worldwide size of the industry (see Table A.1).

Overall, banking assets represent more than 80 percent of Islamic financial assets. However, whereas in Middle East and North Africa (MENA) banking assets by far dominate the landscape, *sukuk*s, funds, and *takaful*

---

[3] CIBAFI is the General Council for Islamic Banks and Financial Institutions. Its web address is www.cibafi.org.
[4] The conclusion of such efforts and attempts at harmonizing financial reporting are critical and should be a priority.
[5] IFSB Financial Stability Report, 2013.

TABLE A.1   Islamic Finance Assets at Year-End 2012 across the World, across Assets (USD Billions)

Assets by Region	Total	Banking Assets	*Sukuks* Outstanding	Islamic Funds Assets	*Takaful* Contributions*
Asia	357.4	171.8	160.3	22.6	2.7
GCC	536.9	434.5	66.3	28.9	7.2
MENA (excluding GCC)	599.4	590.6	1.7	0.2	6.9
Sub-Saharan Africa	19.0	16.9	0.1	1.6	0.4
Others	71.6	59.8	1.0	10.8	0.0
Total USD billions	1,584.3	1,273.6	229.4	64.2	17.2
Shares across assets	100.0%	80.4%	14.5%	4.1%	1.1%

Source: IFSB Financial Stability Report 2013.
* *Takaful* contributions are the monetary payments of insured to the *takaful* operators.

represent more than 50 percent of Islamic financial assets, with a clear dominance of *sukuk*s.

In essence, Islamic finance remains essentially a banking activity and is mainly located in the MENA region, but with significant presence in Asia. Within the MENA region, Islamic financial assets are within the GCC and Iran. Outside the MENA region, Asia has a large profile in the industry. The rest of the world, beyond these two centers, shares less than 10 percent of Islamic financial assets.

While these numbers are large and growing and reflect valuable business activity, they remain of a different order of magnitude than those observed for conventional finance. For example, the assets of Hong Kong–Shanghai Bank Corporation (HSBC) alone represented more than $2.68 trillion at the end of March 2013.[6]

Even with caveats on the number, and relying on a different source, it is clear that Islamic finance has expanded rapidly over recent years. On average, global Islamic financial assets grew at more than 20 percent per year from 2007 to 2012 (see Figure A.1).

However, these global growth rates hide a shift in the weights of different regions in the Islamic finance landscape (see Table A.2). Assets growth has significantly slowed down in Iran and the GCC countries, but to a lesser

---

[6] HSBC was the second largest bank in the world after the Industrial and Commercial Bank of China. The five largest banks of the world had assets in excess of $13.3 billion at the end of March 2013; see www.relbanks.com/worlds-top-banks/assets.

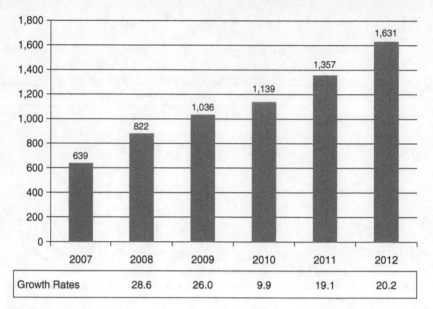

FIGURE A.1   Growth of Global Islamic Financial Assets, 2007–2012 (USD Billions)
Source: Global Islamic Finance Report (GIFR) (2013) at www.gifr.net/publications/
gifr2013/intro.pdf.

extent in the latter. Growth in Malaysia has also slowed down, but experienced a healthy recovery in 2012. In the meantime, Islamic financial assets have exploded in the rest of the world over 2011 and 2012. But again, the noticeable development is the more than doubling in 2011 and impressive 70 percent in 2012 growth in the nontraditional Islamic finance markets.

Looking beyond the aggregate number for countries other than Iran, the GCC countries, and Malaysia, one can separate countries with more than $10 billion from all others (see Table A.3). Again, here the explosion

TABLE A.2   Growth Rates across the World (%)

Countries	2008	2009	2010	2011	2012
Iran	24.68	25.94	10.03	1.72	0.73
GCC	35.11	25.71	9.89	8.38	8.87
Malaysia	29.85	25.29	10.09	9.17	18.32
Other countries	20.27	24.72	10.81	130.08	70.67

Source: Global Islamic Finance Report (GIFR) (2013) at www.gifr.net/publications/
gifr2013/intro.pdf and authors' calculations.

TABLE A.3 Islamic Finance Asset Growth: Emerging Islamic Finance Markets (%)

Other Countries	2008	2009	2010	2011	2012
With $10bn+ assets	18.18	24.36	11.34	41.67	29.41
All others	37.50	27.27	7.14	766.67	119.23

Source: Global Islamic Finance Report (GIFR) (2013) at www.gifr.net/publications/gifr2013/intro.pdf and authors' calculations.

in growth appears more pronounced in those countries where the industry was initially small and is spread more widely—that is, countries with assets less than $10 billion.

The differential in the growth of assets has dented the traditional landscape where Iran, the GCC countries, and Malaysia appeared as the only places where substantial Islamic finance activity was taking place. They do remain the most significant players in the industry, but others are growing in importance. Only Malaysia seems to be maintaining its share of the world market. While most small country markets held barely a 1 percent share of global Islamic finance assets, their share jumped to 10 percent and 17 percent in 2011 and 2012, respectively (see Table A.4).

ISLAMIC BANKING ASSETS

Islamic banking assets have grown at a compounded annual growth rate (CAGR) of 40.3 percent between 2004 and 2011 to reach $1.1 trillion and in 2012 to reach $1.27 trillion (IFSB Financial Stability Report 2013). By the end of 2012, total Islamic banking assets represented 80.4 percent of total Islamic financial assets.

TABLE A.4 Changing Landscape

Countries	2007	2008	2009	2010	2011	2012
Iran	37%	36%	36%	36%	30%	26%
GCC	41%	43%	43%	43%	39%	35%
Malaysia	11%	11%	11%	11%	10%	10%
With $10bn+ assets	10%	9%	9%	9%	11%	12%
Others	1%	1%	1%	1%	10%	17%

Source: Global Islamic Finance Report (GIFR) (2013) at www.gifr.net/publications/gifr2013/intro.pdf and authors' calculations.

TABLE A.5 Share of Islamic Banking Assets in Total Banking Assets, Selected Countries (%)

Countries	2012
GCC	
Bahrain	35.0
Kuwait	42.3
Qatar	22.9
Saudi Arabia	22.7
UAE	12.9
Malaysia	20.0
Indonesia	20.5
Pakistan	7.0
Turkey	5.2
Yemen	33.0

Sources: Central banks, individual institutions, Zawya, The Banker, KFHR KFH-Research: US$1.3 trillion assets of Islamic banks by end of 2012. Yemen data source: central bank of Yemen, 2010; IFSB Financial Stability Report 2013.

One has to note that Islamic banking assets stand at less than 45 percent of total banking assets in most countries of the world with the exception of Iran and Sudan. The highest share is found in Kuwait at 42.3 percent (see Table A.5).

SUKUKS

The *sukuk* market represents 14.5 percent of total Islamic financial assets. The sector is growing at a remarkable pace (see Figure A.2). The growth was driven by the need for securitization among industry players to create market liquidity. *Sukuk* issuances have increased from $6.6 billion in 2004 to reach $131.2 billion at the end of 2012, growing at a CAGR of 60.1 percent (Islamic Finance Information Service [IFIS] Financial Stability Report 2013).

The growth of the primary market was driven by the lower charged return rates compared to those of conventional bonds. This is may be due in part to a perception of lower risks of *sukuk*s as asset-based instruments providing an ownership right to their holders.

The cost of preparation work has also come down significantly, and issues have become more standardized since the first issues on the market.

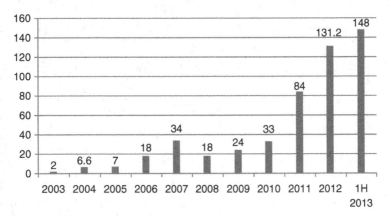

FIGURE A.2 *Sukuk* Market Issuance, 2003–2013 ($ Billions)
Source: Zawya, UFS investment company estimates (www.ufs-federation.com). First half 2013: The New Straits Times Press, Malaysia Berhard, November 24, 2013.

Malaysia continues to be the key player in the *sukuk* market with $104 billion, representing 74 percent of all new issuance in 2012 (see Figure A.3). Saudi Arabia with $10.5 billion, representing 7.5 percent, was followed by United Arab Emirates, Indonesia, Qatar, and Turkey with $6 billion, $6 billion, $5.4 billion, and $2.4 billion, respectively.

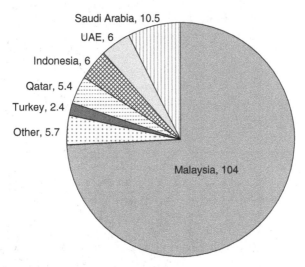

FIGURE A.3 *Sukuk* Issuance by Country, 2012 (USD Millions)
Source: Zawya, UFS investment company estimates (www.ufs-federation.com).

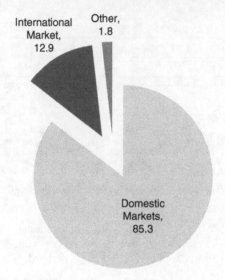

FIGURE A.4   Share of *Sukuk*s by Issue Type, 2012 Issuance (%)
Source: Zawya, UFS investment company estimates, www.ufs-federation.com.

Sovereign *sukuk*s retain their dominance in the market with 66 percent of all issuance, followed by the banks and financial corporations with 10.8 percent.

The *sukuk* market is mostly domestic. Despite the increase in volume, international *sukuk*s amounted to US$18.5 billion or a market share of 12.9 percent in 2012. (See Figures A.4 and A.5.)

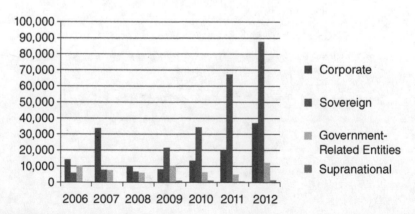

FIGURE A.5   *Sukuk* by Type of Issuer
Source: IFIS *sukuk* database.

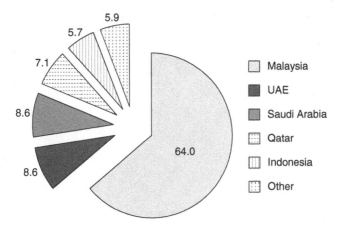

FIGURE A.6   Turnover on *Sukuk* Secondary Markets (%)
Source: Zawya, UFS investment company estimates (www.ufs-federation.com).

The turnover on the secondary market reached $240 billion in 2012. Here also Malaysia is the dominant market with US$154.9 billion or 64 percent of the aggregate, as for the primary market (see Figure A.6). The other markets with significant turnover are the UAE (US$20.9 billion or 8.6 percent), Saudi Arabia (US$20.8 billion or 8.6 percent), Qatar (US$17.3 billion or 7.1 percent), and Indonesia (US$13.9 billion or 5.7 percent). Turnover in the rest of the world is about the size of that in Indonesia.

FUNDS

Islamic funds have seen assets under management grow from US$29.2 billion in 2004 to US$60 billion by end of 2011, representing a growth rate of 10.8 percent, despite the global economic downturn and the sovereign debt crisis in Europe. By the end of October 2012, assets under management had further grown to US$64 billion (IFIS Financial Stability Report 2012). Unlike for *sukuk*s, Saudi Arabia is the leading Islamic funds domiciliation, though Malaysia also retains significant activity. An interesting feature is that close to 20 percent of funds are domiciled in non-Islamic jurisdictions (see Table A.6).

Interestingly, more than half of Islamic funds are commodity funds (see Table A.7). This may reflect the extensive use of commodity markets for liquidity management as well as the materiality requirement in Islamic financial transactions.

Islamic funds need to have special screening mechanisms in selecting their portfolios in order to remain *Shari'a* compliant.

TABLE A.6   Islamic Funds Domiciliation, October 2012

Country	%
Saudi Arabia	40.3
Malaysia	30
Ireland	7.6
United States	5.6
Kuwait	3.7
Pakistan	2.7
South Africa	2.5
Indonesia	2.1
Jersey	2.1
Luxembourg	1.3

Source: IFSB Financial Stability Report 2013.

TABLE A.7   Global Islamic Fund Assets by Asset Class, October 2012

Asset Class	%
Commodities	53.0
Equity	11.6
Mixed assets	15.5
Money market	0.5
Others	2.1
Real estate	6.5
Sukuk	3.6
Trade finance	7.0

Source: IFSB Financial Stability Report 2013.

TAKAFUL

Takaful continues to be the smallest segment of the Islamic finance industry.[7] It has grown from 113 *takaful* operators in 2006 to 195 in 2010. Major players are domiciled in the GCC area, Far East, and Africa (see Table A.8). Contributions to *takaful* operators globally reached $8.3 billion in 2010. The Ernst & Young *Takaful* Report 2012 estimates the global contribution to be $12 billion in 2012 with average growth rate of 20 percent.

[7]See Ernst and & Young (2012), "The World Takaful Report 2012," (www.ey .com/Publication/vwLUAssets/The_World_Takaful_Report_2012/$FILE/Ernst% 20&%20Young's%20The%20World%20Takaful%20Report%202012.pdf).

TABLE A.8 Number of *Takaful* Operators by Region, 2010

Region	Number	%
GCC	77	39.5
Far East	40	20.5
Africa	32	16.5
Middle East (non-Arab)	18	9.2
Indian Subcontinent	12	6.2
Levant	9	4.6
Others	8	3.5

Source: Takaful Re Limited, 6th annual report 2011.

Takaful activity covers activities similar to those covered by conventional insurance operators, namely family and medical insurance, marine and aviation, property and accident, and motor. Apart from Iran, family and medical *takaful* dominates the various markets where *takaful* is present (see Figure A.7).

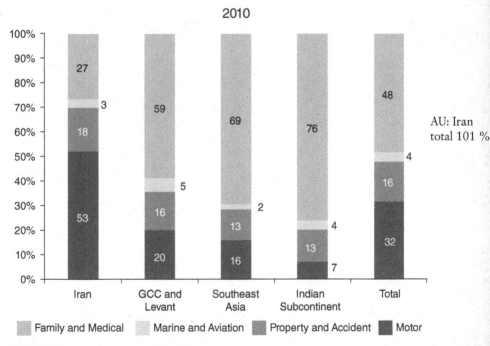

FIGURE A.7 Distribution of *Takaful* Activity across Markets (%)
Source: Ernst & Young, "The World Takaful Report 2012."

References

AAOIFI. 1999. "Statement on the Purpose and Calculation of the Capital Adequacy Ratio for Islamic Banks." Accounting and Auditing Organization for Islamic Financial Institutions, Bahrain, March.

AAOIFI. 2001. "Accounting, Auditing and Governance Standards for Islamic Financial Institutions." Accounting and Auditing Organization for Islamic Financial Institutions, Bahrain, May.

AAOIFI. 2004. Shari'a Standards for Financial Institutions.

Abdel Karim, R. A. 1990. "The Independence of Religious and External Auditors: The Case of Islamic Banks." *Accounting, Auditing & Accountability Journal* 3, no. 3 (March): 34–44.

Abdullah, Mohamed Ridza. 2011. "Development of Islamic Banking in Malaysia." www.ridzalaw.com.my/downloads/2011-klrca_newsletter.pdf.

African Development Bank. 2011. "Islamic Banking and Finance in North Africa." www.afdb.org.

Ahmad, A. 1997. "Structure of Deposits in Selected Islamic Banks." IRTI Research Paper no. 48, Islamic Development Bank, Jeddah.

Ainley, Michael, Ali Mashayekhi, Robert Hicks, Arshadur Rahman, and Ali Ravalia. 2007. *Islamic Finance in the UK: Regulation and Challenges.* London: Financial Services Authority.

Al-Deehani, Talla, Rifaat Ahmed Abdel Karim, and Victor Murinde. 1999. "The Capital Structure of Islamic Banks under the Contractual Obligation of Profit Sharing." *International Journal of Theoretical and Applied Finance* 2 (3): 243–283.

Ali, Salman Syed. 2011. "Islamic Banking in the Mena Region." Islamic Development Bank, Islamic Research and Training Institute, World Bank.

Allen, F., and D. Gale. 1997. "Financial Markets, Intermediaries, and Intertemporal Smoothing." *Journal of Political Economy* 105 (3): 523–546.

Allen, M. and J. Caruana. "Sovereign Wealth Funds: A Work Agenda," International Monetary Fund, Washington, D.C., February 29, 2008.

Alvarez, G.. 2008. Evidence to House Committee on Financial Services, United States Congress, Washington, D.C., March 5, 2008.

Alvi, Ijlal A. 2007. "Increasing the Secondary Market for *Sukuk*s: Overview and Considerations." IIFM website.

Arabianbusiness.com. 2009. "Saudi Banks Post Lower Q4 Profits." January 19. www.arabianbusiness.com/544145-saudi-banks-post-lower-q4-profits.

Archer, S., and R. Abdel Karim. 2007. "Specific Corporate Governance Issues in Islamic Banks." In *Islamic Finance: The Regulatory Challenge*, edited by S. Archer and R. Abdel Karim. Singapore: John Wiley & Sons, Asia.

Archer, S., and T. Ahmed. 2003. "Emerging Standards for Islamic Financial Institutions: The Case of the Accounting and Auditing Organization for Islamic Financial Institutions." Mimeo, World Bank.

Arena, Marco. 2006. "Does Insurance Market Activity Promote Economic Growth? A Cross-Country Study for Industrialized and Developing Countries." World Bank Policy Research Working Paper 4098, December.

AsianBondsOnline. 2009. http://asianbondsonline.adb.org/islamic_finance/structure/overview.php.

Aurangzeb, M. 2002. "Islamisation of the Economy in Pakistan: Past, Present and Future." *Islamic Studies* 41 (4): 675–704.

Ayub, Muhammad. 2007. *Understanding Islamic Finance*. John Wiley and Sons.

Bacha, Obiyathulla I. 2008. "The Islamic Interbank Money Market and a Dual Banking System: The Malaysian Experience." INCEIF the Global University in Islamic Finance; MPRA Paper no. 12699, January. http://mpra.ub.uni-muenchen.de/12699/1/MPRA_paper_12699.pdf.

Badawi, S., and W. Grais. 2007. "Sustainability, Political Risk, and Transparency: Challenges and Solutions for Islamic Microfinance." Harvard Law School Symposium on Islamic Microfinance, April 14.

Baldwin, C., and M. Scott. 1983. "The Resolution of Claims in Financial Distress: The Case of Massey Ferguson." *Journal of Finance* 38:505–516.

The Banker. 2009. "Top 500 Islamic Financial Institutions." FT Business, November. www.mifc.com/index.php?ch=151&pg=735&ac=395&bb=657.

Bank Negara Malaysia. 2002. "Debt Restructuring of Johor Corporation and Its Financially Dependent Subsidiaries." www.bnm.gov.my/index.php?ch=31&pg=221&ac=144&lang=bm.

Bank Negara Malaysia. 2005. "How Does One Measure the Success of a Non-Profit Special Purpose Organisation Like an NPL Resolution Agency? Evaluating Danaharta's Performance." Annual report. www.bnm.gov.my/websites/danaharta.com.my/main/fr/04-Section%20C.pdf.

Bank Negara Malaysia. 2006. Annual report. www.bnm.gov.my/files/publication/ar/en/2006/ar2006_book.pdf.

Bank Negara Malaysia. 2011. "Financial Stability and Payments Systems Report."

Bank Sarasin. 2012. "Islamic Wealth Management Report 2012."

Barth, J., G. Caprio, and R. Levine. 2006. *Rethinking Bank Regulation: Till Angels Govern.* New York: Cambridge University Press.

BCBS. 1999. "Enhancing Corporate Governance for Banking Organizations." Basel Committee on Banking Supervision, Basel, Switzerland.

BCBS. 2002. "Internal Audit and the Supervisor's Relationship with Auditors: A Survey." Basel Committee on Banking Supervision, Basel, Switzerland.

BCBS. 2005. International Convergence of Capital Measurement and Capital Standards: A Revised Framework. (Basel, Ed.) Bank for International Settlements.

Benaissa, N., X. Jopart, and O. Tanrikulu. 2007. "Rethinking Regulation for Islamic Banking." *McKinsey Quarterly.*

Berle, A. A., and G. Means. 1932. *The Modern Corporation and Private Property.* New York: Macmillan.

Bernanke, Ben S. 2007. "Remarks by Chairman" to the Federal Reserve Bank of Atlanta's 2007 Financial Markets Conference, Sea Island, Georgia, May 15. www.federalreserve.gov/newsevents/speech/bernanke 20070515a.htm.

Bhatty, Ajmal. 2007. "The Growth and Global Market for *Takaful.*" Chapter 1 of *Islamic Insurance: Trends, Opportunities and the Future of Takaful,* edited by Jaffer Sohail. London: Euromoney Books.

BlomInvest Bank. 2009. "Islamic Banking in the MENA Region." www .blominvestbank.com/Library/Files/Islamic%20Banking.pdf.

Bollen, Rhys. 2006. "What Is a Deposit (and Why Does It Matter)?" *Journal of Banking and Finance Law and Practice* 17:283.

Briston, R., and A. El-Ashker. 1986. "Religious Audit: Could It Happen Here?" *Accountancy* 98, no. 1118 (October): 120–121.

Büyükdeniz, A. 2006. "Participation Banks in Turkey: An Economic and Social Reality." PowerPoint presentation, Istanbul, August 29.

Cader, S. A. 2007. "The Glass Has Yet to Become Full." *Islamic Finance News* 4 (20): 18–19.

Caprio, Gerard, Jr., and Daniel Klingebiel. 1996. "Bank Insolvency: Bad Luck, Bad Policy, or Bad Banking?" In *Annual World Bank Conference on Development Economics 1996.* Washington, DC: World Bank.

CGAP. 2010. "Financial Access 2010: The State of Financial Inclusion through the Crisis." Consultative Group to Assist the Poor, World Bank Group.

Chapra, M. Umer, and Habib Ahmed. 2002. "Corporate Governance in Islamic Financial Institutions." Occasional Paper no. 6, Islamic Research and Training Institute, Islamic Development Bank, Jeddah.

Chapra, M. Umer, and Tariqullah Khan. 2000. "Regulation and Supervision of Islamic Banks." Occasional Paper no. 3, Islamic Development Bank.

Chen, Yehning. 1999. "Banking Panics: The Role of the First-Come, First-Served Rule and Information Externalities." *Journal of Political Economy* 107:946–968.

Choong, Beng Soon, and Ming-Hua Liu. 2006. "Islamic Banking: Interest-Free or Interest-Based?" http://ssrn.com/abstract=868567.

Čihák, M., and H. Hesse. 2008. "Islamic Banks and Financial Stability: An Empirical Analysis." IMF Working Paper WP/08/16.

Claessens, S. 2003. "Corporate Governance and Development." October. http://ssrn.com/abstract=642721.

Consultative Group to Assist the Poor. 2010. Annual report.

Cordella, T., and E. L. Yeyati. 2002. "Financial Opening, Deposit Insurance, and Risk in a Model of Banking Competition." *European Economic Review* 46:471–485.

Crockett, A. 2008. "Market Liquidity and Financial Stability." *Financial Stability Review* 11:13–17.

Cunningham, A. 2010. "New Guidance on How Islamic Banks May Smooth Return to Investors." www.darienmiddleeast.com/hidden/new-guidance-on-how-islamic-banks-may-smooth-returns-to-investors-2/.

Dar, Humayon, and Talha Ahmed Azami, eds. 2011. "Global Islamic Finance Report." BMB Islamic Publication.

Davies, Brandon. 2011. "Applying Liquidity Rules to Sharia Banking." *Central Banking Journal*, February. www.centralbanking.com/static/central-banking.

Demirgüç-Kunt, A., and E. Detragiache. 1998. "The Determinants of Banking Crises in Developing and Developed Countries." IMF Staff Papers, 45 (March): 81–109.

Demirgüç-Kunt, A., and E. Detragiache. 2002. "Does Deposit Insurance Increase Banking System Stability? An Empirical Investigation." *Journal of Monetary Economics* 49 (7): 1373–1406.

Demirsar, Metin. 1998. "Turkey's Islamic Finance Houses Prepare to Become Banks." *Turkish Daily News*, issue no. 294, August 30. Accessed November 29, 2006, from www.turkishdailynews.fm-tr/archives.php?id=8682.

Derigs, U., and S. Marzban. 2009. "New Strategies and a New Paradigm for *Shariah*-Compliant Portfolio Optimization." *Journal of Banking & Finance* 33:1166–1176. http://tcnh.ntt.edu.vn/images/tapchiqt/48.pdf.

Diamond, D. W., and P. H. Dybvig. 1983. "Bank Runs, Deposit Insurance, and Liquidity." *Journal of Political Economy* 91 (3): 401–419.

Dutton, A., and A. Vause. 2006. "Dispute Resolution Clauses in Islamic Finance Transactions." *Islamic Business and Finance Magazine*, August.

The Economist Intelligence Unit Limited. 2008. *Country Monitor* 16, issue 37 (October 6): 10 (AN 34905428).

El-Gamal, Mahmoud A. 2003. "'Interest' and the Paradox of Contemporary Islamic Law and Finance." Rice University. www.ruf.rice.edu/~elgamal/files/interest.pdf.

El-Gamal, Mahmoud A. 2005. "Islamic Bank Corporate Governance and Regulation: A Call for Mutualization." Rice University, September. www.ruf.rice.edu/~elgamal/files/IBCGR.pdf.

El-Gamal, Mahmoud. 2006. *Islamic Finance: Law, Economics and Practice.* Cambridge: Cambridge University Press.

El-Hawary, D., W. Grais, and Z. Iqbal. 2004. "Regulating Islamic Financial Institutions: The Nature of the Regulated." World Bank Policy Research Working Paper 3227, March.

El Hawary, D., W. Grais, and Z. Iqbal. 2007. "Diversity in the Regulation of Islamic Financial Institutions." *Quarterly Review of Economics and Finance* 46:778–800.

El-Naggar, Hanan I. 2011. "Developing Dual Banking System Regulation in Egypt." www.regulacao.gov.br/publicacoes/artigos/developing-dual-banking-system-regulations-in-egypt.

El Tiby, Amr M. 2011. *Islamic Banking: How to Manage Risk and Improve Profitability.* Wiley Finance. Hoboken, NJ: John Wiley & Sons.

Ernst & Young. 2007. "The Islamic Funds and Investments Report."

Ernst & Young. 2011. "Islamic Funds & Investments Report 2011: Achieving Growth in Challenging Times." www.ey.com/Publication/vwLUAssets/IFIR_2011/$FILE/IFIR_2011.pdf.

Ernst & Young. 2012. "The World Takaful Report." www.ey.com/Publication/vwLUAssets/The_World_Takaful_Report_2012/$FILE/Ernst%20&%20Young's%20The%20World%20Takaful%20Report%202012.pdf.

Errico, L., and M. Farahbaksh. 1998. "Islamic Banking: Issues in Prudential Regulation and Supervision." IMF Working Paper WP/98/30. Washington, DC: International Monetary Fund.

Euroweek. 2009. Issue 1090 (February 6): 64.

Evrensel, Ayşe Y. 2008. "Banking Crisis and Financial Structure: A Survival-Time Analysis." *International Review of Economics and Finance* 17: 589–602.

Fatemi, F., and I. Fooladi. 2006. "Credit Risk Management: A Survey of Practices." *Credit Risk Management* 32 (3): 227–233.

FEE. 2004. "Mandatory Rotation of Audit Firms." Study by the Fédération des Experts Comptables Européens, October.

Fitch Ratings. 2005. "Securitization and *Shari'ah* Law." March.

Fitch Ratings. 2007. "Islamic Banking—Factors in Risk Assessment." March.

Fung, B., J. George, S. Hohl, and G. Ma. 2004. "Public Asset Management Companies in East Asia." Occasional Paper no. 3, Bank for International Settlements (BIS). www.bis.org/fsi/fsipapers03.pdf.

Goodhart, C. 2008. "Liquidity Risk Management." *Financial Stability Review* 11.

Gorton, G., and A. Winton. 2002. "Financial Intermediation." Wharton School, University of Pennsylvania, Financial Institutions Center, March.

Grais, W. 2008. "Islamic Banking: Policy and Institutional Challenges." *Journal of Islamic Economics, Banking and Finance* 4, no. 1 (January–April).

Grais, W. 2009. "Issues in the Corporate Governance of Islamic Financial Services." Presentation at the Fordham Law School Islamic Law and Finance Symposium, February 26.

Grais, W., and Z. Kantur. 2003. "The Changing Financial Landscape: Opportunities and Challenges for the Middle East and North Africa." World Bank Policy Research Working Paper 3050, May.

Grais, W., and A. Kulathunga. 2006. "Capital Structure and Risk in Islamic Financial Services." In *Islamic Finance: The Regulatory Challenge*, edited by S. Archer and R. Abdel Karim. Singapore: John Wiley & Sons, Asia.

Grais, W., and L. Maglione-Piromallo. 2005. "Underlying Trends in Financial Regulatory and Supervisory Regimes." *Arab Bank Review* 7, no. 1 (April).

Grais, W., and M. Pellegrini. 2006a. "Corporate Governance and *Shariah* Compliance in Institutions Offering Islamic Financial Services." World Bank Policy Research Working Paper 4054, November.

Grais, W., and M. Pellegrini. 2006b. "Corporate Governance and Stakeholders' Financial Interests in Institutions Offering Islamic Financial Services." World Bank Policy Research Working Paper 4053, October.

Grais, W., and M. Pellegrini. 2006c. "Corporate Governance in Institutions Offering Islamic Financial Services: Issues and Options." World Bank Policy Research Working Paper 4052, October.

Grais, W., and D. Vittas. 2005. "Institutional Investors, Contractual Savings and Capital Market Development in Egypt, Jordan, Morocco, and Tunisia." In *Money and Finance in the Middle East: Missed Opportunities or Future Prospects?*, edited by Simon Neaime and Nora Ann Colton. Bingley, UK: Emerald Group Publishing.

Grais, W., and Rajhi, W. 2009. "Islamic Financial Institutions, Risks, Contagion, Distress."

Grandmont, R., G. Grant, and F. Silva. 2004. "Beyond the Numbers—Corporate Governance: Implications for Investors." Deutsche Bank, April 1.

Grosfeld, I., and T. Tressel. 2001. "Competition and Corporate Governance: Substitutes or Complements? Evidence from the Warsaw Stock Exchange." DELTA Working Papers 2001-06, DELTA (Ecole Normale Supérieure).

Haron, S., and N. Ahmad. 2000. "The Effects of Conventional Interest Rates and Rate of Profit on Funds Deposited with Islamic Banking

System in Malaysia." *International Journal of Islamic Financial Services* 1, no. 4.

Hasan, M., and J. Dridi. 2010. "The Effects of the Global Crisis on Islamic and Conventional Banks: A Comparative Study." IMF Working Paper WP/10/201, September.

Hassan, Abul, and Antonios Antoniou. 2007. "Equity Fund's Islamic Screening: Effects on Its Financial Performance." www.ibisonline.net.

Hirschman, A. O. 1970. *Exit Voice and Loyalty: Responses to Decline in Firms, Organizations and States*. Cambridge, MA: Harvard University Press.

Hirschman, A. O., and R. R. Nelson. 1976. "Some Uses of the Exit-Voice Approach." *American Economic Review* 66, no. 2 (May): 386–391.

Hoelscher, David S., and Marc Quintyn. 2003. "Managing Systemic Banking Crises." Occasional Paper no. 224, International Monetary Fund.

Honohan, P. 2004a. "The Development Dimension of the FSAP." World Bank, June 14.

Honohan, P. 2004b. "Financial Development, Growth and Poverty: How Close Are the Links?" World Bank Policy Research Working Paper 3203, February.

Hussein, A., and H. Al-Tamimi. 2008. "Implementing Basel II: An Investigation of the UAE Banks' Basel II Preparations." *Journal of Financial Regulation and Compliance* 16 (2): 173–187.

Hussein, K. 2003. "Cost Efficiency in Islamic Banking: The Case of Sudan." Islamic Research and Training Institute, Research Paper 65, Jeddah.

Hussein, K. 2004. "Banking Efficiency in Bahrain: Islamic vs Conventional Banks." Islamic Research and Training Institute, Research Paper 68, Jeddah.

IFIS. 2010. "Is Egypt Going *Takaful*?" December 31. www.securities.com/IFIS/.

IFIS. 2011. "Islamic Finance in Egypt." PDF, www.securities.com/IFIS/.

IFIS. 2012. "Egypt Islamists Draft Code to Boost Islamic Banks." June 12. www.securities.com/IFIS/.

IFIS Analytics. 2008. "*Shariah* Compliant Finance in Egypt." April 21. www.securities.com/IFIS/.

IFSB. 2005. "Capital Adequacy Standard for Institutions (Other Than Insurance Institutions) Offering Only Islamic Financial Services." December. www.ifsb.org.

IFSB. 2006. "Guiding Principles on Corporate Governance for Institutions Offering Only Islamic Financial Services (Excluding Islamic Insurance (*Takaful*) Institutions and Islamic Mutual Funds)." December. www.ifsb.org.

IFSB. 2007a. "Disclosures to Promote Transparency and Market Discipline for Institutions Offering Islamic Financial Services (Excluding Islamic Insurance (*Takaful*) Institutions and Islamic Mutual Funds)." December. www.ifsb.org.

IFSB. 2007b. "Exposure Draft: Capital Adequacy Requirements for «Sukuk» Securitisations and Real Estate Investment." www.ifsb.org/docs/ed_»Sukuk»_english.pdf.

IFSB. 2008. "Technical Note on Issues in Strengthening Liquidity Management of Institutions Offering Islamic Financial Services: The Development of Islamic Money Markets." March. www.ifsb.org/docs/mar2008_liquidity.pdf.

IFSB. 2010. "Guidance Note on the Practice of Smoothing the Profits Payout to Investment Account Holders." December. www.ifsb.org/standard/eng_GN-3_Guidance_Note_on_the_Practice_of_Smoothing.pdf.

IFSB. 2011. "Guidance Note in Connection with the IFSB Capital Adequacy Standard: The Determination of Alpha in the Capital Adequacy Ratio for Institutions (Other Than Insurance Institutions) Offering Only Islamic Financial Services." March. www.ifsb.org.

IIFM. 2010. "*Sukuk* Report: A Comprehensive Study of the International *Sukuk* Market." First edition, www.IIFM.net.

Imam, P., and K. Kpodar. 2010. "Islamic Banking: How Has It Diffused?" IMF Working Paper WP/10/195, August.

IMF. 1998. "Financial Crises: Characteristics and Indicators of Vulnerability." Chapter 4 in *World Economic Outlook*. Washington, DC: International Monetary Fund.

Iqbal, K. 2005. "Liquidity Management of Islamic Financial Institutions in the UAE." HSBC Amanah, Islamic Interbank Money Market. www.iimm.bnm.gov.my/view.php?id=62&dbIndex=0&website_id=14&ex=1211519304&md.

Iqbal, Munawar. 2001. "Islamic and Conventional Banking in the Nineties: A Comparative Study." *Islamic Economic Studies* 8 (2): 1–27.

Iqbal, Z., and A. Mirakhor. 1987. "Islamic Banking." Occasional Paper 49, International Monetary Fund.

Iqbal, Z., and H. Van Greuning. 2008. "Risk Analysis for Islamic Banks." World Bank.

IRTI. 2007. "Framework and Strategies for Development of Islamic Microfinance Services." May.

IsDB, IRTI, and IFSB. 2007. "Islamic Financial Services Industry Development: Ten-Year Framework and Strategies." May.

IslamicBanker.com. 2008. "Islamic Banking: Lessons from the Credit Crisis." www.islamicbanker.com/islamic-banking-lessons-from-the-credit-crisis.html.

"Islamic Finance: Why Islamic Banks Must Offer a Cushion against Collapse." 2008. *Asiamoney* 19, issue 8 (September): 09589309.

Jarrow, R. A. 2008. "Operational Risk." *Journal of Banking & Finance* 32:870–879.

Jobst, Andreas. 2007. The Economics of Islamic Finance and Securitization. IMF Working Paper WP/07/117.

Karim, R., and A. Ali. 1989. "Determinants of the Financial Strategy of Islamic Banks." *Journal of Business Finance and Accounting* 16 (2): 193–212.

Kaufman, G. 1994. "Bank Contagion: A Review of the Theory and Evidence." *Journal of Financial Services Research* 11:123–150.

Khan, M. F., and Feddad. 2004. "The Growth of Islamic Financial Industry: Need for Setting Standards for *Shariah* Application." Paper presented at the Sixth Harvard Forum on Islamic Finance, May.

King, Robert G. and R. Levine. 1993. "Finance and growth : Schumpeter might be right." Policy Research Working Paper Series 1083, The World Bank.

Klingebiel, D. 2001. "Asset Management Companies." In *Resolution of Financial Distress*, edited by S. Claessens, Simeon Djankov, and Ashoka Mody. Washington, DC: World Bank Institute, World Bank.

Kuran, Timur. 1995. "Islamic Economics and the Islamic Sub-Economy." *Journal of Economic Perspectives* 9:155–173.

Lester, Rodney. 2011. "The Insurance Sector in the Middle East and North Africa: Challenges and Development Agenda." World Bank Policy Research Working Paper 5608, March.

Levine, R. 2004. "The Corporate Governance of Banks: A Concise Discussion of Concepts and Evidence." World Bank Policy Research Working Paper 3404.

Levine, R., and S. Zervos. 1998. "Stock Markets, Banks, and Economic Growth." *American Economic Review* 88:537–558.

Llewellyn, D. 1999. "The Economic Rationale for Financial Regulation." Financial Services Authority, April. www.fsa.gov.uk/pubs/occpapers/op01.pdf.

Mako, William P. 2003. "Maximising Value of Nonperforming Assets: Facilitating Out-of-Court Workouts in a Crisis: Lessons from East Asia, 1998–2001." Forum on Asian Insolvency Reform, Asian Development Bank, OECD, World Bank.

Maroun, Y. 2002. "Liquidity Management and Trade Financing." In *Islamic Finance: Innovation and Growth*, edited by R. Abdel Karim and S. Archer, 163–175. London: Euromoney Institutional Investor.

Martin, Matthew. 2008. *MEED: Middle East Economic Digest* 52, issue 47 (November 21): 19.

Mashaal, AbdelBa'ri. 2004. "Strategy for External *Shariah* Supervision." Paper presented at the 4th AAOIFI *Shari'a* conference, Bahrain, October.

Matutes, C., and X. Vives. 2000. "Imperfect Competition, Risk Taking, and Regulation in Banking." *European Economic Review* 44:1–34.

McKinsey & Company. 2011. "Assessing and Mapping the Global Gap in SME Financing: The MENA Case."

McKinsey & Company. 2005. "Tracking an Industry in Transition." Islamic Banking Competitiveness Report, December.

McKinsey & Company. 2007. "CIB 50." August.

McMillen, M. J. T. 2007. "Toward an Effective Legal Framework for Islamic Finance: Securities Laws, Trusts, Enforceability and *Sukuk*." IFSB and IOSCO, April.

Mohieldin, M., Z. Iqbal, A. Rostom, and X. Fu. 2011. "The Role of Islamic Finance in Enhancing Financial Inclusion in Organization of Islamic Cooperation (OIC) Countries." World Bank Staff Policy Research Working Paper 5920, December.

Molyneux, P., and M. Iqbal. 2005. *Banking and Financial Systems in the Arab World*. New York: Palgrave Macmillan.

Moody's. 2006. "A Guide to Rating Islamic Financial Institutions." April.

Muljawan, Dadang, Humayon A. Dar, and Maximilian J. B. Hall. 2004. "A Capital Adequacy Framework for Islamic Banks: The Need to Reconcile Depositors' Risk Aversion with Managers' Risk Taking." *Applied Financial Economics* 14:429–441. www.arabianbusiness.com/search/The+UAE+guaranteed+all+deposits+with+local+banks?x=17&y=9&template=arabianbusiness; www.arabianbusiness.com%2F556374-uae-economy-shows-early-signs-of-recovery---minister.

Obiyathulla, I. B. 2004. "Dual Banking Systems and Interest Rate Risk for Islamic Banks." *Journal of Accounting, Commerce & Finance Islamic Perspective* 8 (182): 1–42.

Obiyathulla, I. B. 2008. "The Islamic Interbank Money Market and a Dual Banking System: The Malaysian Experience." *International Journal of Islamic and Middle Eastern Finance and Management* 1 (3): 210–226.

O'Brien, Justin. 2008. "Barriers to Entry: Foreign Direct Investment and the Regulation of Sovereign Wealth Funds." This paper derives from presentations at the University of California at Berkeley; University of Cambridge; University of Glasgow; University of New Hampshire; Dayton Symposium on Accountability, Ohio; International Monetary Fund, Washington, D.C.; and Lowy Institute for International Policy, Sydney. www.cama.anu.edu.au/Events/swf2008/swf2008_papers/O'Brien_SWF_paper.doc.

OECD (The Organisation for Economic Co-operation and Development). 2004. "OECD Principles of Corporate Governance." Paris, France.

Oh, G., and J. H. Park. 2006. "Creation of a Regional Credit Guarantees Mechanism in Asia." In *Asian Bond Markets: Issues and Prospects*.

Bank for International Settlements, BIS Paper no. 30 (November): 224–240.

Okeahalam, C. 1998. "The Political Economy of Bank Failure and Supervision in the Republic of South Africa." *African Association of Political Science* 3 (2): 29–48.

Olson, Dennis, and Taisier A. Zoubi. 2008. "Using Accounting Ratios to Distinguish between Islamic and Conventional Banks in the GCC Region." *International Journal of Accounting* 43:45–65.

Otiti, Saidat A. 2011. "Evolution of Islamic Banking & Finance." Muslim Public Affairs Center, 2nd series (August). www.mpac-ng.org/archived-article/636-evolution-of-islamic-banking-a-finance.pdf.

Park, D., and C. Rhee. 2006. "Building Infrastructures for the Asian Bond Markets: Settlement and Credit Rating." *Asian Bond Markets: Issues and Prospects*. Bank for International Settlements, Basel. BIS Papers no. 30, 202–221.

Pearce, D. 2011. "Financial Inclusion in the Middle East and North Africa: Analysis and Roadmap Recommendations." World Bank Staff Policy Research Working Paper 5610, March.

Prowse, S. 1998. "Corporate Governance: Emerging Issues and Lessons from East Asia." In *Responding to the Global Financial Crisis, Background Papers/Program of Seminars*, 1998 Annual Meetings of the International Monetary Fund and the World Bank Group. Washington, DC: World Bank.

"Qatar: Little Danger of Systemic Failure." 2008. *Emerging Markets Monitor* 14, issue 32 (November 24): 18.

Quémard, J., and V. Golitin. 2005. "Interest Rate Risk in the French Banking System." *Financial Stability Review*, Banque de France (June): 81–94.

Reinhart, Carmen M., and Kenneth S. Rogoff. 2008. "Is the 2007 U.S. Sub-Prime Financial Crisis So Different? An International Historical Comparison." Harvard University and the NBER. www.economics.harvard.edu/faculty/rogoff/files/Is_The_US_Subprime_Crisis_So_Different.pdf.

Richards, D. A. 2002. "Internal and External Auditors—Inside and Out." www.theiia.org/ecm/print.cfm?doc_id=3648.

Rocha, Roberto R., with Zsofia Aravai and Subika Farazi. 2011. *Financial Access and Stability: A Road Map for the Middle East and North Africa*. Washington, DC: World Bank.

Sahajwala, Ranjana, and P. Van den Berg. 2000. "Supervisory Risk Assessment and Early Warning Systems." Basel Committee on Banking Supervision Working Paper 2. Bank for International Settlements, Basel, Switzerland.

Samolyk, Katherine A. 1994. "Banking Conditions and Regional Economic Performance: Evidence of a Regional Credit Channel." *Journal of Monetary Economics* 34:259–278.

Scott, David F. 2002. "A Practical Guide to Managing Systemic Financial Crises: A Review of Approaches Taken in Indonesia, the Republic of Korea, and Thailand." World Bank Policy Research Working Paper 2843.

Shahul, H., et al. 2004. "Alternative Disclosure and Performance Measures for Islamic Banks." International Islamic University of Malaysia.

Shamseddine, Reem, and Andrew Critchlow. 2008. "Gulf Countries Unveil Measures to Back Banks: U.A.E. Will Guarantee Domestic Deposits and Saudi Arabia Sets Lending Facility as Regional Stock Markets Slip." *Wall Street Journal—Eastern Edition* 252, issue 88 (October 13): A5.

Solé, J. 2007. "Introducing Islamic Banks into Conventional Banking Systems." International Monetary Fund Working Paper WP/07/175. Washington, DC: International Monetary Fund.

Solé, J. 2008. "Prospects and Challenges for Developing Corporate *Sukuk* and Bond Markets: Lessons from a Kuwait Case Study." *International Journal of Islamic and Middle Eastern Finance and Management*.

Standard & Poor's. 2006. "Islamic Finance Outlook 2006: Financial Services Ratings." September.

Starr, M. A., and R. Yilmaz. 2007. "Bank Runs in Emerging-Market Economies: Evidence from Turkey's Special Finans Houses." *Southern Economic Journal* 73 (4): 1112–1132.

Summer, M. 1998. "Does Mandatory Rotation Enhance Auditor Independence?" *Zeitschrift für Wirtschafts- und Sozialwissenschaften* 118 (3): 327–359.

Sundararajan, V. 2006. "Systemic Liquidity Infrastructure and Monetary Policy with Islamic Finance." 3rd Islamic Financial Services Board Summit, Beirut, May 17–18.

Sundararajan, V., and T. Baliño. 1991. "Issues in Recent Banking Crises." In *Banking Crises: Cases and Issues*, edited by V. Sundararajan and T. Balino, 1–59. Washington, DC: International Monetary Fund.

Sundararajan, V., and E. Lucas. 2002. "Islamic Financial Institutions and Products in the Global Financial System: Key Issues in Risk Management and Challenges Ahead." IMF Working Paper WP/02/192. Washington, DC: International Monetary Fund.

Sundararajan, V., David Marston, and Ghiath Shabsigh. 1998. "Monetary Operations and Government Debt Management under Islamic Banking." IMF Working Paper WP/98/144. Washington, DC: International Monetary Fund.

Syed, Salman Aly. 2011. "Islamic Banking in the MENA Region." World Bank, February. http://siteresources.worldbank.org/INTMNAREGTOP POVRED/Resources/MENAFlagshipIslamicFinance2_24_11.pdf.

Tirole, J. 1999. "Corporate Governance." Centre for Economic Policy Research, Discussion Paper no. 2086.

Turk Ariss, R., and S. Yolla. 2007. "Challenges in Implementing Capital Adequacy Guidelines to Islamic Banks." *Journal of Banking Regulation* 9 (1): 46–59.

"UAE: Government Moves to Shore Up Banking Sector." 2008. *Emerging Markets Monitor* 14, issue 28 (October 20): 19 (AN 34881789).

UKIFS. 2012. "Islamic Finance." Financial Markets Series. UK Islamic Finance Secretariat, March.

Usmani, Muhammad Imran Ashraf. 2002. *Meezan Bank's Guide to Islamic Banking*. Karachi: Darul Ishaat.

Usmani, Muhammad Taqi. 2005. *An Introduction to Islamic Finance*. Karachi: Maktaba Ma'ariful Qur'an.

von Hagen, Jürgen, and Tai-kuang Ho. 2007. "Money Market Pressure and the Determinants of Banking Crises." *Journal of Money, Credit and Banking* 39, no. 5 (August).

Whitaker, R. B. 1999. "The Early Stages of Financial Distress." *Journal of Economics and Finance* 23 (2): 123–133.

Wilson, Rodney. 2002. "The Evolution of the Islamic Financial System," in Abdel Karim, Rifaat Ahmed, and Simon Archer: *Islamic Finance: Innovation and Growth*, London, Euromoney Books.

Wilson, R. 2009. "The Development of Islamic Finance in the GCC." www2.lse.ac.uk/government/research/resgroups/kuwait/documents/Wilson.pdf.

World Bank on the Financial Sector Assessment Program, for an overview at http://web.worldbank.org/WBSITE/EXTERNAL/TOPICS/EXTFIN ANCIALSECTOR/0,,contentMDK:22142161~menuPK:6459396~pag ePK:210058~piPK:210062~theSitePK:282885,00.html.

"World Insurance in 2006: Premiums Came Back to Life." 2007. *Sigma* no. 4.

Yasaar Media. 2009. "Islamic Finance in North America." www.yasaarmedia.com.

Zaher, T., and K. Hassan. 2001. "A Comparative Literature Survey of Islamic Finance and Banking." *Financial Markets, Institutions and Instruments* 10:155–199.

Zarqa, Muhammad Anas. 1997. "*Istisna*' Financing of Infrastructure Projects." *Islamic Economic Studies* 4, no. 2 (May). www.isdb.org/irj/go/km/docs/documents/IDBDevelopments/Internet/English/IRTI/CM/downloads/IES_Articles/Vol%204-2..Anas%20Zarqa..ISTISNA%20FINANCING...dp.pdf.

Zawya, Middle East Business Information. 2008. "Islamic Banks Are Sub-Prime Winners." May 3. http://cm3.zawya.com/marketing.cfm?zp&p=/Story.cfm/sidEIU20080401223346006.

Index